The Lion, the Dove,
& the Lamb

The Lion, the Dove, & the Lamb

An Exploration into the Nature of the Christian God as Trinity

REVISED EDITION

A. Bryden Black
Foreword by Alister E. McGrath

WIPF & STOCK · Eugene, Oregon

THE LION, THE DOVE, & THE LAMB, REVISED EDITION
An Exploration into the Nature of the Christian God as Trinity

Copyright © 2018 A. Bryden Black. All rights reserved. Except for brief quotations in critical publications or reviews, no part of this book may be reproduced in any manner without prior written permission from the publisher. Write: Permissions, Wipf and Stock Publishers, 199 W. 8th Ave., Suite 3, Eugene, OR 97401.

Wipf & Stock
An Imprint of Wipf and Stock Publishers
199 W. 8th Ave., Suite 3
Eugene, OR 97401

www.wipfandstock.com

PAPERBACK ISBN: 978-1-5326-7476-1
HARDCOVER ISBN: 978-1-5326-7477-8
EBOOK ISBN: 978-1-5326-7478-5

Scripture quotations marked (NRSV) are taken from the New Revised Standard Version Bible, copyright © 1989, Division of Christian Education of the National Council of the Churches of Christ in the United States of America. Used by permission. All rights reserved.

Scripture quotations marked (NIV) are taken from the Holy Bible, New International Version®, NIV®. Copyright © 1973, 1978, 1984, 2011 by Biblica, Inc.T Used by permission of Zondervan. All rights reserved worldwide. www.zondervan.com The "NIV" and "New International Version" are trademarks registered in the United States Patent and Trademark Office by Biblica, Inc.T.

Scripture quotations marked (ESV) are from the ESV® Bible (The Holy Bible, English Standard Version®), copyright © 2001 by Crossway, a publishing ministry of Good News Publishers. Used by permission. All rights reserved.

Scripture quotations marked (NJPS) are from the Tanakh: The Holy Scriptures: The New JPS Translation according to the Traditional Hebrew Text. Copyright © 1985 by The Jewish Publication Society. Used by permission. All rights reserved.

Figures 6, 7, and 8, illustrating various trinitarian relations, are taken from Robert W. Jenson, *God According to the Gospel: The Triune Identity*. Philadelphia: Fortress Press, 1982. Used by permission—and with grateful thanks. All rights reserved.

Manufactured in the U.S.A.

Every scribe who has been trained for the kingdom of heaven is like the master of a household who brings out of their storeroom new treasures as well as old.

MATT 13:52 NRSV/NIV

Contents

List of Illustrations · ix
Foreword · xi
Preface · xiii
Preface to the Revised Edition · xvii
Acknowledgments · xix
Further Acknowledgments · xxiii
Abbreviations · xxiv

Introduction · 1

one   A Fireside Chat · 5

two   Elementary Trinitarian Speech · 8

three   Joining Some Dots · 12

four   More Dots and Some Colors · 18
    Philippians 2 • John 1 • Revelation 4 & 5 • Luke–Acts

five   A Final Outline and its Colors · 37
    The Lord's Prayer • The *Shema*

six   CAD/CAM – 1: Design · 51
    Some basic philosophy • The Fourth Century Arian Controversy • The Creeds of 325 & 381 • The *homoousion* • The Holy Spirit • *Hypostasis* and *Ousia* • Excursus • And in the Church etc. • *Perichoresis*

seven   CAD/CAM – 2: Manufacture · 89
    Aurelius Augustinus • Relations • On the Holy Spirit • The psychological analogies • The analogies emerge • The question: analogous to what? • Person & Identity • Temporality • The One who has room for us • Revisionary Metaphysics

eight Deconstruction · 140

Personal Atonement • The Anti–Arian Backlash • The Solution of the Church

nine Reconstruction and Reconceiving for Renewal and Reappropriation: 1 · 150

Model of Giver–Gift–Recipient • Its two key forms • Elaborating the Model of GGR • 1.0 The Living God of Love whose Being is in Becoming • 2.0 The ecstatic, epektatic God of Life & Love • 3.0 The Living God's Fullness of Loving Time—and GGR • Interim Conclusion

ten Reconstruction and Reconceiving for Renewal and Reappropriation: 2 · 169

Elaborating definition A • A.1 That . . . event • A.2 Eternally reiterative • A.3: During which • Elaborating definition B • B.1: The history . . . from eternity . . . unto eternity • B.2: Giving • B.3.1: The Father as Giver • B.3.2: The Holy Spirit as Gift • B.3.3: The Son as Recipient • AB.1: Excursus on Reiterative Eventfulness as Eternal Trinitarian Historicality • AB.2: Freedom's Reality • C: The Immanent Trinity

Two Poems as Contemplative Response · 192

Reflecting [on] *In the Self's Place* • Triptych: Timely Meditation, Spatial Sensibility, and Circumincessio

Bibliography · 209
Index of Names · 225
Index of Subjects · 227

List of Illustrations

Figure 1   A diagram of Irenaeus' "The Two Hands of God" · 16

Figure 2   A modified diagram based on the Economy of Salvation · 16

Figure 3   A representation of the Economy derived from Luke–Acts · 33

Figure 4   Israel's Future Hope · 34

Figure 5   The Christian Fulfilment · 34

Figure 6   Traditional trinitarian relations—of origin only · 122

Figure 7   Reciprocal trinitarian relations · 123

Figure 8   Revised reciprocal trinitarian relations · 123

Figure 9   Luke–Acts revised displaying both dominical sacraments · 148

Figure 10 Rublev's Icon of the Trinity (1410) · 190

Foreword

WHEN I WAS AN atheist, back in the late 1960s, I regarded religious people as deluded and irrational souls who believed all sorts of nonsense. The most absurd aspect of Christian belief always seemed to me to be the doctrine of the Trinity. How can God be three and one at the same time? That was just lousy mathematics. It was ridiculous nonsense that a thinking person could not take seriously. When I discovered Christianity as a student at Oxford in the 1970s, I began to explore the landscape of faith. It was an exciting and rewarding process and I found that I was able to make sense of a lot of basic Christian ideas quite quickly. But the doctrine of the Trinity still seemed quite irrational to me. I asked some local clergy to explain it to me. Perhaps I was unlucky or unwise, but it soon became obvious to me that they knew as little about it as I did.

Happily, others were able to provide me with the help I needed. I came across some wonderfully lucid analogies in the writings of C. S. Lewis, which were especially helpful. And as I began to read serious works of theology, I finally realized what the problem was. Those who complain about the "irrationality" of the Trinity are really people who want to limit reality to what reason can manage. They want to reduce God to what we can cope with, when we ought to be expanding our minds to take in the full reality of God.

In the end, it is God who must be allowed to shape our thinking. The contours of our thought need to be adapted to God, not the other way round! The doctrine of the Trinity helps us recapture the vibrant reality of God in our minds and in our hearts. It liberates us from our scaled down and domesticated half-truths about a God who can never be confined to formulae or theories.

Bryden Black's book is just the sort of thing that I looked for (and failed to find) when I was younger—a book that would have helped me grasp what the Trinity was all about, using accessible and engaging images and stories as a way of leading his readers gently into the depths of Trinitarian theology. It's a book that will be welcomed by laity and clergy. Dr Black is obviously a preacher and pastor, and brings his gifts to bear on this central truth of the Christian faith. *The Lion, the Dove, & the Lamb* reassures us that we can trust this way of thinking about God, and helps us to see how it resources and enables the pastoral and missional work of the Christian church. I hope it will help its readers to grasp the deep Trinitarian logic of the Christian faith, and follow through this logic into its outreach and ministry.

Alister McGrath
Oxford University

Preface

THE INTENTION OF A preface is to orientate the reader to approach the text ahead from a particular perspective, to alert them what to look for. In the first instance, as I say at the beginning of Chapter 9, "what we . . . need is adequate translation of the doctrine [of the Trinity] into concrete enrichment of people's actual Christian lives of discipleship". But how do we do this when, as the Roman Catholic theologian, Karl Rahner, said, "despite their orthodox confession of the Trinity, Christians are, in their practical life, almost mere monotheists"?

The reasons for this state of affairs are many and complex; we shall touch upon a few of them in this book, with related material in some of the footnotes. (These footnotes, by the way, while giving references when necessary, are also offered to be pursued as little or as much as any reader might wish.) Essentially however, I sense it comes down to something like this. The nascent Christian church that gave us the NT writings had a series of concrete experiences, which in due time forced the Early Church of the opening centuries, under the sheer pressure of these events, to come up with a new form of language, one that began to bring the God of the Gospel of Jesus, the Messiah of Israel, to human speech. This new way of expressing the kind of deity Christians had come to believe in was eventually enshrined in the Creed of the fourth century, devised at the councils of Nicaea (325) and Constantinople (381). Now fast forward to today. Christians and the church at large are mostly left in some residual manner with this Symbol of the Faith, the Nicene Creed—which, at best, is held in high regard, even if rather abstractly, as folk try to give some kind of formal assent to it—but with little experience or understanding of how all this might specifically impact their own concrete lives. The exact reverse, in other words, of what generated the thing in the first place.

Curiously, providentially, this God of the Gospel in the meantime has not left us as orphans (see John 14:18a). One of the most remarkable theological movements of the twentieth century has been the rise of interest in this very doctrine of the Trinity. This book does not attempt to rehearse this history, nor does it try particularly to evaluate it. Rather, that was the sort of thing I ventured in a doctoral thesis presented in 1988, *The Trinity and the Contemporary Doctrine of God: Towards a new model for understanding the nature of the Christian God*. Others in addition have offered very useful resources. Ted Peters gave us *God as Trinity* in 1993; John Thompson, *Modern Trinitarian Perspectives*, in 1994; and Christoph Schwöbel edited *Trinitarian Theology Today* in 1995. 2002 saw Eerdmans publish *The Trinity* by Roger Olson and Christopher Hall, an historical summary of key contributions to the doctrine with a great bibliography. And lastly, 2011 saw *The Oxford Handbook of the Trinity*, edited by Gilles Emery and Matthew Levering, gather what is perhaps the most comprehensive survey of essays—biblical, historical, and systematic—on the doctrine currently in print. But somehow most of this has not "trickled down" to the person in the pews; they are in effect still "orphans" with regards to this most crucial and formal of all Christian dogmas.

So what's to be done? *The Lion, the Dove, & the Lamb* is my own opening gambit. Please enjoy! And please *enter* hereafter *into* this most glorious of all living truths.

So; *Tolle! Lege!* "Take up and read!" as St Augustine once wrote famously in his *Confessions*. But you will require too a Bible, ready to hand, that most elementary of all Christian resources, for the earlier chapters.

A Note on the title, *The Lion, the Dove, & the Lamb*. A number of years ago I often led a teaching unit on "Christian social justice". The basic material, from which all the conversation flowed, comprised the book of the prophet Amos and Dietrich Bonhoeffer's *Cost of Discipleship*, focusing notably on the Sermon on the Mount. Resources for Amos, the first canonical, writing prophet of the OT, included Alec Motyer's *The Day of the Lion*. The figure of the Lion derives from such verses as 1:2, 3:8, with the Day of the LORD/Yahweh featuring especially in 5:18–20. If the two other symbols of a dove and a lamb are reasonably straight forward, as applied to the Holy Spirit and to Jesus/the Son respectively, seeing the Father and/or the God of Israel as the lion is evoked by Amos via Motyer, and is derived from the basic sense that the missions of Jesus and the Holy Spirit in the NT fulfil, in their specific yet interrelated ways, that essential trait of the OT, the Day of the Lord/Yahweh.

Preface to the Revised Edition

READERS OF THIS BOOK, who are approaching my material for the first time, may wish to know that some people who have read both of the original editions have informed me that, in some cases, *God's Address—Living with the Triune God: A Scripture Workbook* might perhaps turn out to be the easier introduction to things trinitarian. It's ironic—but not atypical of God's ways—that the second book to be published should turn out to be in fact the first one some folk ought to read ahead of the first book. I guess it depends upon how familiar any reader is with either the New Testament itself or some of the earlier centuries of church history. True; *The Lion, the Dove, & the Lamb* does necessarily contain some vital NT material assembled in chapters 4 and 5 before we go into the details of that early church history. These chapters are also deliberately kept to a basic level, showing how those early (Jewish) Christians struggled to interpret and articulate the gospel from the beginning. Either way, yet another approach might very well be to have both books and then mix-and-match them, cutting-and-pasting chapters 4 and 5 after any reader(s) of *God's Address* has/have covered sessions 1-4. How to continue thereafter might depend upon how venturesome one is: either dive into those early centuries of the Christian church in *The Lion, the Dove, & the Lamb*, chapter 6 onwards; or stick with the more familiar territory of the NT. Although perhaps even if one does stick with this second course, one should be warned: the actual way sessions 5-9 of *God's Address* get presented, while covering seemingly familiar NT material well enough, might cause a number of surprises—I am given to understand. So be it! All in all; *Tolle! Lege!* "Take up and read!" Enjoy! And be blessed—and become a richer blessing in your practice of discipleship of the triune God, Father, Son, and Holy Spirit.

Acknowledgments

IT IS ESPECIALLY APPROPRIATE in a book exploring the nature of the Trinity to acknowledge the many people who have contributed to this project, as the seeds of an idea were sown and germinated, as the plant grew and began even to prosper. Now after a good period of time it is offered to the church public in a form that is hopefully fruitful, to itself bear more fruit, to the glory of the God whose Name is Father, Son and Holy Spirit. Consequently, my first acknowledgment is to this very God whose providential ways are so very gracious to his pilgrim people, and to myself no less.

It all began with a typical essay set by our Principal, Jim Hickinbotham, in our final year as ordinands at Wycliffe Hall, Oxford, England. In the way of many such essays, it took the form, "compare and contrast the respective merits of the psychological and social analogies of the Trinity". Curiously, I found the subsequent seminar a frustrating affair, prompting the purchase of a book released that year in English translation (my German not having really graduated much beyond school boy standards). Eberhard Jüngel's *The Doctrine of the Trinity: God's Being is in Becoming* (the first edition of *Gottes Sein ist im Werden. Verantwortliche Rede vom Sein Gottes bei Karl Barth. Eine Paraphrase*, 1964, I single out as the real starting point of our contemporary revival of things trinitarian) embarked me on a journey for which I shall be eternally grateful to Canon Hickinbotham. And there is much more for which to thank my alma mater, Wycliffe Hall. For after eight years of parish ministry in Zimbabwe, which witnessed both the closing years of a guerilla war and the beginning of newly independent government, I was able to return to do postgraduate study under the supervision of Alister McGrath. I well recall his patience, its taking the full first year before our formal sessions together were able to extend much beyond a mere half an hour: I simply ran out of adequate things to discuss profitably! Mercifully, things changed . . . I acknowledge too his kindness in furnishing now his most generous foreword to this small book, where it should be noted, he delightfully paraphrases himself the basic principle advocated by Barth and Jüngel, of our "thinking God's thoughts after him" (*Nachdenken*) and so creating "answering/responsible speech" (*Verantwortliche Rede*) about God on account of divine revelation. Further acknowledgments are due to Geoffrey and Cynthia Shaw, the then Principal and his wife, for the warm welcome extended to my family and myself, who fostered during the mid 1980s a community of staff and students where God was given such rein (reign?) to form folk rich in spirit and intellect. We are fortunate to remain in touch with many friends and colleagues from our times at Wycliffe; so thank you too for our many conversations and shared moments—your "*koinōnia* in the Gospel" no less.

Since submitting in 1988 my doctoral thesis, which tried to gain some purchase upon the then burgeoning revival of the doctrine of the Trinity, this doctrine has rightly become once more the absolute lode star of the Christian Confession. True; some of the explorations offered have encountered as much criticism as others have praise—but that too is the nature of the theological enterprise. I am grateful for having been able to continue to participate in this enterprise in both Melbourne, Australia, and now finally in New Zealand upon our family's return in 2000. There are many names to acknowledge from both countries: Charles Sherlock, Dick McKinney, John Wright, Graham Cole, Randall Prior, Peter Corney, Con Apokis, and Ivor Davidson, Murray Rae, Paul Trebilco, Rod Thompson, Martin Sutherland, John Hitchen, Myk Habets, Lynda Patterson, Don Fergus, and Hugh Bowron, especially, as well as the many other participants of STAANZ (Systematic Theology Association of Aotearoa New Zealand).

And then there's Compass NZ, now reborn after ten plus years as Venn Foundation (see http://www.venn.org.nz/ and thereafter especially the Conference tab). Here the names over the years have become extensive: Paul Henderson, Greg Fleming, Roshan and Lottie Allpress, Mark Strom, Rod Thompson (again), Andrew Shamy, Rachel Kitchens, Sam Bloore, Annette Pereira, Andrew Dwight (with John Fox customarily lurking in the background)—together with countless attendees, whose questing hearts and sharp minds have constantly brought one to the coal face of having to "translate" the Bible's Grand Story and the Christian Tradition into and with cultural forms ever more creatively, and yet hopefully faithfully, in a necessary missionary process of cross-fertilization. Just so, "mission is [truly] the mother of theology" (Martin Kähler). It is especially to this glorious crowd of twenty-first-century Christian disciples and their staunch supporters that I dedicate and offer this book. May you increasingly take delight in the One whose Name is Father, Son, and Holy Spirit, as this God takes delight in you, while you participate ever more fully in the Gospel of Jesus.

Most recently, Matthew Wimer and the team at Wipf & Stock have kindly brought these experiences of mine surrounding the Trinity into published form. My acknowledgment of them is particularly appropriate, since they have been such a competent and gracious bridge between raw manuscript and fine finished product. I and the reading public are in their debt.

In ways known and unknown, all these have contributed towards my ongoing pilgrimage to "remember, understand, and love" ever more richly our triune God, whose Life and Light, Love and Freedom is our human gift and calling. Thank you one and all! Yet last but naturally by no means least, I must acknowledge with immense gratitude and delight my immediate family: my wife Catherine, whose own medical endeavors have on occasion had to accommodate my own, knows well the many sacrifices made, as too do our four children, Anna-Marie, David, Sebastian, and Miriam, plus now two sons-in-law, Michael and Oli; thank you indeed! I hope you have enjoyed it as much as I continue to do! As we've all learned to grow through this "domestic church", it has been above all else a rich awareness of Whose arms truly embrace us that has been our gift, the joyous provision of sharing in nothing less than Father-Son-and-Holy-Spirit, together.

Christchurch, New Zealand
November 2014

Further Acknowledgments

I am grateful to those readers of both this first book of mine and its subsequent follow-up Scriptural Workbook, *God's Address—Living with the Triune God*, published in 2017, for their responses to what I wrote. In many cases, they have helped to improve the clarity of the ideas and so the texts themselves. They have pushed me also to include additional material, the extent of which prompted the possibility of these two revised editions. In particular, I am grateful to Ivor Davidson, Myk Habets and Paul Henderson, whose encouragement tipped the balance in favor of presenting the revisions to Wipf & Stock for publishing. And so lastly, I acknowledge again the staff of Wipf & Stock for their intricate handling of all the revisions: a huge "Thank-you" to them all.

Christchurch, New Zealand
October 2018

Abbreviations

CD	Barth, Karl. *Church Dogmatics*. 4 Vols. Edited by G. W. Bromiley and T. F. Torrance. Edinburgh: T&T Clark, 1956–75.
EVV	The various English versions of the Bible
GNB	Good News Bible
IJST	*International Journal of Systematic Theology*
JB	Jerusalem Bible
JTS	*Journal of Theological Studies*
ModTh	*Modern Theology*
NEB	New English Bible
NPNF	Nicene and Post-Nicene Fathers, Second Series, reprinted Grand Rapids: Eerdmans, 1975ff
NT	New Testament
OT	Old Testament
SJT	*Scottish Journal of Theology*
ST	Jenson, Robert W. *Systematic Theology*. 2 Vols. New York and Oxford: Oxford University Press, 1997/99.
TI	Jenson, Robert W. *God According to the Gospel: The Triune Identity*. Philadelphia: Fortress Press, 1982.

Introduction

As a young boy I spent hours and hours making and painting with care hundreds of plastic models—models of aircraft, from triplanes to space rockets, of all sorts of cars, of boats, from great three-masted cutters to simple patrol boats, even a knight on horse back once. You can imagine the clutter when we eventually moved house! All these scaled models represented their originals. The instructions often prided themselves on the details the manufacturers had managed to achieve. And all for the sake of young boys like myself—or so I thought at the time!

Models can take other forms. As well as being physical representations, made of a variety of materials, they can be forms of speech or mental concepts. In this respect, there is a particular link between models and metaphors; and a great deal of attention has been devoted to trying to establish just how these simple yet sophisticated human tools of communication work. "Our suggestion is that model and metaphor are closely linked; when we use a model, we *regard* one thing or state of affairs in terms of another, and when we use a metaphor, we *speak* of one thing or state of affairs in language suggestive of another."[1]

The point here is that a model need not be a form of speech at all; my airplanes certainly weren't! But in the case of speech, "a model is in essence a sustained and systematic metaphor."[2] Sallie McFague would want to stress that in metaphorical speech we have "two active thoughts which remain in permanent tension or interaction with each other."[3]

---

1. Soskice, *Metaphor*, 50–51, emphasis added.
2. McFague, *Metaphorical Theology*, 67.
3. Ibid., 37; see also 38–39: "Two points are crucial here: the indirect and tentativeness of all judgements and the structural, organizational power of metaphor." This statement sums up the way in which this figure of speech works for McFague. But N. B. Soskice's criticism of McFague regarding her interpretation of Ricoeur's notion that metaphor both "is" and "is not" (*Metaphor*, 88–90). Surely, there is something more

("The garden was awash with a sea of color": this does not mean that it was wet but that like the ever-moving sea, with its immense variety of dancing colors, so all the flowers and leaves together resembled the sea's multicolored display.) Generally therefore, we can say that a model is used to illustrate—"the one thing" by "another"—especially "when we are seeking terminology to deal with abstract states of affairs, entities and relations,"[4] as in both science and religion. We can especially see the power of metaphors when they are used, as is often the case, to interpret the unfamiliar in terms of the more familiar, when the familiar "interacts with" the unfamiliar. In particular, science uses models, and theories associated with them, in order to coordinate our grasp of otherwise diffuse and complicated sets of phenomena—especially when these ideas are novel, when the objects of study are fresh discoveries. In this way we are able to structure and order our world.[5] Similarly, theology helps us to understand certain experiences through the use of models.

We need some examples to illustrate these points. In science, we nowadays view the everyday thing we call "light" by means of two basic models. The one sees light behaving as if it were like waves (back to the sea again!); the other sees light as if it were bundles of energy called photons—a bit like a rapid fire machine gun with many bullets. Our CD players—fixed or dangling from our necks—and DVD machines then use a special form of light known as lasers, where these bullets are not scattered like some bird scaring device in a field of wheat, but are most precisely focused and coherently formed from a well-controlled source to make the waves well up together so much more strongly (the word "laser" is itself actually an acronym).

McFague is correct in saying that "the root metaphor or original model" in Christian theology is that of "personal relation."[6] God is said to be in relationship with creation, and specifically in personal relationship with this human creature. The form of this relationship is described by a series of models found in the normative writings of the Judeo-Christian experience, the Bible. The very terms "creation" and "redemption" are such models, while other examples like "covenant" or "adoption" also spring to mind. God the creator is like an artist or a potter; God is like

---

permanent about metaphor: it really can and does *re*-describe, even if often surprise!

4. Soskice, *Metaphor*, 95.

5. As well as McFague, *Metaphorical Theology*, 83–90, see Torrance, "Integration of Form," 61–105.

6. McFague, *Metaphorical Theology*, 104.

someone buying back an otherwise enslaved person or an entire people; God makes us his/her very own children such is the intensity of the care God holds for us. And when we come to trinitarian theology we are concerned with "the language of relationality *par excellence*."[7] We are saying that not only is God in relationship with humankind, but that this *external* relating—God to the world and to humans—has its "basis and prototype" (Karl Barth) *internally*, within God's very self and being.

Modeling this relationship, which is found in both God's external relationship with the human world and within God's very own being, is what this book is all about. How can we think and speak of God's relationship with us that does sufficient justice to the otherwise complicated idea of "Trinity"? I mean to say, any child at school knows that one and three are different numbers. And the phrases "three-in-one" and "one-in-three" are arithmetical nonsense. But down the centuries some rather intelligent people have dared to hold to the traditional doctrine of the Trinity as if they would die for it. Indeed, some people *have* died for this belief! And they still do . . . What *are* we to make of all this? Can we imagine a particular model, along the lines of science's waves and photons, that will help us understand—and so, please, experience (more fully)—God's relationship with us and our relationship with God. That's our goal in writing this small book.

A final introductory series of comments on how we shall be proceeding. The opening chapters are brief and tell a true story. Chapter 3 briefly sketches the reasons for the rise of trinitarian dogma. Chapter 4 then changes gear a little, starting to address some of the more complicated New Testament material, as it seeks to show how the NT church looked upon the significance of Jesus. Chapter 6 sees another gear change, signaled by the change in the title's metaphor. Here we've to tell something of the story of the missionary impact of the gospel of Jesus as Lord upon Hellenistic culture. Both these pairs of chapters (4 and 5, 6 and 7) can be seen as introductory hermeneutical exercises, suggesting how early (Jewish) Christians and classical Greco-Roman ones respectively struggled to interpret and articulate the gospel. Chapter 8 spells out an ongoing consequence of the initial settlement of Christian dogma. Finally, chapters 9 and 10 comprise two systematic treatments that interlock, presenting the proposed model of the Trinity "at work." They summarize how the model functions by exploring more fully key features of the nature of the

---

7. LaCugna, "Re-Conceiving," 13.

Christian God as Trinity by means of the model's depictions of the triune deity. All along we offer questions for reflection after each chapter, which may be used individually or in groups.

one

A Fireside Chat

It was a typical August night in Christchurch: cold, wet, and windy! Fortunately the elements outside were countered by the fire we had stoked up in our wood burner. Inside, the two of us sat on opposite small sofas in front of the mantlepiece, as other members of the family made arrangements for the evening meal.

"Would you like something to drink before we eat?" I ask my ninety-year-old mother-in-law, as she slowly sits down.

"No thank you; not yet."

Mary lives with us, in her own "howsheen," as she calls it, in typical Irish style. Most evenings she walks gingerly across the front courtyard to join us for the main family meal. That is, if we can manage a main meal together, before extracurricula activities scatter members of the family to the four winds: orchestras; debates; indoor soccer; professional enhancement sessions—you name it. Such is the lot of the modern urban family.

"And so, how was your day, then?" she asks me.

"Well, I've finally proofread my book with all its footnotes, etc. Quite a laborious and finicky job really."

"No one told me you're writing a book!" she retorts. She prides herself on keeping up with things. There is always a struggle for sections of the newspaper in our home!

"You should hear Mim on the subject!" say I. Our youngest daughter, Miriam, had for the past few weeks complained that her homework was not being discussed enough. Of course, she did not quite put it that way: "As if you haven't enough already on your plate without the *extra* work of *writing a book*!" She was right on both counts though . . .

"What's it about?" she asks.

"Oh, an academic study of the Trinity," I answer.

"But that's just a *mystery of faith*," she replies. "How can anyone say anything much about *that*?" On the one hand, she was replying as any "good Catholic" would, especially one who has such a lively faith as she. Yet on the other hand, she was quietly telling this son-in-law that perhaps there might be better uses for his time . . .

Undaunted, I typically rose to the challenge. Ours is nothing if not a robust and fond relationship. It has to be with us all living within the same *kraal*!

"Well, true enough—in the *final* analysis. But there *is also plenty* that *can* be said meanwhile, if only we can learn to speak it properly," I reply.

"What do you mean?" she asks. My wife, Cathy, reckons Mary should have been a lawyer, such is her sharp, interrogatory wit. But her family couldn't have possibly entertained such ideas at the beginning of the last century, especially in Ireland and of the eldest child of eight children. She had become a nurse, training at the Mater in Dublin.

At this point I had to find out how preparations for the meal were going: how long had we to go before eating, and so how long had I got before others were going to join the conversation. Mim had laid the table; Seb had done the bins; and Dave had just staggered back from uni footy practice—despite the weather! (Our eldest daughter is a teacher of maths, among other things, in Melbourne, her having stayed to complete her double degree there before we'd returned to Christchurch in 2000.) I had approximately four minutes. "That'll be enough," I say to Mary. I launched forth, as I had often done in confirmation classes, with teenagers and/or adult candidates who had come to Christian faith later in life.

Questions for Reflection

1. "A mystery of faith": What do you think might be the balance between acknowledging the true mystery of God on the one hand, and yet faith also seeking genuine understanding on the other?

2. Down the centuries one definition of theology has been just that, faith seeking understanding.[1] Yet even here it is not just a case of any old human faith, as if it were "faith in faith" almost. Rather, authentic Christian faith has its true Object—"God with us"; "the Word become flesh"; "God [was] in Christ, reconciling the world to himself." So; as we attend carefully to Jesus, then we might be able to apprehend more of God's Ways with us. What understanding might you have of your own faith and God's Ways?

---

1. This definition is derived from the second century BC Greek translation of Isaiah 7:9 (which differs somewhat from the standard Hebrew version), "If you do not believe, you will not understand," which in turn was translated into Latin at the end of the fourth century AD. Thereafter, Augustine, who wrote in Latin, was very fond of this verse and used it often: "Unless you believe, you shall not understand." His practice gave rise to the expression, "faith seeking understanding."

two

Elementary Trinitarian Speech

BEFORE I RELATE MY typical precis of things trinitarian, I should also explain that Mary has been living with us now for nearly five years. The original intention had been for both her husband, Robert, and her to live with us, to spend their final days in the relative safety and comfort of Christchurch, as opposed to Harare in Zimbabwe, which was descending into increasing states of anarchy and political tyranny—no fit place for old folks at all. But sadly Robert, after a marriage of fifty-four years, and life together in the one house they had built in 1953, had died after a long illness before the family cottage had been completed, and we had moved into the new main house. She had come by herself, but nonetheless to the huge relief of all concerned.

"Before you married your beloved Robert, what was the old fashioned word for your unmarried state?" I ask.

"I was a spinster, I suppose," she immediately replies.

"And Robert was a footloose and fancy-free bachelor boy," says I, laughing. She musters a smile and a twinkle—for I know I am treading on holy ground here, which was going to get holier still before we were done.

"And when you finally got married after the war and all, what did you become and what did he become? What are the names for each of you?"

"Wife and husband, of course!"

"Exactly! Within the reality of marriage, there are precisely husbands and wives," says I. "The word 'wife' *implies* the word 'husband,' and vice versa, as and when two people get married. This is what 'marriage' means. And good old Christian tradition—after the story of Genesis which Jesus takes up too—declares that these 'two' *become* 'one' in the single business of marriage. Nothing too complicated or mysterious about that really. Well, at *one* level any way!"

"Now, when Robert died"—and the ground suddenly became exquisitely holy and painful and beautiful all at the one time—"what were you now called, now that the marriage no longer existed?"

"I'm a widow now," she says slowly, with quiet dignity. And we both pause briefly to ponder the enormity of it all . . .

"And it's remarkably similar with the trinitarian God," I say. "The very word 'God' means, in the Christian scheme of things, that there are three identities to the divine reality. Within the reality of marriage—what makes marriage marriage—*are* the mutually constituting persons of husband-and-wife, wife-and-husband, with the wife uniquely complementing the husband and the husband uniquely complementing the wife, so too within the triune God there simply *are* Father-Son-and-Holy-Spirit. These 'persons' are all necessarily bound up together in their specifically complementary relationships one with the other. The problem is—and has been for many a century if the truth be known, given the 'slipperiness' of the third one, the Holy Spirit—how to have, how to express, three and only three such 'persons' necessarily tied and related uniquely to one another. And not just in any old way, any old fashion or other, but according to how God has actually gone about showing *himself*—if I can use that male term of the moment—*to be, to exist in his unique divine manner of being*."

"The story of Jesus, as recounted in the pages of Scripture, gives us a model of how God is necessarily related as *two* such 'persons.' The word 'Father' implies the word 'Son,' and 'Son' implies 'Father'—just as the word 'child' has to convey necessarily 'parent.' Well, usually, if we forget about modern hi-tech non-human forms of reproduction, for the moment. Is there a way of describing and so speaking about God's being among us which links together all *three, and* only *these three*, 'persons'? That's the sixty-four thousand dollar question!"

"And I suppose you're going to tell me there is!" she throws out.

"Yes! Exactly! Nor am I making it up. There, from the pages of the Bible, we can discern a specific pattern of how these three divine identities actually operate, as and when Jesus comes among us and does and says what he does. There's a given flow, as it were, to God's varied but joint activity on earth. Notice how Jesus is conceived by the power of the Spirit in Mary's womb. Notice especially the events at the Jordan during Jesus' baptism: the Father sends the Holy Spirit to rest upon Jesus, calling him in that very process 'beloved Son.' Then, throughout Jesus' ministry, he is enabled to be the messiah he is, the human being he is, the very identity he is, because of the Holy Spirit given by the Father. Notice even how the letter to the Hebrews states that Jesus offered himself to the Father 'through the eternal Spirit' (9:14). Supremely, we see Jesus being resurrected by the Father through the power of the Holy Spirit (Rom 1:4). And once Jesus has ascended to the supreme executive position of God—as God's 'Right Hand Man'—so he then pours out, shares, this same Holy One with us (Acts 2:32–33). We too become sons and daughters, children of the one heavenly Father in *the* Son, Jesus, due to our sharing *the* Gift of the Holy Spirit. Do you follow?"

"To be sure; all three are doing what *each* one does, in their *own* way—I think—but all together at one and the same time, jointly," she answers briefly. The meal was just about on the table . . .

"And what they are all doing can be summarized through the single idea of 'giving.' We have the Father as the Giver, the Holy Spirit as the Gift, and Jesus the Son as the Recipient. All three are required for 'giving' to be a single, complete, and entire reality—and only these three form, are necessary for constituting, what 'giving' or 'donation' is all about. Instead of husbands-and-wives in the marriage thing, we have in the divine reality, completely and fully, Giver-Gift-Recipient (or GGR for short). And this scheme follows a crucial pattern of the divine activity when God comes to earth. That's what 'God' means: the event of God giving himself to himself. Or as I say more formally in my book, the reiterative event during which God gives himself to himself. It's like God 'repeats' Godself during his own self-determining and self-fulfilling life of self-relating being."

Just as I was possibly losing her with the technicalities of the last expression, Mim calls out—in her inimitable school French accent, "à table!"—a phrase she picked up when we went as a family to Europe and visited our dear old friends whom my family had known for over forty years. "Bring Granny will you . . ." I got up from my sofa and helped Mary shuffle her way through the arch that divides the family room from the kitchen area where we usually eat. As we made it slowly across the room, she summarized her reaction: "very interesting . . ." To which I was not quite sure how to respond, but knew she'd be "pondering" it most of the night, like her namesake, Jesus' mother.

Questions for Reflection

3. "To ponder": twice in Luke's gospel we see Mary pondering/thinking deeply upon the Ways of God (2:19, 51). What sorts of things have you pondered over in your faith journey so far? What do you yourself bring to such pondering? And how are you expecting this book to add grist to this mill, this pondering, this milling of trinitarian theology, of faith seeking understanding?

three

Joining Some Dots

I suspect many a reader can recall when, as a child, they were given a coloring book. Some pages were blank for a free-for-all, swirling and scribbling at will, with whatever colors and shapes that took their fancy. Then some other pages had a string of numbers printed on them, scattered—or so it seemed at first—all around the page. The trick was to find the number 1, and then number 2, and so on, joining the numbered dots, one after the other. Eventually, specific shapes began to emerge, and a picture along with them: an old woman on a chair, a cat with her kittens, a dog with a bone. The sense of discovery was exciting and fun—and tricky! For sticking to the proper sequence of dots and forming the correct shapes sometimes did not quite work out as it should . . . Another exercise, on other pages of the book, was to be presented with a black and white outline picture already formed, but with numbers this time within sections of outlined shapes: 1 = black; 2 = yellow; 3 = blue; 4 = red; and so on. So pick up the relevant crayon and fill in the bits, little by little. This too could be tricky, sticking to the allotted areas and keeping the colors within the designated boundaries: no blurring of the colors, which if it occurred distorted the proper kaleidoscopic outcome.

This chapter will look at some potentially tricky features of the doctrine of the Trinity. And I have deliberately chosen such elementary analogies to illustrate the kinds of tricky things that sometimes (often?) go wrong when people try to understand what this doctrine is itself trying to portray. The picture becomes unduly distorted or jumbled when we do not pay careful enough attention to joining the dots or coloring in properly with the right crayon. But before we open the "coloring book" and set to work, it would be advisable to outline some basic things about doctrine itself, about what it is that doctrine generally is seeking to achieve within Christianity.

An initial way into this discussion is to compare the relationship between doctrine and dogma, and between doctrine and theology. For by and large these three aspects of the Christian intellectual task—although in fact doctrine has wider functions and sources than simply the intellectual[1]—are often not carefully distinguished enough, even if there is a clear link among them.

A Russian church historian by the name of Bolotov has distinguished three levels of authority with regards to the Christian faith as follows:

1. Dogmas, to which all believers are obliged to adhere.
2. "Theologoumena," being beliefs and their expressions which are probable, and so authoritative, but not absolutely in the form of 1.
3. Theological opinions, which may be useful/helpful but lack due authority—until/unless for reasons of need they come into focus and are adopted by e.g., a church council.

At all three levels, theology, in a general sense, has been at work. Yet the results of this work within a specific community, the church, has been elevated to the point where this church community now seeks to firmly and formally *identify itself* by adherence to certain doctrinal formulae as *dogmas*. An example is the Nicene Creed, which was composed by two fourth-century church councils, the one at Nicaea in 325 and the other at Constantinople in 381. Formally promulgated by yet another council in 451 at Chalcedon, this creed performs a number of key functions. (Later chapters will go into the story of the emergence of this creed in much greater detail; the following is sufficient for the moment.)

In 325 at Nicaea the bishops of the church and other representatives concluded that Jesus of Nazareth, while being *a particular human being*, born "from/of the Virgin Mary" and "crucified under Pontius Pilate," who both comes into existence and now dies like any other, and so is a specific human actor in the drama of history, was and is nevertheless *simultaneously God*. To distinguish his identity from God more generally, they used the parental metaphor of Father-and-Son, stating that

---

1. See for example McGrath, *Genesis of Doctrine*, and at a more introductory level, McGrath, *Understanding Doctrine*.

this Son was "*homoousios* with the Father." The first metaphor was taken straight from the New Testament: e.g. Matt 11:25–27 and John's gospel. The second, non-biblical word, coined from the philosophical language of the day, was put to service to achieve two key things. Jesus' identity, while that of a human creature on the one hand, was and is nevertheless also divine on the other hand; he stands on the *other side* of the creature/Creator divide *as Creator*, "begotten (of the Father), not made." But while Jesus was and is "wholly God" ("God of God, Light of Light, true God of true God"), he is not all there is to "God"; there is more to the divine reality than Jesus alone. And this "more" the creed goes on to spell out, firstly as "Father Almighty," and then subsequently, after more controversial decades, in 381 at Constantinople, as "the Holy Spirit, the Lord, the giver of life, who proceeds from the Father, who with the Father and the Son is co-worshipped and co-glorified." "Deity" is now to be viewed as being formally constituted by the dynamic relationships among these three. "Dogma" has been established.[2]

Nor should we see this fourth century move by the early church to be a novelty. Quite the opposite in fact is the case. For we can now say categorically more happened in the hearts and minds of the earliest Christians in the first twenty to thirty years of the church (approximately AD 30–60, i.e., the very first generation) than happened thereafter in 350 years. For at root, we have right from the earliest documents of the New Testament expressions that grant due honor to Jesus *as if he were "somehow"* on a par *with Yahweh*, the One and Only God of the Jews (Deut 6:4)—and so is *worthy of all worship*. It is the business of worship, and worship from within originally a Jewish context what's more, that gives us the key to unlock how it was that the earliest followers of Jesus came to place him alongside the God of the Covenant of the Hebrew Scriptures.[3] In other words, the dogmatic creeds of the fourth century

---

2. See Lonergan, *Way to Nicea*, viii: "[A]nte-Nicene thought was propelled by two distinct though related determinants. The explicit issue was christological, and to this the major writers explicitly adverted. But underpinning it and going forward without any explicit advertence on anyone's part, there was a far profounder matter: the emergence and the development of dogma, which began indeed at Nicea but continued down the centuries." See too Jenson, *ST 1*, VI, 35–9.

3. It would take us longer than we have space for here to substantiate this line of thinking. Suffice to mention four resources: Hengel, *Son of God*; Dunn, *Making*; Bauckham, *God Crucified*; Hurtado, *Lord Jesus Christ*; Bauckham amplifies his study in *Jesus and the God of Israel*. To be sure; Dunn, *Did the First Christians Worship Jesus?* makes some subtle qualifications to this simple summary given here.

were only formally acknowledging, and in language appropriate to their cultural setting,⁴ what was already known concretely and experientially to be the case among members of the NT church.

From the point of view of our analogies with which we began this chapter, a number of dots have been made to appear on the page by all these moves. Dot number one is that this Jesus, who tramped around Palestine in the first decades of the first century, getting dust between his toes, and who seemed for all intents and purposes to be a human being, was and is, in fact, divine, the Creator. Alongside is dot two, quickly to be joined to dot one, for we cannot separate these two dots. Indeed; there's a third dot also next door to be joined up just as quickly. All together now, these three dots, when joined, create a "space," to be colored in, as properly and formally establishing what Christians *mean* by the word G–O–D. The Nicene Creed declares one crucial dogmatic stance of the Christian faith: "God" = "Father–Son–and–Holy–Spirit."

Just as crucial though is the conclusion reached by the later council at Chalcedon. Here they sought to address not so much the problem of what constitutes deity, of how to bring to speech and thought the significance of Jesus for understanding "God," but how to think Jesus as being both–divine–and–human *all at once*; that is, of his being "one and the same" person, Jesus, who is simultaneously human–and–divine. Here the problem was less the question of the Trinity as the question of Christology—or was it? For I am reminded at just this point of a remark made by Bishop Stephen Neill. That the doctrine of the Trinity is not so much about the nature of God as about the identity of a particular human being—that he was/is God; and concomitantly, Christology is not so much about the nature of Christ as about God—that God is free/able to become a human being. This dual comment reinforces the fact that trinitarian and christological concerns are the flip–side of each other. It is this very fact that enables me to propose our new trinitarian model. For it is by attending carefully to the pattern of the divine activity in the historical mission of the human being, Jesus, that we are able to construct the model for understanding trinitarian deity that I am proposing. Moreover, this pattern of divine activity involves comprehensively the Father, the Holy Spirit, and the Son; all three "persons" are to be traced, and traced all together, in the mission of Jesus and its aftermath. And when they are

---

4. For a technical essay, which summarizes much of the story, see Pannenberg, "Appropriation," 119–83.

so traced, we may come up with the GGR model I have briefly sketched already above.

Speaking of "tracing patterns" leads to one final point. Irenaeus, who was Bishop of Lyons AD c. 130–c. 200, spoke of God's own two "hands," "his Word and his Wisdom, the Son and the Spirit" (*Adversus Haereses*, 4.20.1), by whose *direct mediation* God engaged the world of which he was the Creator, Ruler, and Redeemer. It is by means of this Word-and-Spirit that he has established the divine Economy,[5] the programme of salvation to which Scripture is the unique and specific written witness. The first figure below begins to set out the picture. But things are not quite as straightforward as Irenaeus initially expresses it; or rather, the seeming parallel between this first diagram and the notion of "two divine hands" is only partially the case. For God's economy of salvation is more complex in its execution. Diagrammatically, we need to add two key elements: (1) the Father sends the Son *in the power of the Holy Spirit* is the first thing; (2) next, we also need to note the Father sends the Spirit *through the Son*. Galatians 4:4–6 captures an element of this added richness, which we shall be examining later. The point of all this is to recognise that my model primarily focusses on the second diagram's left-hand side. How we might trace the pattern of the right-hand side, with God's sending the Spirit through the Son, we shall have to address differently and later.

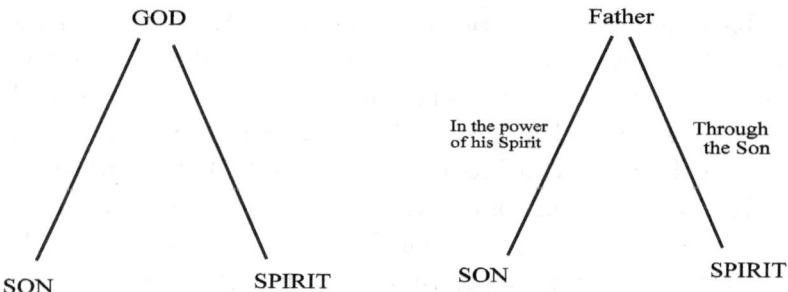

Figure 1: A diagram of Irenaeus' "The Two Hands of God"

Figure 2: A modified diagram based on the Economy of Salvation

5. Sanders, *Triune God*, constructs his entire approach around these two communicative divine missions of Word and Spirit, as expressed in the Incarnation and Pentecost. Figure 1 encapsulates this approach. Figure 2 supplements elements which appear to be overlooked by Sanders however, given his singular emphasis on these two distinct missions. This is unfortunate, as his book is among the very best introductions to the doctrine of the Trinity available.

> **Questions for Reflection**
>
> 4. "Dogma": Nowadays it's considered pretty non-PC to be "dogmatic." Yet we also extol the right of everyone to their "opinions," it would seem. What's really going on here? For what it's worth, my own opinion (*sic*) is that the root question is one of authority. Built into that word "authority" is the word "author": questions of authority raise issues of *sources*; where do we get certain key notions *from*? Christian dogma is ranked where it is due to the church's recognition that here we have to do with *God's revelation. Lose this idea,* that the Christian faith is actually not just "a good idea," but is rather a response to who God is and what he has done—what *he* has *initiated*—and it's pretty well all over.
>
>   What do you think? Why? How might you *legitimate/justify* your opinions?

four

More Dots and Some Colors

THIS CHAPTER SEEKS TO summarize two sets of answers to two sets of basic questions that understandably quickly arose as Christianity spread across the ancient Mediterranean world. For, as we said in the previous chapter, more happened in the hearts and minds of the earliest Christians in the first twenty to thirty years of the church, in the very first generation, than happened thereafter in 350 years. The first set has to do with Jesus and his identity, and the second, being the corollary, with thereafter the new understanding of deity this provoked, which we term Trinity.

Built into Israelite and so Jewish understandings of the world is a certain sense of *history*. The God of the Israelites, who gave his name as "Yahweh" according to Exodus chapter 3 and Moses' encounter with the burning bush, was preeminently seen to be the Lord of history. Indeed, the name has about it a certain futuristic sense: "you will know I am Yahweh (Who I Am), as and when I myself perform such and so."[1] While, to be sure, this understanding took centuries to develop (with Isaiah 40-66 being an absolute standout section to ponder, which the earliest Christians seem to have squeezed for all their worth), it entailed supremely the following. God, as the Creator of all the world and Lord of all the nations, who had also called the People of Israel for a special role among the nations of the world, would, in due time and in his own way, duly establish his purposes for the world he has made and continues to sustain—*despite* and *precisely in the face of* all obstacles to the contrary.

---

1. The temptation to make this opening section an extensive piece of biblical theology is great; but I shall desist. See only Zimmerli, *I am Yahweh*, and LaCocque and Ricoeur, "Exodus 3:14," 307–61.

The world's history would eventually reach its fulfillment, in this world. Yet this belief was, for all that, pretty hard to hold onto in the face of actual events during the last, say, four hundred years leading up to the time of Jesus' birth. One effect of this profound ambivalence which pervaded the Jewish nation, who both felt utterly called of God and yet who had, on the surface at least, not much to show for it, was a strong, emerging sense of *expectation*.

The prophets of old had, in their day, spoken of Yahweh having his own unique day—some time, eventually, up ahead, on the distant horizon of human history. But *here and now* things are reaching a *climax*—**this** *was the Christian claim*! This is why the earliest accounts of the significance of Jesus' story and mission all seek to tie his identity in with an overarching narrative of God's relationship with the world, and how that relationship specifically pans out through Israel. Whether it is the beginning of Mark's gospel, 1:1–15, which is quite probably the earliest example of this form of Jesus–gospel–biography, or a slice of an early Christian creed-like confession used by Paul in his letter to the Galatians 4:4–6, the crux is this: the Creator God and Lord of History is *now* decisively *on the move*. "Somehow" Yahweh is bringing all things together through this unique agent, Jesus of Nazareth: all wrongs will be righted and everything will become appropriately aligned, with the true nature of the world coming to pass; God will be openly viewed by all people as *the* Source and Author of all, with his being in a fresh and lively, sovereign relationship with human beings. The universal scope of the gospel message quickly meant problems with the parent, Judaism. Yet it was also from within this very mother religion that the earliest followers first took their bearings (indeed, had to take their bearings), seeking to understand what had happened in their midst, and how it had come to pass this way. What Christians term the Old Testament + the Apocrypha was the written resource, the interpretive grid they brought to bear upon these events (see e.g. Luke 24:27, 44).[2]

To cut a long and complicated story short (which very story and its reconstruction(s) puts bread on the tables of NT scholars and populists alike!), I will select some key parts of the NT to show what was afoot in those early days of Christianity's development. Firstly we will look at Philippians 2:6–11, then John 1:1–18, and lastly the book of Revelation, chapters 4 and 5, as these focus on Jesus and his relationship with God

2. See Childs' wonderful opening chapter, "Early Reception," 1–31; the demanding but rewarding Watson, *Paul,* and notably Hays, *Echoes.*

as his "Father." We will then conclude this chapter with an overview of the two volume work known as Luke–Acts and elements of Paul's letters to show how God was active via *both* this man Jesus *and* the Holy Spirit *together*. Indeed; it is this very joint activity of Son-and-Spirit that prompted Irenaeus towards the end of the second century to speak of God's two "hands," "his Word and Wisdom, the Son and the Spirit" (*Adv. Haer.* 4.20.1), as we've seen.

Philippians 2:6–11

Much ink has been spilt by scholars and commentators over the years in their attempts to unpack the significance of these verses in this late letter of Paul's to a Christian community he founded in 49 or the early 50s (see the story in Acts 16).[3] In a way, it is a thank–you letter, written in response to a gift they had sent by the hand of Epaphroditus (Phil 2:25–30, 4:10–20), and who himself was part of their gift as an assistant for Paul while he was in prison (possibly in Rome). Yet, being Paul, their apostle in the faith, whose ministry among them meant a unique "partnership in the Gospel" (Phil 1:5), it could not be a mere note! No; such was their joint "citizenship in heaven" (Phil 3:20–21), embraced with eagerly anticipated "joy" on account of Jesus' completed task when he came to fulfill his heavenly Father's mission, that Paul simply had to convey far more than his thanks for a gift. And what he conveyed we today too are recipients and heirs of.

Naturally, this passage, which reads every bit like a hymn such is its poetic structure, and which Paul either composes himself or adapts from an existing source, has an immediate context. Paul places the hymn where he does as part of an overall argument, which in this case runs from Phil 2:1 down to v. 13. For Paul is not only concerned his dear friends in Philippi appreciate properly their own struggles with *outsiders* which they presently find themselves experiencing (this he does by conveying his own experience and understanding of his own problematic situation, 1:12–30); he wishes above all else that they embody properly *among themselves* the gospel and so *truly* "participate in it" (1:5). To the

---

3. See especially Martin, *Hymn of Christ*, and Martin and Dodd, *Where Christology Began*. See too Wright, "Jesus Christ is Lord," 56–98, and "The One God of Israel, Freshly Revealed," esp. 680–89: "Paul's christological revision of Israel's monotheism of divine identity has taken place at its key eschatological moment. *This is what it looked like when YHWH returned to Zion*" (683 emphasis original).

fore is Paul's desire for the Christians of Philippi to be united. But how might such unity be an appropriate expression of the very gospel of Jesus? For there is unity, and there is unity, different forms of unity based on different understandings of the nature of the world, of reality itself even.

Paul offers a strong fourfold appeal: "if . . . then . . ." (2:1). Each of the conditions alone is a key feature of the Christian life; together they multiply Paul's sense of urgency. For unity in the gospel is absolutely paramount in his mind. So too is the result: "Think alike. Love alike. Be of one soul. Be of one mind." And Paul's "joy" in his friends, who are also his apostolic children in the faith, will be "complete." Yet he is not yet done. Six consequences arise. "Rivalry" has already been mentioned, in 1:17; then "vain-glory" is the exact opposite to a number of references to appropriate Godlike glory, in 1:11, 2:11, 4:19 and 20. These two negatives are then countered by the next four positives: appropriately, "act rather with humility" starts the list;[4] which means "considering others better than yourselves"; so that "each of you must look not to your own interests, but [rather] to the interests of others."

And why all this? Because this way or "mind-set" (this is a crucial word/motif in this letter: 1:7; 2:2 (twice), 5; 3:15 (twice), 19; 4:2, 10 (twice) expresses especially the Humble Way of Christ, in whom the Philippians, *as Christians*, have their very existence, v. 5 (NEB): "Let your bearing towards one another arise out of your life in Christ Jesus." Here we have a reference to baptism/incorporation "into Christ Jesus," who himself supremely demonstrates such [encouragement to] humility and unselfishness, and which we now have displayed in this hymn to Christ with due majesty and glory.

The thrust of vv. 6-11 is this. Contrary to what one might have expected (as being the implication of being "in the form of God," of being in possession of all the characteristics and qualities belonging to God), Jesus refused to take advantage of/"exploit" [the NRSV has the translation correct among all the EVV] his divine status for himself, but rather

---

4. Already in the OT the note is struck: God chooses the unimportant and the insignificant for his plans (1 Kgs 18:23; Ps 119:67, 71; Jdt 9:11; Wis 2:3); God saves the lowly and humble (Ps 18:27); God looks upon the lowly (Ps 113:7-9); God pays attention to the prayers of the lowly (Ps 102:17); God gives grace to the lowly while he opposes scoffers (see Isa 2:11; Ezek 17:24). Lowliness and humility are thus evaluated as positive virtues by the Bible, especially as they affect the way in which people behave towards others and in which they approach God (see Isa 57:15). Jesus simply brings all this to its supreme climax, and all of which is in *stark contrast* to the classical Greco-Roman world which effectively despised humility.

precisely took the significance of that status to mean his pursuing a life of self-abnegation and humility. For he "emptied himself, taking the form of a slave," in total obedience to the true calling of humanity—as was supposed to be the case with firstly Adam, and then Israel; for Adam *did* "grasp" at what was not his by right, while Israel also failed to live up to its calling, which was to be the means of addressing Adam's disobedience/fault.

Just so (v. 9), in *vindication* of Jesus' path of obedient, redemptive suffering and shameful, penal death—as being indeed the most *appropriate* vehicle for *both* the divine self-revelation, of *God's* true holy love in action, *and human* existence, rather than being merely some reward or recompense for his labors: "therefore (that is why) God" freely and sovereignly declares this human being to be indeed *on a par with himself*, the Creator of all the earth and everything in it, and Ruler of all history and all peoples.

We need to note the two verbs with Jesus as subject—"empty/pour out" and "humbled"—in the first part, and then the two with God as subject—"super-exalt and bestow/confer"—in the second, as they divide up the hymn perfectly, designating too its basic meaning.

A full Christology is compressed into one here. As well as being the authentic revelation of God, Jesus declares the true nature and destiny of humanity (so e.g., Pss 8 and 110, Gen 1, and Dan 7). The Lord of all has become the humble and humiliated Servant of all: this is the revelation of Jesus. For only the Servant of all may be the sovereign Lord of all, such is the true nature and identity of the God of "grace and truth."

It is well worth noting the following details.

"It is He Who . . ." would be a formal beginning. "Consider" (NIV), "regard" (NRSV), "count" (RSV), "consider/reckon" (GNB), "deem," is the same Greek word as both 2:3 and 3:7, 8, and then 2:25. NRSV's "exploited" makes much better sense than "grasped" (NIV) or "snatched" (NEB) or "by force" (GNB). The JB's "cling to" seems to suggest that his "emptying himself" (v. 7) means somehow his divinity was "given up/surrendered"—which is exactly wrong; the summary above suggests quite the opposite: that vv. 7–8 supremely *reveal* the true significance of "deity," *affirmed* by the events of vv. 9–11.

"But": implies the sheer *contrast* with v. 6. There's a certain irony to "likeness" and "appearance"—for what are *real* people like, how might we "recognize" them, who has seen a *real* human being? "Servant": literally, slave (as in 1:1 as well), which is reinforced by "death on a cross," since crucifixion was reserved in Roman law for both slaves and Roman traitors. Such humiliation results from Jesus' "humility" (see too 2:3, which verse puns as well with "empty"). "Emptied" echoes "poured out his soul to death" (Isa 53:12), since Jesus' death was *his* choice, his act of obedience, while death is *our* no-escaping-fate.

V. 9 "Super-exaltation": Paul compounds verbs with *hyper* often [20/28 in the NT]; here uniquely with "exalt" as the greatest possible superlative! Note also "exalt" echoes once more Isaiah, here 52:13. The "Name above every name" suggests to Jewish ears the "all excelling Name of Yahweh"—which is then spelt out explicitly in vv. 10–11; see below. John 17:11–12, 24, together with 8:58, express similar ideas to vv. 9–11.

There's a *twofold* purpose to God's action, as summarized earlier. (See, too, Acts 2:36 and 16:18; and *especially* Ps 110:1, the most quoted piece of the OT in NT, which is the basic background here.)

V. 10 is the ultimate sticking point for any Jehovah's Witness! *See Isa 45:18–25 and 48:11* where Yahweh's Glory is singularly his and his alone.[5] So; what's the hymn doing *ascribing this now* to the human being, Jesus, as the bearer of this singular Name and its uniquely associated Glory?

V. 11 "Lord" is literally *kyrios* in the Greek. Yet this is crucial, since the Septuagint Greek translation of the Hebrew OT used this word of YHWH, the very point behind the Isaiah references. See, too, Rom 10:9–13; 1 Cor 11:23; 12:3; 16:22.

And when we come to "glory," we need to see that Jesus has now *redefined* this *uniquely divine* trait. For the upshot of the entire hymn is that, via the exalted Name of Yahweh—the now shared Name—the identity of "Jesus" and the identity of "God" are to be seen to constitute one another.[6]

---

5. For a detailed examination of the significance of these verses, see Goldingay and Payne, *Isaiah*, 2:49–62, 134–35; and North, *Second Isaiah*, 155–62, 130 re 43:25's similar "monotheistic formula" to 48:11.

6. Hill, *Paul and the Trinity*, importantly directs us to Paul's "'bi-directionality' of God-talk" (and subsequently the "tri-directionality" of such God-talk with the inclusion of the Holy Spirit) with his two seminal chapters, "God in relation to Jesus," and "Jesus in relation to God," 49–75 and 77–134. "In order to identify Jesus, it is necessary to refer to God, *but also*, in order to identify God it is necessary to refer to Jesus. *Mutuality*, rather than a unilateral movement (in either direction), is the watchword here," 49–50, emphasis original. Hill will go on to stress also the *"asymmetry"* within such mutuality of the Father-Son relationship, which allows for "the full interdependence of 'God the Father' and 'Jesus Christ' on one another for the distinct identities of each but *not* their *interchangeability*," 135, emphasis original. See also the Excursus, pages 70–77.

Rounding off the immediate context, we conclude by reviewing the significance of 2:12–13, which ties in with vv. 1–4, all of which has Paul exhorting his friends to live a life of *mutual submission among themselves* after the example of Jesus, into whom after all they have been baptized (so v. 5).

"Well then, my beloved friends . . ." Note the way Paul links the paragraphs, and his form of intimate address. The gist is: "Obediently embrace *again* the demands of the Gospel as you *once* did *and* through me . . ."; see 1:27 for the first mention of the idea of "presence/absence." "Work out" has the ring of "thoroughness/completion" about it—which *is* achievable: "for God . . ." grants both the "desire" and the "power" (literally, "work" once more).

"Working out/in" is deliberately cooperative; it importantly parallels as well the dynamic mutuality of Father and Jesus/Son, whose own work is supremely "salvation" (see 1:19, 28).

For the distinctive phrase, "fear and trembling," see 1 Cor 2:3, 2 Cor 7:15, Eph 6:5, and Eph 5:18–21, all of which describe a vital form of person-to-person stance, that of humility, as per the very Savior himself.

God's exaltation of Jesus *affirms* his *act of humbly emptying himself* to be indeed *the form of fullest divine revelation*: what are the implications of this "kenoticism" (self-emptying) for the Christian understanding of the *very nature* of God?

John 1:1–18

The opening prologue to the Fourth Gospel is just far too rich and expansive in its meaning for us to pick up on every detail here.[7] Instead, I'll be noting only those key elements that impact upon our main topic of the doctrine of the Trinity and how it emerged, and its significance for us.

There have been many attempts to explain how these 18 verses—and even if it is in fact these verses or less—might have been arranged. For my money, the best approach is to see them as broadly having a hymnic form, with some interpolations, and being constructed around a staircase literary pattern. This means firstly that the writer has taken a pre-existing hymn to Christ as Wisdom, patterned on the OT and echoing forcibly

---

7. See Hengel, "Prologue," 265–94. Generally, see Thompson, *God of the Gospel of John*, esp.189–226, chapter 5, "The Worship of God."

Gen 1:1 and Wisdom's role in Creation. The first five verses in particular are especially tightly formed:

> In the beginning was the Word,
> and the Word was with God,
> and what God was, the Word was;
> This One was with God in the beginning.

Then we have:

> All things came into being through him,
> and without him not one thing came into being.
> What has come into being in him was life,
> and the life was the light of all people.
> The light shines in the darkness,
> and the darkness has not overcome/mastered it.[8]

The second noun of each line becomes the first of the next line, building as a stairway; yet overall the opening two verses also double back on themselves to form another structure known as a chiasm, where the central idea (here "God") is accentuated, by having ideas and words both before and after arranged in parallel, either as a complement or contrast.

Next we should note how the very first phrase picks up on a key philosophical issue for the Hellenistic world: ἐν ἀρχῇ = *en archē*/in the beginning. For they debated endlessly the question of what was/is the First Principle or Source of All Things, the Unoriginate Origin of All. Then we can add to this the common enough usage of λόγος = *logos*/word to often depict that very thing that bound together the cosmos and all things within it, as well as referring to the rational element in humans. And so, we have a writer who seeks deliberately, through his judicious use of common words and ideas, to bridge the Jewish world of the OT and ancient Mediterranean culture.

Thereafter we have: "the Word *was*" being parallel to "the Word *became*"; "the Word was *with (pros) God*" being parallel to "dwelt *among (en) us*"; and, "the Word was *God*" being parallel to "the Word became *flesh*." These shifts are striking. For the truth of the God of the Christian Scriptures is, as we saw earlier in the Stephen Neill quote, that he is free to become a human being. The sheer actuality of the Incarnation indicates

---

8. Translation taken from Culpepper, *Gospel and Letters of John*, 113, with "mastered" added from Moffat's translation.

the divine possibility. The significance of this is crucial. For it is often suggested the idea of the Incarnation, of God's becoming human, is like trying to square a circle—which is supposed to be impossible in principle. Yet perhaps what is wrongheaded is this very approach, the assumption about what constitutes deity at all at all. Rather than *predefine* deity as being the *opposite* of the finite world as we experience it, the gospel simply declares the fact, the reality, the actuality of Jesus being divine—from which basis or premise we are to think and speak and live thereafter. The infinite God has become this human being, Jesus; the Creator of all has become this creature.

This line of thinking propels us quite quickly down the line of having to construct some kind of trinitarian idea or concept. But we also need to be quite nuanced as well. While Jesus is wholly God, no one Person alone is all there is to God; there is "more" to deity than this Jesus. Which drives us to have to consider both "the Father" and "the Holy Spirit" as *also* constituting deity. The trick then becomes how to think all three together—as one yet three, as three yet one . . . The Christian faith remains resolutely monotheistic even as it simultaneously declares the full deity of Jesus, who is also fully human.

We are not quite done even now with this glorious prologue. Two further features should concern us. Firstly, like any good Jewish writer who knows well his OT, John not only echoes Wisdom Literature to depict Jesus' identity, but also uses profound temple imagery, imagery which will reappear throughout the Fourth Gospel to make additional points. When the EVV translate (v. 14): "and the Word became flesh and dwelt among us, and we beheld his glory . . .," we miss the literal echo when the word "dwell" is actually "tabernacled." For the Tabernacle of Exodus was the original *dwelling place* of the divine *glory*—so Exod 25:8, 29:44–46, and Exod 40:34–35. Thereafter of course we have both the Solomonic temple, 1 Kgs 8, and the visionary temple of Ezekiel, chapters 40–48, as part of this OT imagery. All this declares with great profundity and brevity how Jesus is simply the *meeting place* between Yahweh and people hereafter; this is the point of the gospel; in Jesus, heaven and earth overlap and are now being brought together.[9] Moreover, such a meeting

---

9. Perrin, *Jesus the Temple*, importantly situates Jesus' ministry in the context of first century Jewish counter-temple movements. It also claims this was Jesus' own view of himself, that he was the true fulfillment of all that the temple and its cultus represented. See too Black, *God's Address*, 13–15, 18–19, and notably Beale, *The Temple and the Church's Mission*, which elaborates well Perrin's thesis.

place is from now on the place of blessing, "full of grace and truth," where this expression captures the archetypal blessing of Exod 34:6 (see too Mic 7:18-19), via the key covenant terms *hesed* (steadfast-love/mercy) and *'emet* (faithfulness/truth/constancy) in Hebrew, which stand behind the two Greek terms.

Yet there is, secondly, another key feature to highlight. Perhaps too it is the highlight of the entire thing—if we run with the suggestion the entire 18 verses are arranged via a chiasmic pattern. Here the center becomes Jesus giving people the "power/authority/right to become children of God" (v. 12b, own translation):

> But to as many as received him,
> he gave to them power/authority/the right to become children of God,
> to those who believed in his Name.

In the first instance, "to receive Jesus" is to *welcome* him as the Logos. Yet this is further amplified by the subsequent expression "to believe in his Name." This kind of language is unique to John's Gospel and stresses the unique identity of Jesus: he and he alone bears the divine Name, since the Father "has given [Jesus *his*] Name" (John 17:11-12).[10] It is on this basis that Jesus may in turn have the authority/power/right to grant those who believe in him, as the very Son of God, adoption into his own unique relationship with the Father, sharing that relationship with them.

Just so, the Glory of the Father is notably, when the full drama of the Fourth Gospel has run its course and the Hour of Glory has come,[11] the begetting of many additional sons and daughters (τέκνα/*tekna* = children) from among humanity, through *the* Son (υἱός/*huios*), Jesus, and the gift of the Holy Spirit. They are granted "eternal life," which is nothing less than their dwelling in/with the Father and the Son in the Spirit, and this God's dwelling in/among them (see especially 13:3—17:26; 20:21-22; and see too therefore Rev 21:3, 22-24). More formally, we may say that

---

10. See especially Soulen, *Divine Name(s)*, 201-6.

11. John's gospel has two parts to it, chapters 1-12, which we may term the Book of Signs, and chapters 13-20, the Book of Glory; chapter 21 is an epilogue. The signs are premonitions of glory, six chosen miracles, each signifying an aspect of the rich meaning of the Hour of Glory. This Hour occurs when Jesus is "lifted up," which has a typical double meaning for John: both suspended above the ground on a Roman scaffold in crucifixion, and raised from the tomb by the Father on Easter Day. Together, this twin event fulfills Jesus' mission from his Father, the reason he was "sent into the world." The center of the chiasm that is the prologue also ties in directly with John 20:30-31.

the destiny of human beings is nothing less than to participate in the life and light, the love and freedom of the triune Godhead, "sharing the divine nature" (2 Pet 1:4), an idea beloved of the Eastern Orthodox Church.

Revelation 4 and 5

The book of Revelation or Apocalypse is certainly a curious book to many modern minds. Even postmoderns, who are supposedly more open to re-enchantments and suchlike mythologies, while they might revel in its often unusual symbolism do not truly comply with its exclusive conclusions. For the theological "bottom line" clashes horridly with any who try to evade it (as would be characteristic of much of postmodernity): God wins; we worship! Yet, *which* God, is not an idle question. And the answer is abundantly clear: the God of the Lord Jesus Christ—and none other!

The heart of the entire text lies in the two scenes presented side by side in chapters 4 and 5. That they are side by side is crucial; that they employ language repeated in both scenes is also crucial. Chapter 4 employs typical language used of Jews to describe the holiness of the God of Israel, who is seen as Creator and Lord of all the earth, as well as the electing God of Israel. The word "throne" occurs again and again such is the sovereignty of this God, whose appearance echoes Ezekiel's dramatic opening visions.[12] The "Holy holy holy" (4:8) captures another prophetic vision, that of Isa 6. Other characteristics recall Yahweh's descent upon Mt. Sinai in Exodus. One could continue. All in all, the majestic language is clearly traditional for anyone in the know. And the response is equally clear:

> And whenever the living creatures give glory and honour and thanks to him who is seated on the throne, who lives forever and ever, the twenty four elders fall down before him who is seated on the throne and worship him who lives forever and ever. They cast their crowns before the throne, saying,
>
> "Worthy are you, our Lord and God,

---

12. While Ezekiel is seminal for the throne room scenes of Rev 4–5, the background to the throne motif as a whole is rich and complex. See notably Gallusz, *Throne Motif*, who offers a thoroughgoing examination of the significance of the throne motif in the entire Book of Revelation, both regarding the background to understanding this symbol of God's sovereignty, and how it coordinates much of the structure and content of the Book itself. This is a glorious resource for those who wish to dig deeply into how early NT writers viewed Jesus to be on a par with Yahweh, and why.

> to receive glory and honour and power,
> for you created all things,
> And by your will they existed and were created" (4:9–11 ESV).

The fundamental calculus of monotheism is soundly declared: this One and solely this One is worthy *of* all worship *by* all of creation *due to* this One's creative purposes *for* all of creation. Along the way, there is a clear distinction made between this One, "Who was and is and is to come," and all other beings who are only creatures (see too 22:8–9). The very identities of God on the one hand and of creatures on the other are coordinated via this business of worship.

Yet having established this bold vision, we come immediately to another in chapter 5—and it is frankly most surprising; indeed, there's a twofold surprise! Firstly, the conclusion runs exactly parallel to the previous one, replicating the language, but tying now "the Lamb" *together with* the Lord God of all Creation:

> Then I looked and heard the voice of many angels, numbering thousands upon thousands, and ten thousand times ten thousand. They encircled the throne and the living creatures and the elders. In a loud voice they sang:
>
> "Worthy is the Lamb, who was slain,
> to receive power and wealth and wisdom and
> strength and honour and glory and praise!"
>
> Then I heard every creature in heaven and on earth and under the earth and on the sea, and all that is in them, singing:
>
> "To him who sits on the throne and to the Lamb
> be praise and honour and glory and power,
> for ever and ever!"
>
> The four living creatures said, "Amen," and the elders fell down and worshipped (5:11–14 NIV).

Every living creature imaginable accords *both* the Lamb *and* the Creator *equal* worth, equal "praise and honour and glory and power, forever and ever!" This is the first stunning conclusion. And the second is like it, but perhaps even more stunning.

One of the elders *says* to John, "Do not weep! Behold, the *Lion* of the tribe of *Judah*, the Root of *David*, has *triumphed/conquered*. He is *able to open* the scroll and its seven seals" (NIV modified). This said, with all its inferences of majesty and power and strength, John however next *sees* "between the throne and the four living creatures and among the elders *a*

Lamb standing as if it had been *slaughtered*, having seven horns and seven eyes, which are the seven spirits of God sent out into all the earth." The most profound paradox of all is clear: the creature destined for sacrifice, weak and helpless, nonetheless now *stands*, and stands amidst the *throne*, having *complete strength and wisdom*.

The conclusion is, as I say, stunning: the identity of the Lord God of all creation, to whom all worship is due, is now inextricably associated with *this slain-Lamb*. The *crucified* Jesus, whom God has exalted to his "right hand," to sit on God's sovereign throne, is now himself definitively identified by and with God; he it is, and no other, who now executes God's sovereign purposes for the entire world, "opening the seals of the book." The sheer pressure of these conclusions drives the early church to seek for language with which to articulate this mystery: that there's this human being who is on a par with God; that "God" henceforth equates in some way with this crucified-yet-risen Jesus.[13] And note finally: not just Jesus' teaching or his mission or his life, but with Jesus' very Person; for to see the Person of Jesus is to see God; *he* defines and displays the reality of absolute worth; NB John 20:28 then!

It's not therefore surprising to note Revelation's icing on the cake, as it were. At the outset of the book, after the epistolary introduction, vv. 1–7, we have God declare: "I am the Alpha and the Omega," says the Lord God, "who is and who was and who is to come, the Almighty" (1:8, NIV). Then again at 21:6 (NIV) we have God again say, "I am the Alpha and the Omega, the Beginning and the End . . ." God's embrace of the entire creation as the universal Creator could not be clearer. These titles act as bookends to the text itself, echoing the likes of Isa 44:6 (NRSV)—"I am the first [before all things] and I am the last [after all things]. Besides me there is no god." Yet this very form of language is found *also* on the lips of *Jesus* at both the beginning and the end of the book: "I am the First and the Last. I am the Living One; I was dead, and behold I am alive for ever and ever! And I hold the keys of death and Hades" (1:17–18 NIV). What is also unequivocal is the identity of the speaker here: only Jesus can be so described as having been dead and yet also raised, to live eternally. And again:

> Behold, I am coming soon! My reward is with me, and I will give to everyone according to what he has done. I am the Alpha

---

13. Martin Luther would conclude: *crux probat omnia*—the cross is the criterion for evaluating everything. See McGrath, *Luther's Theology of the Cross*, 219.

and the Omega, the First and the Last, the Beginning and the End . . .

I, Jesus, have sent my angel to give you this testimony for the churches. I am the Root and the Offspring of David, and the bright Morning Star (Rev 22:12–16 NIV).

God's identity, as the Lord God of all creation, all space-time, the entire cosmos, who rules over all the nations, now embraces the *crucified* human being, Jesus of Nazareth. This is the stunning conclusion of the last book of the Bible as it artfully crafts its powerful symbolic universe, declaring its most notable "rebirth of images" (Austin Farrer).

Luke–Acts

However, these conclusions, as clear as they may be, are neither the last word nor the only word. For we've also to include the Holy Spirit, the Spirit of Jesus, in this view of deity. To help us begin to see how we might do this, we turn to Luke–Acts, to note once again the sheer pattern of the narrative, of how "God" is said to engage with his world by means of both Jesus and the Spirit, together. For the initial feature of Luke's portrait of Jesus to highlight is how, in the words of Walter Kasper, he presents "a pneumatologically orientated Christology".[14] This means everything about Jesus, from conception to ascension, and even thereafter, is on account of the Holy Spirit. Luke exhibits this theme by starting both volumes in ways that suggest they are somehow in parallel to one another.

In the first place, the angel's answer to Mary's question reads (Luke 1:35 ESV):

> The Holy Spirit will come upon you,
> and the power of the Most High will overshadow you;
> therefore the child to be born will be called holy—
> Son of God.

When we come to Acts 1:8, with its definitive agenda for the second volume, we see again the crucial use of the same language:

> You will receive power when the Holy Spirit comes upon you;
> and you will be my witness in Jerusalem,
> and in all Judea and Samaria,

---

14. Kasper, *Jesus*, 249; see 267 for the alternative expression, "a Christology in a pneumatological perspective."

and to the ends of the earth.

This is especially so when we note that Luke uses the rare, unusual compound verb ἐπέρχομαι (*epi* + *erchomai* = upon + to come), while also ringing the changes with the words "Holy Spirit" and "power" in both places. Fascinatingly, we are not quite done with the parallels. For when Mary visits her cousin Elizabeth, she prophesies with the words of the Magnificat (Luke 1:46–55). When the Holy Spirit similarly comes upon those gathered in the Upper Room at Pentecost, their response is also "to tell [the crowd] in [their] own languages the mighty works of God" (Acts 2:11 own translation).

It's important then to understand the way these two volumes function together. James Dunn has suggested we may view Luke's gospel, vol. 1, as depicting Jesus as "the Man of the Spirit," and then vol. 2, the Acts of the Apostles, as depicting Jesus now as "the Lord of the Spirit."[15] How this comes about, how these volumes are joined together, in effect, is deftly done by Luke. For we need to notice the story of the ascension is told *twice*, once at the *conclusion* of the gospel, and again as the *introduction* to Acts. This is because the ascension is a *hinge event*: it marks the end of Jesus' own earthly career—he is a human glorified, in the presence of the eternal Father; and it initiates the disciples (and the whole church) into sharing what he has done. In the language of the Fourth Gospel (John 1:32–34), the One on whom the Spirit has descended/come down and remained [to be Man of the Spirit] has become the One who baptizes in the Holy Spirit [as Lord of the Spirit]. Yet it is exactly at this point that we should be most careful regarding just this "baptismal" language. For John's testimony is remarkably similar to Acts 2:33 in fact: "Exalted to the right hand of God, he has received from the Father the promise of the Holy Spirit, and has poured out what you now see and hear" (NIV)—once we have stopped being hung up on "baptism in the Holy Spirit" language.

In Luke 24:49 the Spirit is called "the Father's promise" and is associated with "power." Then reading the full introduction to Acts, 1:1–11, Acts 1:4 repeats the language of promise, and v. 5 takes up John's prediction of Luke 3:16, but reverses an active verb into a passive, leaving the subject, the baptizing one, unspecified for now. Then as we've seen, Acts 1:8 deliberately echoes Luke 1:35, repeating the words "Holy Spirit" and "power" and "come upon." Lastly, we must note at crucial stages in the book of Acts the activity of the Spirit is depicted by Luke's ringing the changes once more

---

15. See Dunn, *Baptism*, 41, and *Jesus and the Spirit*.

with his words. He uses *eight different phrases* overall: baptize in the Holy Spirit; the Holy Spirit comes upon; being filled with the Holy Spirit; pour out the Holy Spirit; receive (the gift of) the Holy Spirit; give (the gift of) the Holy Spirit; the Holy Spirit falls upon; the promise of the Holy Spirit. That is, we need not and should not get too hung up on the actual *expression* "baptism in/with the Holy Spirit." What is crucial is the actual *reality* to which the expression refers, notably in terms of the summary description offered in Acts 2:38–39, with its full picture of Christian initiation. Jesus, the Lord of the Holy Spirit, incorporates people into his saving work, which is his very own Person; Jesus baptizes people with the Holy Spirit into his Body; people are baptized into Jesus with/by the Holy Spirit (to echo the language of Paul, see below).

A diagram represents reasonably well this entire picture of Luke–Acts.

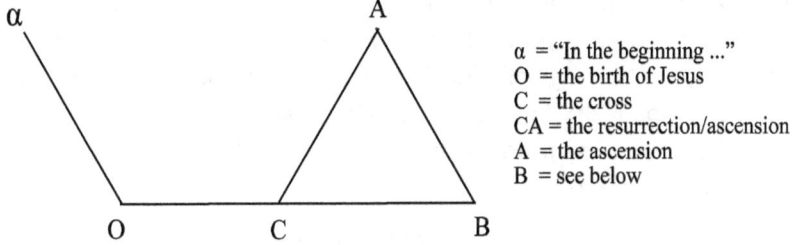

α = "In the beginning ..."
O = the birth of Jesus
C = the cross
CA = the resurrection/ascension
A = the ascension
B = see below

Figure 3: A representation of the Economy derived from Luke–Acts

With αO being parallel to AB, as we've said, ABC = the "overwhelming/drenching" work of the Holy Spirit whereby we are "put into" Jesus' entire work, OCA (Acts 2:33, 38–39, Rom 6:3, 1 Cor 12:13, Col 2:9–12). B = the rite of water baptism. (The English word "baptism" comes directly from the Greek word *baptizein* = to immerse, drench, overwhelm, plunge, dip, put into.) In other words, what Jesus did formally in his own life in a substitutionary and representative manner is now actualised for each person/household who comes to him. A kind of "recycling" occurs, as Jesus "immerses" people into himself with/by means of the Holy Spirit, *the self-same One* who enabled his own mission.

It is important to see all this as the ministry of the glorified Jesus Christ, in the presence of the eternal Father, through the eternal Holy Spirit (see Heb 9:14). Otherwise, to indicate diagrammatically a supposed "movement backwards in time," the line BC (for the disciples some 35 years and less, for ourselves c. 2,000), and to see all the events of Jesus' career in the power of the Spirit from conception to exaltation as "telescoped into a single happening" is confusing gibberish.

Yet something like this has to be said and is meaningful when we see the transcendent Lord of History breaking into history and himself becoming an actor in the drama (*the* Singular Actor!) and proleptically and programmatically establishing his sovereign rule. On the one hand, there are three elements or phases to the climax of the economy of salvation: the events of Jesus' mission; the ensuing era of the church; the Parousia (which repeats key features of Tom Wright's scheme of "Five Acts" in the Divine Story: Creation, Fall, Israel, Jesus, and Church).[16] On the other hand, this division is to a large degree more analytical than real. For the experience of the church since Pentecost is a "recycling" of what has *already* happened to our substitute and representative human being, Jesus; and the Parousia or Second Coming is the Unveiling and Appearing of what *already* is the case "in Christ Jesus" (see e.g. Col 3:3–4, 1 Pet 1:3–9). While the Old Age is still with us, although passing away and destined to perish, the New Age of God's Future has arrived/begun to arrive and those in union with Christ *can share in it already*.

A pair of diagrams will help to show how the NT takes OT expectations and revamps them:

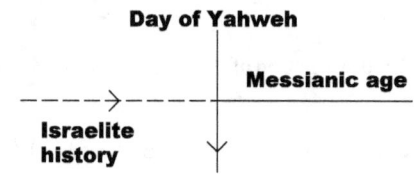

Figure 4: Israel's Future Hope

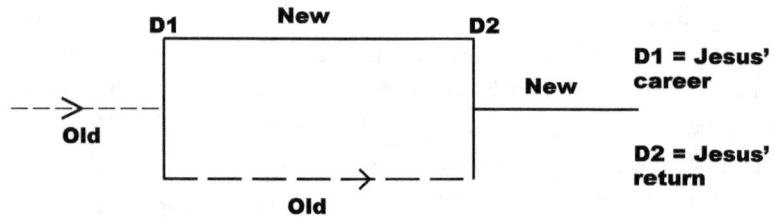

Figure 5: The Christian Fulfilment

---

16. See esp. Bartholomew and Goheen, *Drama of Scripture*, which nicely builds on Wright's Five Act scheme, introduced in *NT and People of God*, 141–43.

The doctrine of the Trinity then becomes a summary concept, a compressed way of summarizing *who* it is that *acts* in the *way* he has and does in the missions of Jesus and of the Holy Spirit—all of which activity is now embodied in and with and through the church, the Place where God's Presence seeks to dwell (see e.g., Eph 2:11–22, as well as all that has been said in this chapter).[17] Nor is it at all surprising that the trinitarian Name—Father Son and Holy Spirit (as in Matt 28:19)—has its initial location in the church's rite of initiation. For when folk are baptized, they are publicly declaring this is the One whom they will follow henceforth—and if necessary die for. This is the One, among the great field of claimants to deity around the world, who is truly the Lord. For he has now *demonstrated* it!

Our journey so far has established a number of key dots and shapes, which we have begun to extensively color in. There is one more key element of the NT which we have held back however, and which we must now bring to the fore. It has to do with prayer (and worship), and warrants its own distinctive chapter, even if we have actually begun to speak about it somewhat already here.

---

17. Gordon Fee offers us one of the very best summaries of what this means: see Fee, *God's Empowering Presence*.

Questions for Reflection

5. "God's exaltation of Jesus affirms his act of humbly emptying himself to be indeed the form of fullest divine revelation: what are the implications of this 'kenoticism' (self-emptying) for the Christian understanding of the very nature of God?" As we ponder the significance of this question, ask yourself a range of questions about how we reach *any* understanding of God's nature? What sorts of things *count* towards our being able to draw conclusions about God's nature?

6. While this chapter assembles a few specific NT texts, it is also true to say the entire NT has about it a certain "logic," a certain "scope," a "grammar" even, all of which underscores trinitarian thinking. Can you think of examples of where this appears? E.g., Jesus' entry into Jerusalem;[18] or Eph 1:3–14, with its threefold appeal to praise the divine glory.

---

18. To explore this theme further, see Soulen, *Divine Name(s)*, 164–73, and Wright, *Victory*, 651–53 (with countless references to earlier sections re the Temple and Yahweh's Return to Zion, e.g., 201–9); re Messiahship in particular, see *People of God*, 310–20, as well as *Victory*, 477–539.

five

A Final Outline and Its Colors

FOR MANY CENTURIES AND in every land, countless people have pondered the question, Who is God? Not just, What is God, but Who? One approach to the answer I have found rather helpful is this: God is the One to Whom one prays/we pray.

But *why* might one pray—to God? To any "god" at all? Why pray *to this particular* God/god/goddess? *What* is it about *this specific* deity that solicits your belief, that makes you turn to them in prayer? For what *kind* of *salvation* might this God/god/goddess *offer* you, their supplicant? In short: what does it *mean* for *this* deity "N" to "save" in *this* way?

This basic line of questioning is a very helpful way *to distinguish claimants to deity* among the *field of religious options*. For example, why pray to Diana/Artemis of the Ephesians (Acts 19 and the pastoral letters), often associated with deer, as the goddess of hunting, and of women's child-bearing, and so something of a mother–goddess? Why choose Horus of the Egyptians, god of war and protection? Or Kali, Shiva's consort, goddess of time and death? Or Buddha the Compassionate One? Or even Maui, a demi-god of the Maori peoples, whose canoe is said to be the South Island.

Following this scheme, we should note the Bible is no exception. "I am Yahweh your God, who brought you out of Egypt, out of the land of slavery. You shall have no other gods before me" is how the Ten Commandments, the due summary of the Torah/the Law, begins (Exod 20:2–3, and see Exod 3:15b). From the point of view of the NT, we have further insight, as Jesus specifically gives his followers a pattern of prayer we call the Lord's Prayer. This is found in two places, and so in two slightly different forms.

The Lord's Prayer

Luke 11:2–4 (ESV) gives us:

> Father, hallowed be your name.
> Your kingdom come.
> Give us each day our daily bread,
> and forgive us our sins,
> for we ourselves forgive everyone who is indebted to us.
> And lead us not into temptation.

Matt 6:9–13 (ESV) has:

> Our Father in heaven,
> hallowed be your name.
> Your kingdom come,
> your will be done,
> on earth as it is in heaven.
> Give us this day our daily bread,
> and forgive us our debts,
> as we also have forgiven our debtors.
> And lead us not into temptation,
> but deliver us from evil.

The two differing settings are insightful as well. The Matthean setting we call the Sermon on the Mount (Matt 5–7), while Luke places his prayer in the body of teaching that has Jesus on his journey from Galilee to Jerusalem (Luke 9–19). Given these two contexts, the temptation is now to set about an extensive exegesis of each. But I shall desist, saying only this much, before we focus upon the Lucan form in particular, as this offers us immediate insight into matters of the Trinity.

Matthew's Sermon on the Mount is most artfully constructed, drawing together a wide selection of Jesus' teaching.[1] Indeed, it constitutes the first such body of teaching in the gospel, where there are deliberately

---

1. The literature on the Sermon on the Mount is vast, ranging from simple introductions to the exquisitely rich. I shall offer only four: Greenman et al., eds, *Sermon on the Mount*; Stott, *Message*; Patte, *Discipleship*; Green, *Matthew*.

five such blocks, chapters 5–7, chapter 10, chapter 13, chapter 18, and chapters 23–25, each concluding with the same formula. What is so elegant about the Sermon is the way Matthew places the Lord's Prayer at the center of a chiasmic pattern. Thereafter this literary structure, with the central item being the most important, has sections before and afterwards complementing it in a most artful way, each petition of the prayer paralleling a subsection of teaching. A diagram represents the results:

A – Hallowed be your Name (5:3–12)

  B – Your Kingdom come (5:13–16)

    C – Your Will be done (5:17–48)

      D – Jewish piety (6:1) – Alms giving (6:2–4), Prayer (6:5–8)

        The Center: The Lord's Prayer and Forgiveness

      D' – Jewish piety (cont) – Fasting (6:16–18)

    C' – Give us today our daily bread

    (6:19–34, 7:7–11; see Mark 11:22–24)

  B' – Forgive us our debts, as we also have forgiven . . .

  (7:1–12, 6:14–15; see Mark 11:25)

A' – Lead us not into temptation, but deliver us . . . (7:13–23 [7:6?])

The very Lord's Prayer, as lain out petition by petition, is to find its natural expression, and fulfillment even, in the way Jesus spells it out, subunit by subunit, in the Sermon on the Mount, climaxing in the parable of the two builders. That is, our prayerfully coming to "our Father" (which word is used 17 times of God throughout the Sermon) "in secret" (Matt 6:5–8) is the very heartbeat of our "visible" life of discipleship "before the world" (5:13–16). More fulsomely and formally, we may not face the world in mission unless we have first faced our God in worship; yet the authenticity of our worship is tested by the reality of our mission. This last way of putting it has deliberate trinitarian overtones, which we will pick up when we have examined the Lucan form of the Lord's Prayer.

In Luke 9:51—19:48 Jesus is on a journey to Jerusalem, during which he teaches a good deal: on Christian discipleship, its cost, and the need for humility; on the Coming Kingdom of God, and therefore judgment, mercy, and eternal life; and the heart of it all, on his relationship with his and Israel's God. Chapter 11 opens with Jesus at prayer. Luke's portrait of Jesus often depicts him at prayer (Luke 6:12, 9:18,28–9, 23:34,46, and compare these with Matthew and Mark), and he explicitly links prayer and the Holy Spirit (3:21–2, comparing this baptismal story with those of Matt 3 and Mark 1; Acts 1:14, and chapter 2, the day of Pentecost). As we have already seen, with Jesus as the Man of the Spirit, this neatly ties all three elements together: Jesus, prayer, and the Holy Spirit.

When the disciples ask Jesus, "Teach us to pray," there is much going on. Clearly there's something special about Jesus' relationship with God, which they've observed and which is the source of his authority and power, his wisdom and compassion. Then his disciples realize as well that, with their becoming increasingly a distinctive community, centered on Jesus, they too are to express their relationship to God in a distinctive way.

The prayer in Luke addresses God less formally than in Matthew. The single word, "Father," almost certainly echoes the Aramaic "Abba!" on Jesus' own lips (Mark 14:36). Then, with only two petitions regarding God, the first focused upon ourselves, regarding present material sustenance day after day, becomes the central request of the prayer, balanced as it is by two further requests. The one covers past wrongs and the other future trials. All in all, the shape of the prayer is of two sets of requests: firstly, for us to get involved in God's business (especially when filled out by Matthew's extra petition with the expression, "your will be done, on earth as in heaven"), and then secondly, for God to get involved in ours, past, present, and future.

There is however another perspective upon the Lord's Prayer, which colors its entire meaning. For it may be placed within an explicitly first century Jewish context, with a strong eschatological flavor, one which views furthermore these decisive actions of Yahweh as a "New Exodus."[2] This then impacts the interpretation of each of the six petitions, even the very first. In fact, the first ceases to be a mere exhortation for God to be generally honored as such. Instead, it takes its cue from the driving force that would see Yahweh specifically "hallow his Name" as Ezekiel foretold in the following way (36:22–28, NJPS):

> Say to the House of Israel: Thus said the Lord GOD: Not for your sake will I act, O House of Israel, but *for My holy name*, which

---

2. For all the exegetical details of what follows, see Pitre, *Jesus*, chapter 3, "The New Manna," 148–250.

you have caused to be profaned among the nations to which you have come. I will *sanctify My great name* which has been profaned among the nations—among whom you have caused it to be profaned. And the nations shall know that I am the LORD—declares the Lord GOD—when I *manifest My holiness* before their eyes *through you*. I will take you from among the nations and gather you from all the countries, and I will *bring you back to your own land*. I will sprinkle clean water upon you, and you shall be clean: I will cleanse you from all your uncleanness and from all your fetishes. And I will give you a new heart and put a new spirit into you: I will remove the heart of stone from your body and give you a heart of flesh; and I will put My spirit into you. Thus I will cause you to follow My laws and faithfully to observe My rules. Then you shall dwell in the *land* which I gave to your fathers, and *you shall be My people and I will be your God*. (emphases added)

Here we have language which invokes the "land," a "new covenant," and so another, "new exodus," all specifically resulting in "hallowing/sanctifying/making holy God's name", and this through Israel. Nor does this famous new covenant passage stand alone. The very next chapter of Ezekiel, 37:11–14 (NJPS), continues:

And He said to me, "O mortal, these bones are the whole House of Israel. They say, 'Our bones are dried up, our hope is gone; we are doomed.' Prophesy, therefore, and say to them: Thus said the Lord GOD: I am going to open your graves and lift you out of the graves, O My people, and *bring you to the land of Israel. You shall know*, O My people, that *I am the LORD*, when I have opened your graves and lifted you out of your graves. I will put My breath into you and you *shall live again*, and I will set you upon your *own soil*. Then *you shall know that I the LORD* have spoken and have acted"—declares the LORD. (emphases added)

Once more the language is powerfully evocative—"you shall know I am Yahweh"—with the *reviving* of God's people explicitly once more in "the land of Israel," which is their "own soil." And so the first petition of the Lord's Prayer, from the lips of Jesus the first century Jew, directs us towards an eschatological reading, one which renews key OT motifs of covenant and exodus. Yet there is more to be said in this respect.

The very form of address at the start of the prayer, "Our Father in heaven" (Matt 6:9), or simply "Father" (Luke 11:2), similarly invokes a prophetic vision of the future when God would decisively act to honor his Name (see again the opening paragraphs of chapter four above). Both Isa 63:11–17 and Jer 3:16–19 have Yahweh addressed as "Our/My Father", and furthermore, this appellation is in the context of invoking God to remember the exodus of old precisely to bring about a new exodus of the people into the land again. Nor are we quite done even now. Jer 3:17 speaks directly of "all the nations" coming to Jerusalem, such is Yahweh's decisive demonstration of his sovereignty. This echoes too Micah 4:1–8 (see too Isa 2:2–5), which climaxes with an explicit reference to "dominion/sovereignty" returning to Zion (v. 8), the content of the second petition of the Lord's Prayer.

We could continue to enrich the first century eschatological coloring of the entire Prayer, but this might take us far from our own particular study. Only one final feature is worth noting here, with the center of Luke's prayer being concerned with "bread" as we've already noted above. For how might the setting of a "new exodus" shed light upon the otherwise problematic exegesis of this bread as ἐπιούσιος (*epiousios*: both Luke 11:3 and Matt 6:11). As Brant Pitre elaborates,[3] the meaning of the request to "give us each day (Matthew)/this day (Luke) our *epiousios* bread" has been hotly debated down the centuries. For all that, situating it firmly in the context of Exod 16 and the manna from heaven sheds direct light upon this conundrum. If indeed we read the Lord's Prayer, and this petition in particular, from the point of view of the primordial hope for a new exodus, "*then the petition for the [new, eschatological] manna of the kingdom of God stands at the very center of Jesus' and his disciples' hopes for the future.*"[4] And finally, just as the exodus of old was beset with trials and temptations of its own, so too especially will the near-future arrival of the fulfilment of God's final promises have their attendant evils, delivery from which Christians must surely pray. Once again, the bold eschatological coloring adds meaning to *all* the petitions.

The rest of Luke's presentation of the Lord's Prayer, vv. 5–8 and vv. 9–13, then amplifies the business of prayer. First, there's a typical parable, unique to Luke's gospel, depicting Middle Eastern life.[5] It is constructed in two parts: What will surely not happen (5–7), *versus* "I tell you" what will indeed happen, because there is a question of honor at stake (8). The setting is of any village community into whose midst comes a traveller

---

3. Ibid., 171–93, the details of which are well worth exploring in their own right.

4. Ibid., 191, emphasis original.

5. For a helpful analysis of this section of the pericope, see Bailey, "Exegesis of Luke 11:5–13," 119–41.

(note this nice touch given the overall setting, Jesus on his own journey to Jerusalem). Hospitality is the key thereafter. Both the friend and then the neighbor have the village's community name to safeguard and so must honor this unexpected visitor. The excuses are just that, excuses—"how ridiculous!" The difficult word, ἀναίδεια (*anaideia*), v. 8, is hard to translate, for is the connotation here negative or positive? Does the sleeping neighbor act out of his sense of shame, that is, to avoid the scandal of refusing hospitality, or is the one making the request the focus? The various EVV suggest one approach or another: persistence, boldness, impudence, importunity. But perhaps its very ambiguity allows us to hedge our bets, and so put the stress of the parable's punchline *both* on us who pray *and* on the God to whom we pray (re the latter, see the paired parable in Luke 18:1–8). Finally, note the request for "three loaves" of bread (N.B. this echoes the prayer's own center, v. 3), due to his having "nothing to set before" the visitor, is countered by the neighbor who "gives him as much as [ὅσων/ *hosōn*] he needs." So the neighbor in fact supplies *everything* required! Note vv. 5, 7, 8: "lend, give :: give, give" leads into the remaining verses of the entire section, all of which reinforces the point of the prayer—that we would receive, in order then to pass on to others, for their benefit.

Vv. 9–13 are parallelled more or less in Matt 7:7–11, with one crucial difference, the conclusion. The verses are made up of a three-part poem in three stanzas, which may be lain out as follows:

Ask, and it will be *given* to **you** (present tense continuous)   *Second person*
    Seek, and you shall find
        Knock, and it shall be opened to you

For **everyone** who *asks* receives   *Third person*
    and the one who seeks finds
        and to the knocker it shall be opened

And who among you[6]
    if the son *asks* the father for bread
        will he *give* him a stone?

---

6. The Greek of v. 11 τίνα δὲ ἐξ ὑμῶν (*tina de ex humōn*) parallels τίς ἐξ ὑμῶν (*tis ex humōn*) of v. 5, often not accentuated in EVV.

>   or a fish, instead of a fish
>   will he *give* him a snake (eel)?
>   or if he *asks* for an egg
>   will he *give* him a scorpion?
>
> If therefore
>   **You** being evil   *Second person*
>   you know good gifts
>   to *give* to your children
>
>   How much more the Father   *Third person*
>   out of heaven Holy Spirit
>   shall *give* to **those** *asking* him

Giver   }
Gift   } repeated three times, in each stanza
    Recipient   }

The last point is the most interesting when we recall our model of chapter 2, when we noted the pattern of Giver–Gift–Recipient re the Trinity. For what makes Jesus the Man of the Spirit, and so the One who especially prays in the power of the Holy Spirit (as Luke paints his portrait of Jesus), is the fact he is first the Recipient of the Gift of the Spirit from his Father, the Giver. Then, when he becomes Lord of the Spirit, he is able to share precisely the selfsame Holy Spirit, the Father's promise to his disciples. In other words, when we note both the introductory sentence, "One day Jesus was praying," and the conclusion, "How much more shall the heavenly Father give the Holy Spirit to those who ask him," then we may see they act as a pair of literary "bookends," sandwiching the entire section and highlighting what are its chief contents. Jesus' followers and disciples may now share this Spirit of Sonship/Adoption whereby they too cry "Abba! Father!" in prayer. The picture is perhaps not quite as sophisticated theologically as Paul's or John's (e.g., Rom 8:15–6, Gal 4:4–6, and John 1:12, chapters 14–17), but the end result is similar: this most intimate and profound relationship with God as Father is what Jesus supremely comes to grant us human beings.

Nor should we miss drawing here a key conclusion regarding the nature of the triune God. The Trinity is itself already and always in a divine conversation. "God" = a *conversation*, among Father, Son, and Holy Spirit. What we are privileged to see in Luke 11 is a snap-shot of the disciples eavesdropping upon this divine conversation; and then we are being shown how we too may *join the conversation*! This is the heart of the form of "salvation" the Trinity brings, the essential reason we might pray to *this* triune God, whose "Name [is] Father, Son, and Holy Spirit" (Matt 28:19).[7]

Christian prayer is to the Father with and through the Son in the grace and power/authority of the Holy Spirit. The prepositions of this summary in relation to each Person are absolutely crucial. They enable us to see how the doctrine of the Trinity is not some creed to which we must give formal assent should we wish to be "orthodox"—even if it appears to be sheer mystification! Rather, we are enabled to become actually caught up into a living and lively concern, as we invoke in prayer and worship the One whose Name is "Father, Son, and Holy Spirit." Trinitarianism is either an operational reality or it is nothing at all! Then "mission" too is an explicitly trinitarian thing. For the church's mission is none other than *our* participation in the *Missio Dei* as it is called, the Father's sending the Son and the Spirit into the world, to fulfill the divine purposes for the world (see the likes of John 20:21-22).[8]

The Shema

We close off this chapter by looking at a final text from the NT, 1 Cor 8:4-6, drawing as well some conclusions regarding worship itself. In addition, I have deliberately chosen to conclude with this brief but seminal text from 1 Cor 8, since it forms a crucial link between the gathered NT material of these last two chapters and our next chapter on the story of the Nicene Creed.[9]

---

7. For those who wish to pursue such intricacies, see Soulen, *Divine Name(s)*, for how one might relate the OT Name of Yahweh and this NT Name of "Father, Son, and Holy Spirit"—yet not without debate, for see Sanders, "A Name," 22-27, et al, 28-64, with replies by Soulen, 65-80, esp. his responses to Jenson and MacDonald, 77-8. See further below, chapter 7, re "Person and Identity."

8. For those interested in pursuing this idea of *Missio Dei*, see Wright, *Mission of God*; and most fulsomely, Flett, *Witness of God*, who examines especially the nuances of Barth's original German missional vocabulary, thereby establishing an important corrective to this oft used yet imprecise phrase, and so grounding it in the triune God, and thereafter seeing it reflected suitably in the entire church.

9. See esp. Blaising, "Creedal Formation," 371-88, and Soulen, *Divine Name(s)*,

The *Shema* is the quintessential confessional Jewish prayer of traditional, orthodox Judaism. Its name is derived from the first word in Hebrew of the text of Deut 6:4, which reads (literally), "Hear you, Israel, Yahweh our God, Yahweh is one," although some translate the last clause "Yahweh alone." The last letters of the first and last words of this verse are written in Hebrew Bibles in oversized script, to form the Hebrew word "witness," indicating by this verse that Jews testify to the oneness and uniqueness of their God, differentiating God from polytheism both quantitatively and qualitatively.

Liturgical development by the second century AD caused the *Shema* to consist of Deut 6:4–9, plus 11:13–21, and Num 15:37–41, together with special benedictions to be recited every morning and evening (based on Deut 6:7). For devout Jews, the *Shema* is written on parchments enclosed in the *phylacteries* and *mezuzah* (small boxes tied to a man's forehead and left upper arm, and the small, long container fixed to a doorpost with scrolls inside). As a watchword of faith and faithfulness, the *Shema* constitutes the climax of sayings recited before death; as a result, it was also recited during martyrdom. Jesus identified the *Shema* as the first commandment in the Law (Mark 12:29).

All in all therefore, we can say the *Shema* represents the highest appreciation of Jewish worship, with its identification of Jewry's One true God, on the lips of good faithful Jews. And so, just what does Paul think he is up to when he writes in 1 Cor 8:4–6, deliberately echoing this very *Shema*:

> So then, about eating food sacrificed to idols: We know that an idol is nothing at all in the world and that there is no God but one. For even if there are so-called gods, whether in heaven or on earth (as indeed there are many "gods" and many "lords"), yet for us there is but one God, the Father, from whom all things came and for whom we live; and there is but one Lord, Jesus Christ, through whom all things came and through whom we live (NIV).

What *is* going on? To paraphrase slightly, to underscore the question:

> To return to the topic of eating meat associated with idols, then, we share your knowledge that "An idol has no real existence," and that "There is no God but One." For even if there really exist, for the sake of argument, so-called gods, whether in heaven

---

40–41, 46.

or on earth, as indeed there are many "gods" and many "lords," yet for us there is one God, the Father, from whom all things take their origin and who is the goal of our existence, and one Lord Jesus Christ, through whom all things come and who is the means of our existence.[10]

"The Corinthians' point will be that since there is no reality to an idol because there is no God but one, how can we be faulted for eating meals at the temples, since the gods represented by these idols do not in fact exist?"[11] For all the logic of their case, however, the prior verses, 1–3, show how Paul insists that true *love* for one another surpasses any such spiritual *knowledge*. For even if technically such knowing and understanding of the world might grant certain "rights" (see the use of ἐξουσία (*exousia*) in 8:9 and 9:4, and ἔξεστιν (*exestin*) in 6:12 and 10:23), the practical outcome of such knowledge is rather a sense of self-importance and self-inflation (one almost inevitably feels a sense of spiritual superiority, having such a purchase upon things!) *versus* a genuine "building up" of one another. For in the final analysis, true knowing is in fact a being known—and that by God (v. 3), who is love itself.

Yet such a divine love is only revealed and known in the very fact of Jesus Christ's death and resurrection; what Jesus embodies is nothing less than the divine love itself in action, which climaxes in Golgotha and Easter morning. Yet as we've seen all along in these pages, the claim that God is uniquely involved through, and even identifies himself with this Jesus of Nazareth, propels us to have to reconfigure the meaning of the word "God." For if "God" is now known uniquely by reference to Jesus, any such knowledge impels the knower when duly related to its object to similarly reflect the sorts of humility and nonexploitative behavior exhibited by Jesus (back to Phil 2). For, finally, personal knowledge of persons, divine no less than human, necessarily implies a mutual self-emptying on behalf of each other—such is the sheer logic of personal intersubjectivity when subjects are known as objects by other subjects, in the light of the Trinity.

---

10. Thiselton, *First Epistle to the Corinthians*, 613. This magisterial work, together with Fee's commentary, *First Epistle to the Corinthians*, offer the best of exegetical insights. See too Wright, "The One God of Israel," esp. 661–70: "It has recently been customary, and for good reason, to examine 1 Corinthians 8:6 as one of the key texts in which Paul's christologically revised monotheism comes to sharp and startling expression" (661).

11. Fee, *First Epistle to the Corinthians*, 371.

All of which is an extended commentary on the now expanded *Shema* that Paul so naturally slips into. For when he unpacks the assumption held by both himself and the Corinthians, that "There is no God but one" (v. 4), he is forced by the sheer gospel's revelation (with which of course he began earlier in chapters 1–4 of 1 Cor) to bind talk of "one God, the Father" with the concomitant notion of "one Lord, Jesus Christ" (v. 6)—even if he also steers a quite specific path by means of the prepositions once again, please note, with due attention to *how* each is related to creation's "all things." The implications of this for a Christianized Jewish Rabbi are just staggering! "It should be quite clear that Paul is including the Lord Jesus Christ in the unique divine identity. He is redefining monotheism as christological monotheism."[12]

"No one can say 'Jesus is Lord!' except by/through the agency of the Holy Spirit," says Paul in 1 Cor 12:3. Nor is this "One Lord" (8:6)—recalling what we noted in Phil 2 that the word for "Lord," *kyrios* in Greek, was used in the Septuagint translation for YHWH—merely alongside and/or in competition with the "One God." There are not "two gods" or "powers" here! Rather, we need to see the incomparable God of Israel (so Isa 45:18–25 again) as being necessarily in an inextricable relationship with this Jesus of Nazareth. For furthermore, when Jesus during his earthly mission claimed to have himself a singularly unique relationship with his God, Yahweh of Israel, whom he invoked as "Abba! Father!," this claim is verified and vindicated by God's exaltation of him as per Phil 2. Jesus is intrinsic to Yahweh's identity, and vice versa—that's the upshot of all this confessional logic in Paul's writings. Consequently, when the later church fathers, like Athanasius, homed in on the explicit *relational* language of "Father" and "Son," they were only pursuing the logic already found in the NT itself—even as they pushed it out to its logical conclusion, that the Son is *eternally* "with the Father" (so too John 1:1). But such a logic is no mere piece of knowledge, as we've seen: it's real purpose is one of confessional worship—as per the *Shema* itself! We are back to our section on Rev 4–5. And *this* "God" is therefore in stark contrast to all the "many gods" and "many lords" (8:5) both of Paul's day and the background of Isa 40–55. Yahweh and Yahweh alone is both Creator and Savior/Redeemer of all the world, from whom and for whom are "all things," as declared and demonstrated through Jesus, his Son and Lord, *the* singular divine-human mediator, who is fully human yet also fully divine.

12. Bauckham, *Jesus and the God of Israel*, 28; the entire section, 26–30, is especially helpful re this revamped *Shema* of Paul's.

Trinitarian language, to conclude this chapter therefore, is the *very milieu* of Christian prayer and worship. The Holy Spirit enables us to invoke and confess and duly acknowledge Jesus as Lord, on a par with Yahweh his Father, to the full honor and glory and praise of God. Furthermore, this very act has the effect also of embracing us *within* the self-same relationship Jesus has with his Father: we too cry "Abba! Father!" in the Spirit. This Luke and Paul endorse in their separate ways. Yet in the end what all this does is to ensure "we live *for* him, who is the *goal* of our existence" (see above): trinitarian speech reveals the heart of Christian discipleship, "the foundation for the community which is living . . . as the kingdom–people in the midst of the pagan world."[13]

What this chapter and the previous one have done is to try to show how very early all this understanding actually was among the nascent Christian church, who were responsible for producing what became the NT writings. The doctrine of the Trinity is no later invention of the church. It is rather the deepest and best interpretation by the church of Who God is, as he has come among us in Christ Jesus and the Holy Spirit. This is Who the historical church actually encountered and experienced; and their response was inevitable, under the sheer pressure of this experience. There's one final thing to note: this interpretation is duly offered us no less than by means of and through the Scriptures of Christianity's mother religion, Judaism. It is they which offered the NT writers no less their key interpretative grid, the way to understand what had happened among them and continues to happen among us (e.g. note 2, chapter four again). In the end, we may not separate OT from NT. As St Augustine once said: "The New Testament is hidden [Latin: *latet*] in the Old; the Old is made accessible [*patet*] by the New."

---

13. See Vickers, *Invocation and Assent*, esp. 1–23, where he rightly locates trinitarian speech in its setting of Christian initiation, which itself gave rise to the early church's Rule of Faith, the due form of Christian discipleship. And see once more Wright, "The One God of Israel," 663: "To pray the *Shema* was to embrace the yoke of God's kingdom, to commit oneself to God's purposes on earth as in heaven, whatever it might cost. It was to invoke, and declare one's loyalty to, the One God who had revealed himself in action at the Exodus and was now giving his people their inheritance. Paul uses the *Shema* in this passage in exactly this way, not as a detached statement of dogma, not as a 'spiritual' aside, not simply in order to swat away the 'many "gods" and many "lords"' of the previous verse, but in order to be *the foundation for the community which is living, or which Paul is teaching to live, as the kingdom–people in the midst of the pagan world*" (emphasis added).

Questions for Reflection

7. When you start to pray, what words exactly do you use to address God? What does this say about how you view God and the kind of relationship you have with God/God has with you?

8. When did you first learn the Lord's Prayer? And how do you use it now? Are there other ways of using it?

9. With the parable of Luke 11:5–8 in mind, what has been your experience of praying?

10. If the Lord's Prayer is first about *our* getting involved in God's business, and then *God* getting involved in ours (so that all may be transformed from glory into glory; so Matthew).

    What is the pattern of your own praying? And how might such mutual concern in prayer reflect the divine conversation among the Trinity? And now in an explicit eschatological mode: If *God's* business is the hallowing of his Name through the coming of his kingdom and will, how does this impact all of *our* business?

11. "Trinitarian speech reveals the heart of Christian discipleship," "the foundation for the community which is living . . . as the kingdom-people in the midst of the pagan world." With our very lives being an act of worship, try to memorize the Christianized *Shema* of Rabbi Paul, the Apostle, using it as a brief prayer in your own personal devotions.

six

CAD/CAM—1
Design

THE TITLE OF THIS chapter is no less metaphorical than our previous ones, derived as they were from the world of kindergarten. But now we step up considerably our approach: Computer Aided Design/Computer Aided Manufacture racks up the possibilities way beyond a toddler's scribbling on bits of paper! The number of footnotes from now on speaks for itself as well. I already hinted at something of this towards the close of the last chapter, mentioning the names of Athanasius and Augustine. Athanasius of Alexandria (c. 296–373) was a key player in the Arian controversy, which will be a major focus of this chapter. Augustine, Bishop of Hippo (354–430), was a towering figure around the dissolution of the Roman Empire. His voluminous writings laid the foundations for Latin, Western Christianity over many centuries, and his *De Trinitate* remains an absolute classic, which he began to write around 399 and completed some twenty-plus years later. We shall come to him and *De Trinitate* in our next chapter.

Some Basic Philosophy

We begin this chapter in what might seem a curious way to some people. For we need to appreciate some basic philosophy, appropriating some of its classical terms, all of which formed the perennial language of the ancient Greco-Roman world.[1]

1. See again the essay by Pannenberg, "Appropriation."

Consider how we conceptualize reality, dividing everything up into categories, classifying items, answering the questions, "What is/how is it so-and-so?" Groups of things holding something in common are higher up a scale of categories than those with more particular traits. Yet, all these vaguely similar items possess "tableness," for example. Their *nature* or *essence* in this case, *that which* each item *possesses* in common, is the same, namely "tableness," even if such things as their number, their size, their color, their relations to other items, their location, and so on, are variable, or "accidental." *That which* items *essentially possess*, and those things *themselves* that *possess/do the possessing* of sundry categories were termed "secondary" and "primary substances" respectively in the Hellenistic world. A primary substance (*substantia* in Latin, οὐσία (*ousia*) in Greek) constitutes the logical subject (*this* so-and-so), and secondary substance (e.g., tableness), together with whatever accidents may be the case, form the predicate or everything that follows. Another word used for itemised subjects was ὑπόστασις (*hypostasis*)—but just to confuse us, it was also used to refer to essence as well on occasion. Both major terms will concern us with the doctrine of the Trinity in due course.

An example: our (coffee, adjectival modifier) table [subject] is: 1.2 m long, and 80 cm wide; it [subject] has: four turned legs, and is made of Kauri wood, stained a light brown; it [subject] was: made by a local carpenter for us in 2002; it [subject] is: placed in the center of our lounge. Everything after the colon is pure accident, for such things could be different, and in other cases are indeed so. For I could go on to describe other "tables" in our home, picking out their respective features, all arranged in, say, an insurance list: subject followed by predicate in each case, each predicate assuming "tableness," alongside their respective, other, variable categories, all of which distinguish and pick out "*which* table." Then I could list our "pictures" in the same way: a Monet, a Picasso, a Rembrandt . . . just kidding! But you get the point by now.

When the ancient Mediterranean world wanted to speak of deity it naturally went about the process in the same philosophical way—but with a crucial prejudice, an *assumption* about what constituted deity at all. All of our world is subject to change and decay, chance, and death, they said; it and its constituents are all *finite*. Deity *by definition* is infinite; it is eternal, by *definition*: or so the Greeks deemed to be the case. In addition, while some Greco-Roman philosophies disagreed, (neo) Platonism, the most perennial of them all, defined deity firstly as "immaterial," and secondly as "simple"; that is, God is not "good" or "wise," they are not *qualities* of deity; rather God is Goodness and Wisdom *per se*. "Of course," we are quite quick to say. But what if this "classical deity" runs into the claim that a particular human being, a finite, material creature of space and time, with dust between his toes and sweat on his brow, is "somehow" "God"—despite furthermore the crucially perceived problem of his *dying*! What happens to our "God-talk" now? Christology and the doctrine of the Trinity are just the historical consequences of this necessary wrestling with the Christian faith as it crosses boundaries in the mission of the church into the ancient Greco-Roman cultural context.[2]

Attempts to explain Jesus in relation to such God-talk began in a more systematic fashion (after the likes of the NT authors, that is) and in earnest by the start of the second century. Collectively, writers known as the apologists sought to convey the faith as a missionary exercise into the pagan world.[3] Justin Martyr (c. 100–c. 165) is one of the more prominent members of this group. He uses what we might term a Logos theology, citing the role of reason generally among humans, and linking that with the Logos as found in Jesus the Word and in the world. Then there's Irenaeus of Lyon (c. 130–200), whose *Adversus Haereses* run to five volumes or books. While his main focus was on apostolic tradition and the Rule of Faith, as these answered various *Gnostic* claims (we'll come back to this word soon), for our purposes we need to note again his idea of God's two "own hands," "his Word and his Wisdom, the Son and the Spirit" (*Adv. Haer.* 4.20.1), who themselves mediate God's actions in creation and history, what he also called "the economy of salvation" (3.23.1).[4] Lastly, we note the subtle, concise expression, detailing the Father-Son relation: "All saw the Father in the Son; for the Father is the invisible [ἀόρατον (*a-oraton*)] of the Son, the Son the visible [ὁρατὸν (*horaton*)] of the Father" (4.6.5).

Key to the development of the doctrine of the Trinity is Tertullian of North Africa (c. 160–c. 225), who was the first to coin the word *Trinitas*

---

2. The situation is made more complex however by the invasion of Greece's culture already into Judaism at the time of Alexander the Great, 332 BC onwards. See Hengel, *Judaism and Hellenism*.

3. Most helpful here is Grant, *Greek Apologists*.

4. This expression, "the economy," became an important piece of shorthand, first employed by Ignatius of Antioch in his Letter to the Ephesians (20). It's also helpful and important to see its etymology. *Oikos* is Greek for household, *oikonomia* then becoming the administration of that household, notably through its *oikonomos* or steward. See especially Ephesians 1–3, where a whole lot of words, both nouns and verbs (to build), use this *oiko*-root.

of the entire Godhead, and to employ *persona* of each divine person.[5] He was also responsible for the two key Latin terms, *persona* and *substantia*. The first originally came from the theatre and referred to an actor's mask, and so therefore to the role a person played. The Latin word, *persona*, was itself supposed to derive from the Greek, πρόσωπον (*prosōpon*), which means face or mask. The second was meant to convey especially the unity of the One God whose Monarchy was revealed through the drama of redemption via precisely the roles of Son and Spirit, whose *personae* were thus "different although not separate" (*discreti non separati*), "distinct yet not divided" (*distincti non divisi*) from the unity (*Adversus Praxean* 9).[6] Of course, this language was fluid at this stage and not exact; nor was Tertullian consistent in all his usage of these terms. We need to note especially the very possibility of interpreting such talk from the point of view of Sabellianism,[7] which sees these roles as being only manifested in the economy or "dispensation" of salvation; they are viewed as being not *intrinsic* to God's very essence but were mere appearances.

Then there's an important intellectual group in Alexandria, who include Clement (active around 200) and Origen (c. 185–255), and who begin to appropriate more fully the *lingua franca* of the day, Neo-Platonism. Origen especially comes up with the notion of the Son's "eternal generation" from the Father—which was somewhat muddied, however, due to his notion also of eternal creation. It was especially the perceived tension between these two in the fourth century that was a major trigger for debate and necessary resolution. Lastly, we need to note his use of the

---

5. See Daniélou, "Tertullian's System," 3:361–66.

6. These translations of *Adversus Praxean* 9 are taken from McGrath, *Christian Theology*, 250.

7. Sabellius's views are represented only in the writings of his opponents, as his own writings have not survived. But why oppose his trinitarian ideas; what were they? God is said to act in the economy in such a way that we see now the Father, and now the Son, and now the Holy Spirit. Each appears as a manifestation of the One God; each is a mode of the One God's Being. This last expression gives rise to another name for this entire set of ideas, modalism. The key point is that each person of the Trinity is only an *appearance* in this world, in the economy of salvation; God in God's very own Being does not have these distinctions at all. Importantly, a common way of trying to explain Trinitarianism nowadays makes a similar mistake, by ascribing certain functions to each person, and then by creating what tries to be an alternative Name out of them: Creator, Redeemer, and Sanctifier or Life-Giver. But this cannot be an adequate Name for the Trinity, since God's Being must be seen to be *eternally* triune; and if eternally so, then in a way that does *not* assume the need to even create or redeem or give life to others. We shall meet this important issue again later.

term ὑπόστασις (*hypostasis* = subsistence/essence/entity) of each person, Father, Son and Holy Spirit—although here again there was a later difficulty, due to Origen's *ranking* them according to the traditional *glacis* or chain-of-being metaphysic, so that *subordination* was integral to his understanding of "divinity": Father > Son > Spirit.[8]

The Fourth-Century Arian Controversy[9]

Fast forward now to the opening decades of the fourth century, when we meet Arius, who was a presbyter in the church of Alexandria during the first third of that century (he died in 336). While his life before his rise to prominence in 318 is obscure (he was probably born around 256 in Libya and was a reasonably influential member of the wider Alexandrian church), that year saw his clash with the bishop of Alexandria, named Alexander, who excommunicated both him and some close followers. However, they were allowed to practice their presbyterate of a congregation by some bishops of Palestine, despite formal condemnation by an Alexandrian synod of 321 of their doctrinal views. Yet doctrine is not the only feature of this controversy! Alexandria was at this time a large, complex city, with a number of churches scattered over defined districts, all with their respective leadership. The bishop, while respected *beyond* the city in the wider region of the eastern Mediterranean, nevertheless was no monarchial figure *within* the city itself. Yet again, while "respect" for the bishop of Alexandria was acknowledged by many, such respect was not allowed to be to the detriment or loss of *other* local synods and bishops and *their* influence either. And so Arius appealed by letter to another influential bishop, Eusebius of Nicomedia, in NW Turkey.

There began rounds of hostile correspondence and jockeying for support, each canvassing ways of expressing their beliefs *and* justifying their actions. Legitimation moreover was sought by a *number* of

---

8. For further details on Origen's views on the nature of the Son vis-à-vis the Trinity, see Daniélou, "Origen," 2:375–86. Overall, this book is a useful resource for the earlier Apologists, Irenaeus, Justin, and Clement, as well as Origen; but, because of its thematic approach, referencing all the relevant sections is complex, and so is avoided here.

9. The literature is vast, but amongst it all, generally from the simple to the more complex, see: Chadwick, *The Early Church*; Bray, *Creeds, Councils and Christ*; Wilken, *Spirit of Early Christian Thought*; Kelly, *Early Christian Doctrines*; Grillmeier, *Christ in Christian Tradition*; Young, *From Nicaea to Chalcedon*; Hanson, *Search for the Christian Doctrine of God*; Ayres, *Nicaea and its Legacy*; Anatolios, *Retrieving Nicaea*.

traditional means:[10] scriptural exegesis, recourse to differing schools of philosophical thought and/or ascetical and/or "charismatic" practices, to Rules of Faith, even to martyrdom or fidelity under persecution, and consequent notions of "holiness."[11] Similarly, the range of themes debated was diverse, even if in the end they circled around a multifaceted center—Christian life and faith focused on the One True God, no less. Just so, questions of worship, of the nature of salvation, of Christ's (mediatorial) role in that salvation, and lastly conceptions of the relationship between God and created reality—all are involved and implicate each other. Enter on stage, finally, imperial, political tensions as well, including an eventual war between Licinius and Constantine (321–24), with the latter emerging victor. All this affects mere doctrine, as the church and churches become involved in having to take sides (for survival and against continued persecution, no less than doctrine). Constantine too has to take sides eventually—if only to establish some *peace and unity* among his subjects! Hence the call for the Council of Nicaea in 325.

But this was merely the beginning of a long, tortuous drama, stretching over time and space, from 325 to 381 and across most of the Mediterranean world. The Arian controversy, as we now call it, combined a rich mixture of elements as suggested: the ecclesiastical and the political, employing virtually all means, fair and foul, the intellectual and the physical—and the spiritual too! No sooner was one faction in ascendency than another aspect of the delicate equation of power and ideas would

---

10. Pelikan, *Credo*, 125, suggests four key "factors"—exegesis, prayer, polemics, and politics—which make up part II's subsequent four chapters, each elaborating their respective factor.

11. See Ayres, *Nicaea*, chapters 11–13 for a most significant section within his overall study of pro-Nicene theology, since it focuses on the development of a specific "culture" and *habitus*, with its concomitant "life of the mind" during the fourth century: i.e., cultivated practices of intellect and body result in due purification of body and mind and so communion with and in Jesus Christ and so life within the triune God. Chapter 13 in particular address the necessary scriptural reading habits and goals as well, 335–41. For according to Ayres, understanding, production and confession of Nicene creedal orthodoxy was a function of a strategic development of a quite specific theological imagination coupled with a necessary way/form of life—this is Ayres' thesis, based on what he terms a "dual-focus anthropology," 326: "where problems with unsanctified human thinking and action—and the cure for those problems—are described by exploring how human beings should possess a trained soul that animates the body and attends to their joint τέλος (telos) in the divine presence through contemplation of God."

shift the balance.[12] The two individuals, Arius and Alexander (who died in 328), were soon forgotten, as this arch-heretical struggle took on quintessential scope, "*Arianism*" versus *Orthodox Catholic Faith*. Perhaps only the name of Athanasius, who succeeded Alexander as bishop in 328, and who himself experienced exile from Alexandria *five times* during his long, forty-six-year episcopacy (he died May 2, 373), stands out individually from the massive tangle of events.

Two vital features of this history need highlighting at this point. First, when the narrative of Scripture, or the Christian story, comes to be viewed from another, more conceptual framework (as a means of interpretation and/or elucidation), not just *any* set of ideas (philosophical, cultural, or whatever) will do. Rather, we need to be able to *trace* a direct line from what the Scriptures *infer*—but do not explicitly state—to those controlling ideas or concepts or philosophy.[13] Then, secondly, it will not do just to throw biblical texts around and at each other. The inference(s) of Scripture—what Athanasius would term Scripture's *dianoia* or "mind"— need to tie in with *how* Scripture is actually *read and used* within the community of faith, along with other canonical means of grace issuing in salvation; that is, within the church's essential setting of *worship and witness, its entire life* (see again the reference to Ayres' thesis, note 11 above). For not only is Jesus remembered as the central actor of the drama as told in the story; his Living Presence is proclaimed as being here–and–now, both in the world/cosmos and especially among his people, in such a way that he is worthy of all worship and adoration, being the Lord of "all things"—and this despite whatever the future consequences might be for either life or limb, or metaphysical philosophy! Again and again Athanasius made this point: if the church falsely worships the Son as being on a par with the Father, then that is truly idolatry; yet that is what the church from its very origins has been actually doing—worshipping the Son alongside the Father! Draw the right and only conclusion then![14] At the core of all positions in the struggle was the key question: how to satisfy

---

12. As Jerome wrote after the Council of Rimini, in Italy in 359, "The world groaned to find itself Arian."

13. See esp. Yeago, "NT and Nicene Dogma," 153, emphases original: "[T]he ancient theologians were right . . . that the Nicene *homoousion* is neither imposed *on* the New Testament texts, nor distantly deduced *from* the texts, but rather describes a pattern of judgements present *in* the texts, in the texture of scriptural discourse concerning Jesus and the God of Israel."

14. See Athanasius, *De Incarnatione Verbi Dei*, and Anatolios, *Athanasius*, esp. 83–86 re "eusebeia," that basic tenet of "piety" or godliness/worship.

the Scriptural affirmation of Jesus' singular Lordship, and so the church's acknowledgement of this, his primacy in worship, with perceived understandings of God's absolute transcendence, above "all things."

The Latin tag, *lex orandi, lex credendi* ("the law of worship is the principle of belief"), was used to sum up this last point. (While this tag may still formally stand, its contemporary applicability however has been severely compromised by the sheer variety of forms of worship, culturally and globally, all of which do *not* reflect similar beliefs necessarily.) Fundamentally then, we must be able to trace this discernible line of connection and/or development from existential encounter and belief and worship through confession to conceptual hermeneutical formulation, all as an integrated whole. Trinitarian doctrine is a "summary concept" (Eberhard Jüngel) of the Catholic Church's entire existence and life, since Jesus' Lordship creates an entire Way of New Life, with the Creed being its primary "symbol"—which is why, for example, it is often sung rather than just said during the course of a church service.[15]

Consequently, there is a final caution and question to ponder here. With varying conceptual frameworks being employed to aid interpretation (down the centuries), with the occasional cultural blindness too, what is the relationship between right faith and right practice, especially the exercise of ecclesial love? Is a creed therefore not *more* a canonical tool aiding communal practice, than a criterion of right understanding, an epistemic tool to access due knowledge, as many a modern understanding of reason might have it?[16]

---

15. See Steiner, *Real Presences*, 216–17, 218: "Music and the metaphysical, in the root sense of that term, music and religious feeling, have been virtually inseparable. It is in and through music that we are in the presence of the logically, of the verbally inexpressible but wholly palpable energy in being that communicates to our senses and to our reflection of what little we can grasp of the naked wonder of life. I take music to be the naming of the naming of life . . . Music makes utterly substantive what I have sought to suggest of the real presence of meaning where that presence cannot be analytically shown or paraphrased. Music brings to our daily lives an immediate encounter with a logic of sense other than that of reason. It is, precisely, the truest name we have for the logic at work in the springs of being that generate vital forms."

16. See for example Abraham, *Canon and Criterion*, who makes this point with extensive historical material and persuasion.

The Creeds of 325 and 381

We need now to present some *formal theological conclusions* of this crucial fourth century saga, encapsulated in the Nicene-Constantinopolitan Creeds of 325 and 381. But first the Creeds themselves.

An Edict of Constantine, dated May 23, formally convened the bishops of the empire (numbers estimate between 250 and 300) at Nicaea, in modern NW Turkey. In the event, they met until the end of July, presided over by Ossius bishop of Cordova, who was the Emperor's adviser on Christian matters and the church, even though Constantine himself was present and also spoke. The famous conclusion of their hard fought debates from this first ecumenical council is embodied in the following creed:[17]

> We believe in One God, the Father, Almighty/the ruler of all, the maker of all things, visible and invisible; and in one Lord, Jesus Christ the Son of God, begotten as the only Son out of the Father, that is out of the substance [*ousia*] of the Father, God from God, light from light, true God from true God, begotten not made, *homoousios* with the Father, through whom all things came to be, things in heaven and things in earth; who, for the sake of us human beings and our salvation, descended and became flesh, became human, suffered, and rose on the third day, ascended into the heavens and is coming to judge living and dead; and in the Holy Spirit.
>
> As for those who say, "There was when he was not," or "he did not exist before he was begotten," or "he came into being out of non-existence," or who fantasize that the Son of God is [made] from some other *hypostasis* or *ousia*, or that he is created or mutable or changeable, such people the catholic and apostolic church anathematizes.[18]

The ink was barely dry when confusion set in. As we've seen, both politics, imperial as well as ecclesiastical, and doctrine were causes; so too were the considerable *semantic differences* among the philosophical stances of the bishops. The ever acrimonious and often violent toing and froing between Nicaea and the final settlement of Constantinople was

---

17. It is helpful to see the parallels between this 325 Creed and Paul's *Shema*, both re structure and certain key phrases. See again Blaising, "Creedal Formation" and Soulen, *Divine Name(s)*, note 9, chapter five.

18. This translation is not taken from a single source but is a redaction of a number of English texts in relation to the Greek.

assuaged as much as anything else by *eventual agreement on what terms to use for what aspects of God's reality and nature*—as well as the necessary favor of pro-Nicene emperors East and West. Indeed, it was the explicitly pro-Nicene Theodosius who summoned the Council at Constantinople in May 381.

The approximate 150 bishops who attended met until July, formally concluding a number of canons and confirming certain Catholic, that is, Nicene, bishops in their sees. Notable among them was Gregory of Nazianzus, one of the three Cappadocian fathers—Basil of Caesarea and his younger brother Gregory of Nyssa being the other two—who was the legitimate bishop of Constantinople itself. Yet there is a problem: did the treatise (*tomos*) mentioned in a letter sent to Rome in 382 actually mean the Creed formally only promulgated at *Chalcedon in 451*, with its number of *additions* to the creed of Nicaea? Or should we see these additions as being part of the Council's general affirmation of the Nicene Creed, which affirmation they formulated both in a canon, number 1, and by inserting, in the *spirit* of Nicaea, precisely those further items which addressed matters that Nicaea itself had no immediate cause to meet? In their eyes, their full Constantinopolitan Creed did not *replace* the earlier Nicene version; it merely reaffirmed it, awaiting a fuller gathering of both East and West for its official endorsement (which finally came, as mentioned, in 451).

> We believe in one God, the Father, the Almighty/the ruler of all, maker of heaven and earth, of all that is, seen and unseen.
> And in one Lord, Jesus Christ, the only Son of God, begotten of the Father before all ages, Light from Light, true God from true God, begotten, not made, of one Being (*homoousion*) with the Father; through him all things were made. For us all (men/humans) and for our salvation he came down from heaven, and became incarnate by (the power of) the Holy Spirit and from the Virgin Mary, and was made man/human. For our sake he was crucified under Pontius Pilate; he suffered (death) and was buried. On the third day he rose (again) from the dead in accordance with the scriptures, and ascended into heaven and is seated at the right hand of the Father, and will come again in glory to judge the living and the dead, and his kingdom will have no end.
> And in the Holy Spirit, the Lord, the giver of life, who proceeds from the Father, who with the Father and the Son is

co-worshipped and co-glorified, who has spoken through the Prophets.

(We believe) in one holy catholic and apostolic church. We (acknowledge) confess one baptism for the forgiveness of sins. We look for the resurrection of the dead, and the life of the (world) age to come. Amen.[19]

The Homoousion

The key to the settlement of the Nicene Creed is the *homoousion*,[20] as it is called. The Creed's conclusion, that Jesus is indeed "God of God, Light of Light, very God of very God, begotten not made, of one being with the Father (ὁμοούσιον τῷ πατρί/*homoousion tō patri*)," introduces an essential formulation without which we simply may not do sufficient justice to the identity of the God who redeems us through Jesus. Such is the reality and significance of the gospel events, "the things that have been brought to pass among us" (Luke 1:1), that we've to construct—and that *is* the right word—new vocabulary that breaks new ground. Nor should this surprise us really: it's the same with any scientific breakthrough, which frequently comes up with new and often outlandish forms of speech, new models or paradigms, to render the thing intelligible at all. Such is the *homoousion* also.

> It was a decisive step in the deeper understanding of the Gospel, giving precise expression to the all-important relation between the incarnate Son and God the Father, which they [the Ecumenical Council Fathers] made in obedience to God's saving revelation in Jesus Christ and in continuity with the apostolic tradition upon which the church could not go back. With it a giant step was taken in grasping and giving expression to the internal relation of the incarnate Son to the Father, and thereby to the ontological substructure and coherence of the Gospel. It proved to be an inerasable and irreversible event in the history of Christian theology.[21]

---

19. This translation mostly follows that found in World Council of Churches, *Confessing the One Faith*, 10–12.

20. For a thorough explication of this term and its implications, see Torrance's introduction in *The Incarnation*, xi–xxii.

21. Torrance, *Christian Doctrine of God*, ix–x. And see again Yeago, note 13 above.

To see the real import of such a claim as this by Tom Torrance, we might ask the questions: What historically was the principle of the *homoousion* addressing? For what problem does it offer the solution? The answer, in a word, is "*dualism.*"[22] Ancient Greek culture, the *lingua franca* of the ancient Mediterranean world, presupposed that deity was simply everything that this world was not, as we've hinted earlier. Just as this world is ever changing, decaying, and finite, so "God," by definition, is deemed to be immutable, eternal, and infinite. And just so, *never shall the twain meet*: *that's* the assumption; a form of transcendence is absolute. Consequently indeed, forms of Hellenistic philosophy, of which the Gnostics were the most popular, speculated upon an entire series or grades of intermediary realities, or shades/degrees of being between the One True God and this mundane human existence of ours: in this way, Ultimate Reality is not to be soiled in any way at all by us lot! Enter *into this context* the gospel of Jesus, and the temptation is strong merely to appoint Christ amidst this throng of intermediary figures, which is what Gnostic Christianity tried to do, and against which the likes of Irenaeus objected so strongly.

There is of course an important missiological question lurking here; and Pannenberg's seminal essay already mentioned above (note 4, chapter three, and note 1 above) is especially helpful. For when crossing boundaries in mission, the church still has to translate the gospel into terms that will be intelligible to those who have not heard it before. Evangelists have to appropriate some elements of the local culture to make themselves heard, even as they might disavow other features of that culture.

And so, to make a complicated story brief, let us note only this: when it came to rendering the gospel of Jesus into language borrowed from ancient Hellenism, the church pushed the terms ready-to-hand literally over the brink; they stretched the language of the day and the thought-world it conveyed to its very breaking point. As Robert Jenson observes, "As a piece of trinitarian language, *hypostasis* is merely an item of linguistic debris knocked from Hellenistic philosophy by collision with Yahweh,"[23] the God and Father of Jesus Christ. He might just as easily have used any of the perennial language available, like *ousia*, to make his

---

22. For a helpful summary of this classical view of things, which has a range of consequences, philosophical, social, ethical, etc., see Strom, *Reframing Paul*, part 1, "Primary Reality and Everyday Reality: Ancient Frames for a Split World," 23–69.

23. Jenson, *TI*, 108; and "Second Locus," 138.

point.²⁴ For, and this is the point, given the assumption that the infinite Creator is deemed not able to mix with finite creation, let alone actually to become a creature in the midst of this world, how then might we couch the essential Christian claim we have already met—that the Word has indeed *become flesh* and dwelt among us, that Jesus is to be seen as *intrinsic* to Yahweh's identity? In a nutshell, dear old Arius, and those who loyally thought like him in the fourth century, simply could not stomach the tension raised by the question! Jesus, they tried to say, was the *very greatest link* in the intermediary chain of entities *between* the Ultimate Origin of "All Things" and ourselves. That is, if push comes to shove, Jesus' identity falls *this side* of the great divide between the One True Unoriginate Creator and all the rest of created reality; he quite simply is the very greatest of everything else there is ever going to be . . . but *not actually* GOD! If we must talk of divine unity, then the most we may manage is to convey a supreme unity of *will* between Father and Son—but *not* any unity of Actual Divine Being.

So *feel* the *problem* folks! Rowan Williams has offered us one of the very best assessments of this quintessential dilemma for the early church.²⁵ He identifies Arius as in fact a good old conservative, a good old Hellenistic thinker trying to fight a last ditch, rearguard action against these revolutionaries who want to upset the entire worldview of the Ancient Mediterranean. And the likes of Athanasius did this upsetting by saying things like this:

> It would be more godly and more accurate or true to signify God from the Son and call Him Father, than to name God from his works only and call him Unoriginate.²⁶

---

24. See Stead, *Divine Substance*, for an extensive examination of the term, *ousia/substantia*.

25. See Williams, *Arius*. Leithart, *Athanasius*, 17–25, "Motivations of Arian Theology," in chapter 1, "Evangelizing Metaphysics," is also an excellent summary.

26. Athanasius, "Four Discourses against the Arians–Discourse 1," IX, 34 in *NPNF IV*, 326. Underscoring this point, Torrance, *Trinitarian Faith*, repeats this quote, 49, and then says more fulsomely later, 87: "while God was always Father, he was not always Creator or Maker." That is, to call God "Father" *implies there is* a "Son" with whom the Father is *essentially* in relation, whereas there might *never* have been a creation *at all*, to signify God as either its "Origin," or as therefore "Unoriginate." Both Athanasius and Torrance are making inordinately crucial points, soon to be amplified, given the sorts of assumptions at play, both then and now.

That is, if we listen obediently to the words of Jesus, and acknowledge them as indeed words from his Father and his God, all such God-talk becomes necessarily *relational* from now on. We simply may not conceive of God the Father without seeing simultaneously God the Son; the two necessarily constitute each other, in the fullest divine sense; there is never one without the other. They are *homoousios*—"of the same substance"; *the divine nature is essentially relational.* Just so, that anathema pronounced at the Council of Nicaea we noted above immediately after the Creed.[27] In other words, our entire language, and the worldview it depicts, has to undergo not only radical repentance (or *metanoia* in Greek) but as Athanasius puts it, an entire *dianoia*, as we've said before. To translate this into twenty-first-century scientific language, our entire mental apparatus has to undergo a *root paradigm shift*. We've to see that, while on the one hand, deity *by definition* is unique and indivisible, and while on the other hand, the *essential and absolute divide* between the Creator's Being and all contingent created being (the Creed's "all things"), brought into existence "out of nothing"/*ex nihilo* by the Creator, warrants no mediating degrees or levels of being,[28] yet the *triune* God *himself is supremely free to transcend his transcendence*. The one who is "beyond all being" (Athanasius) comes graciously and concretely in his Word *among his creation*. Indeed; even while he was never "far from it before" or "distant," this Word now "enters the world in a new way, stooping to our level in His love and Self-revealing to us."[29] As Karl Barth would express it many centuries later: "We cannot imagine any possibility or actuality or ordering of our knowledge of God apart from that which God Himself has established.

---

27. Athanasius pursues just this logic of the anathema in "Four Discourses against the Arians - Discourse 1," *NPNF IV*, VII, 25 and IV, 12, 321 and 313. And see Rusch, *Trinitarian Controversy*, 88 and 74–75.

28. E.g., Gregory of Nyssa, "On the Holy Spirit," 3, in *NPNF V*, 316: "When once our minds have grasped the idea of Deity, we accept by the implication of that very name the perfection in it of every conceivable thing that befits the Deity. Deity, in fact, exhibits perfection in every line in which the good can be found. If it fails and comes short of perfection in any single point, in that point the conception of Deity will be impaired, so that it cannot, therein, be or be called Deity at all." Just so, true devotion and glory may be ascribed to both Son and Holy Spirit, who with the Father share divine Being.

29. *De Incarnatione Verbi Dei*, 33. This Nicene understanding upends the very idea of classical transcendence and/or the immense *distance* between God the Creator and his creation: the triune God is ever fully *present* to and in his world. Just so, *everything* hinges around this destruction of any "dualism."

We cannot think of being able to explain our knowledge of God in any way from itself instead of its object."[30]

Putting it most succinctly, the actuality determines the possibility; what God has actually established in and through and with Jesus of Nazareth in our space-time world determines what is in fact possible thereafter to say and think and, finally, even be. For the triune God himself has set up the very way we may know him at all, and that is through Jesus, Word-become-flesh, and in the Holy Spirit.[31]

In this light, the principle of the *homoousion*, that Jesus the Son and his Father are essentially one in their very Being, is the direct opposite of the Hellenistic philosophical premise or assumption we call "dualism." Just as our obedience to careful observations of how the planets in fact/ actually go around the sun gives rise to what we term the Copernican revolution, upsetting the traditional Ptolemaic view of things, so too faithful acknowledgement of and adherence to what has transpired in Christ Jesus means we have to ditch any form of dualism and affirm the *homoousion*—no matter how revolutionary! This is an absolute prerequisite. And the practice is no mere piece of antiquarianism, to be relegated to patristic studies of the early church: dualism is alive and well in our twenty-first century, and as equally destructive of the gospel as any Hellenism once was! How so?

It is curious how common dualism actually is. Most New Age spiritualities nowadays assume one form of dualism or another, with their ways of seeing reality which split the "really key aspects" from "lesser features." Yet the consequences of such splitting are not universal: either one may *ignore* such "lesser" levels of reality, *squandering* their use wantonly; or there's the opposite, the "lesser" must be treated with an *ascetic rigor* since what *really* counts is ever "above" us. For ethics is always a function of some form of metaphysics or other. Nor may we lay all the blame at the fad of contemporary spiritualities. Immanuel Kant (1724–1804) has bequeathed not only a philosophical legacy, but also a more widespread cultural one that would split practical matters from the theoretical, limiting often the role of reason to mere instrumentality. Add to this now the huge success of modern technology, and the temptation in many Western Christian circles has been to reduce much theological debate to

---

30. Barth, *CD* II/1, 41. And note Roberts, "Karl Barth," 84: "The claim made by Barth is that the Trinity is not a merely formal explanation of revelation but its ontological enabling, the real possibility behind the revealed reality."

31. See Torrance, "Epistemological Relevance," 165–92.

mere ethics, as if the Christian faith were supremely a case of ethics only: after all, it might be said, what of our Lord's two commandments that summarize the Law?

Nor is this last paragraph a digression away from our topic. Such legacies have impacted trinitarian thinking these past few hundred years, reducing any theoretical notions to "mere monotheism,"[32] to a view of deity that is "unipersonal," if personal at all.[33] For Christian faith to resist such dualism (once more), it would have to offer instead a robust enough ontology, one premised upon an incarnational view of creation, which has been lovingly brought into existence and sustained and redeemed by the triune God, and which will be treated in a quite specific manner by those who both are to be its stewards and are themselves an integral part of it. Ethics in such a theoretical undertaking is still important, to be sure; but it now finds itself the natural outcome of a particular view of the human person, one which furthermore finds its true identity as a reflection of the triune Godhead, in whose Image humanity was made and is now being recreated in Christ Jesus, in loving freedom and truth.

The Holy Spirit

All of which talk, however, presupposes one crucial facet of trinitarianism, the Holy Spirit, for which we return once more to the fourth century, in order to round off our discussion and conclusions of the two creeds. The first thing to note is Constantinople expands the Third Article considerably beyond the mere statement of 325: "and in the Holy Spirit." Yet the language of that expansion is quite careful, reflecting some of the debates surrounding the nature of the Holy Spirit in the intervening decades. There is no equivalent directly of the *homoousion*. Rather, having quoted John 15:26, "who proceeds from the Father," and so avoiding any thought of there possibly being two "generated sons," the Creed follows Basil of Caesarea's lead in his treatise *De Spiritu Sancto* (On the Holy

---

32. Rahner, *Trinity*, 10: "Despite their orthodox confession of the Trinity, Christians are, in their practical life, almost mere monotheists."

33. See Kasper, *God*, 285, where he considers such a unipersonal notion an Enlightenment invention and not Christian at all—one furthermore that would later become susceptible to such atheistic denials as those of a Feuerbach or a Marx, especially after the rise of Deistic understandings of "God," yet another form of dualism. And further, see Vickers, *Invocation and Assent*, esp. the summary commencing chapter 6, 169–71.

Spirit),[34] written around 374, simply asserting of the Spirit, "who with the Father and the Son is co-worshipped and co-glorified." Once more, the actual worshipping experience and life of the Christian community is the primary context of its intellectual reflections upon the One who is so worshipped as Lord of all. For if indeed the Holy Spirit is supremely "the Lord and Giver of Life," then of course he should be honored as being on a par with God the Father and God the Son. There is quite simply no room for any gradation at all in the Divine Being: "full glory may be given" (Basil) to each and all of the three persons of the Trinity. This argument, of there being no possibility of a "hierarchy of Being" within the life of God, is also emphasised by Basil's brother, Gregory of Nyssa, in his debates with a certain Eunomius, who took up a war of words against Basil and Gregory. Yet if the nature of deity is *sheer infinitude* (as Gregory argued), with "the one divine *ousia*, the *varied* sharing of which distinguishes Father, Son and Spirit, and the varied *sharing* of which qualifies their joint act as God,"[35] how may there possibly be any gradation among them in that being: infinity is infinity, and by definition permits no grades (no "before" or "after")!

Hypostasis and Ousia

In the process of these debates another clarification emerges, just hinted at. *Hypostasis* now becomes distinguishable from *ousia*, with the former being used to identify each of the three divine persons, each of whose τρόπος ὑπάρξεως/*tropos hyparxeōs* (mode/manner of existence/subsistence), as the three Cappadocians averred, then underscores their specific identities. As Basil says in *De Spiritu Sancto*:

---

34. See his opening comment, "On the Holy Spirit," *NPNF VIII*, I.3, regarding the wording of the doxology, and subsequently, chapters XIX–XXVI, stressing the appropriateness of according the Spirit full honor and glory: 3, and 30–40 respectively. Gregory of Nazianzus repeats the idea: "For if he is not to be worshipped, how can he deify me by baptism? But if he is to be worshipped, surely he is an object of adoration, and if an object of adoration, he must be God; the one is linked to the other, a truly golden and saving chain" ("Fifth Theological Oration: On the Holy Spirit," in *NPNF VII*, 327).

35. Jenson, *TI*, 166, emphases in the text. This quote is from chapter 5, "Triune Infinity," all of which is most seminal, setting up Jenson's own trinitarian theology, which he pursues later in *Unbaptized God* and his *Systematic Theology*, all of which we shall pursue in earnest later.

> Thus the way of the knowledge of God lies from One Spirit through the One Son to the One Father, and conversely the natural Goodness and the inherent Holiness and the royal Dignity extend from the Father through the Only-begotten to the Spirit. Thus there is both acknowledgment of the *hypostases* (plural) and the true dogma of the Monarchy is not lost.[36]

Another way of expressing these ideas comes from his brother Gregory of Nyssa:

> Every activity which pervades from God to creation and is named according to our manifold designs starts off from the Father, proceeds through the Son, and is completed by the Holy Spirit. On account of this, the name of the activity is not divided into the multitude of those who are active. . . . Therefore then, the holy Trinity works every activity according to the manner stated, not divided according to the number of the *hypostases*, but one certain motion and disposition of goodwill occurs, proceeding from the Father through the Son to the Spirit.[37]

In these ways we are able to speak of there being firstly true *unity* of divine action or monarchy by means of secondly *each* person's *specific* identity, or as they would say later in Latin, the *proprium* of each divine person.

In our own day, one of the pioneers of the current revival of interest in the doctrine of the Trinity, Karl Rahner, has emphasised the distinctive *hypostasis* of each person most forcibly by saying: "Grace gives rise to not-appropriated relations of divine persons to man."[38] That is, when we look closely at the economy of salvation, we need to pay most careful attention to two key elements which impact greatly our appreciation of God's triune nature. On the one hand, it is the proper and peculiar nature of the *Son* to enter into a hypostatic union, to become the Incarnate One, assuming human nature. Likewise on the other hand, the *Holy Spirit* is specifically the One who, in a "quasi–formal" as opposed to "efficient" way,[39] causes humans to participate in the very life of God. Or again, not-

---

36. Basil of Caesarea, "On the Holy Spirit," in *NPNF VIII*, 29. See esp. "Letter XXXVIII," ibid., 137–41, although this is commonly attributed nowadays to Gregory of Nyssa.

37. Gregory of Nyssa, "Concerning we should think of saying that There are Not Three Gods—To Ablabius," in Rusch, *Trinitarian Controversy*, 149–61 at 155.

38. Rahner, *Trinity*, 25.

39. See e.g., ibid., 13, 36, for this scholastic distinction and its implications, and

ing a key feature of the entire NT, the Holy Spirit is the *eschatological* gift of the Messianic Age. Paying close attention to this, we may then pick up on the fact of the *Spirit's* being the ἀρραβών/*arrabōn* (down payment or guarantee) of our future redemption (2 Cor 1:22; Eph 1:14). And he *may be* this towards us his creatures, since he *is* among the triune Godhead God's very own Unsurpassable Futurity,[40] as well as being the quintessential expression of the "desire" and "delight" between the Father and the Son. The contrary experiment was sometimes entertained in the Middle Ages, speculating whether either the Father or the Spirit may have become the Incarnate One.[41] Frankly, such speculations actually miss the point of the entire Nicene endeavor and victory, and Rahner is to be commended for highlighting this for us.

What all this understanding of the Trinity reveals may be summed up like this, quoting the initiator of today's revival of the Trinity, Karl Barth (1886–1968): "What [God] is in revelation He is antecedently in Himself. And what He is antecedently in Himself He is in revelation. Within the deepest depths of deity, as the final thing to be said about Him, God is God the Spirit as He is God the Father and God the Son."[42]

Or as T. F. Torrance put it in the editors' preface to the very first volume of Karl Barth's *Church Dogmatics*: it is "Barth's determination to move behind an 'economic' to an 'immanent' (i.e., an ontological) Trinity." The entire point of the creedal victory over the various forms of Arianism that sought to dominate during the fourth century is just this. God as we experience and encounter him during the unfolding of the mission of Jesus and its aftermath in the life of the church through the Holy Spirit—God *pro nobis*, "for/towards us," as theology would now summarize—is in reality none other than the eternal God *in se*, as he is in himself. To be sure; there's more to God in himself than that which he has (currently) revealed. When Karl Rahner states his *Grundaxiom* or basic

---

Foundations of Christian Faith, 120–22. The distinction lies at the heart of other contemporary theologians' insistence that we are concerned with *uncreated grace directly* and not *created grace* via *intermediaries* (as some older schemes of theology were wont to say), which impacts profoundly our trinitarianism and christology, as well as pneumatology. Some of the significance of this will be taken up later.

40. Talk of divine Futurity and God's Unsurpassability are expressions devised by Robert Jenson, whose trinitarian theology addresses the key issue of temporality. See *TI*, and *Unbaptized God*, esp. chapters 8–10, and *ST 1*. We shall come to all of this soon enough.

41. See even Aquinas, *Summa Theologiae*, III q.3, in 8 articles, esp. art.8.

42. Barth, *CD* I/1, 466.

methodological principle, "the economic Trinity is the immanent Trinity and the immanent Trinity is the economic Trinity,"[43] it is the vice versa of the second part that is suspect, since it *collapses* God's very Eternal Being *into* the economy, reducing that Eternal Being *to* the economy—which of course is false. Nevertheless, Rahner is onto something crucial, and what that is Barth expresses more felicitously—and necessarily.

Excursus[44]

These last few paragraphs prompt a brief series of comments upon the legitimacy or otherwise of viewing the *Imago Dei* as necessarily gendered because reflective of the Trinity in some way. After all, the first mention of "the image and likeness" of God, after which humankind is made/created, would appear to promote explicitly a gendered view of things.

> And God said, "Let us make man in our image, after our likeness. They shall rule the fish of the sea, the birds of the sky, the cattle, the whole earth, and all the creeping things that creep on earth."
> And God created (the) man in His image,
> in the image of God He created him;
> male and female [nouns] He created them.
> God blessed them and God said to them, "Be fertile and increase, fill the earth and master it; and rule the fish of the sea, the birds of the sky, and all the living things that creep on earth" (Gen 1:26–28 NJPS).

Following the cue of Janet Martin Soskice:

> We must also say that sexual difference is not, or should not be, a matter of theological indifference. Genesis 1 suggests that sexual difference has something to tell us, not just about human beings, but about God in whose image they are made, male and

---

43. Rahner, *Trinity*, 22.

44. In times past this excursus would not have been necessary. Today's contemporary postmodern confusion, however, with its tendency towards gross plasticity and horrendous fragmentation, all of which bear down upon the human in our inordinately disorientated state, requires the matter to be raised. In addition, given the introductory nature of this book, we cannot deal adequately with this complex issue. We may not for example address either positively or negatively the likes of Sarah Coakley's seminal ideas, found in e.g. "Re-thinking Gregory," 431–43; "Gender Reconsidered," 133–42; and *God, Sexuality, and the Self*, nor the reviews, headed by Rogers, in the book symposium, 552–99. What we can do is to signal something of a way forward.

female. The unresolved question then is: where, why, and how does sexual difference make a difference?[45]

If the two terms "male and female" are poetically parallel to "the image" in v. 27, and so interpret each other according to the rules of Hebrew poetry, then there is a *prima facie* case for beginning to draw the conclusion that the gendered form in which we encounter humanity (*adam* in the Hebrew) has necessarily something to do with humanity's nature. Humans are to be found as either men or women; and together they constitute what being created *imago Dei* is all about, even as the tradition would aver each individual human being as a bearer of the divine image.[46] True; the narrative of Genesis 1 has to be complemented by the narrative of Gen 2–3, without which there is an incomplete view; and we shall turn to briefly examine Gen 2 shortly.

But first we have to consider whether "image" and "likeness" are synonyms, or whether there are significant shifts of meaning between them. Initially, one might be tempted to see the repetition as more lyrical than substantive, as being yet another example of the repetitions found throughout vv. 26–30, and indeed the entire narrative. Lexical work however soon yields some results. The first word denotes a sculpture or statue, a material image that represents something else. The second word too conveys the sense of representation but more directly or immediately, something is like something else, pure and simple; nor does it have any attenuated sense of being only alike and not the same. Putting these together and establishing the meaning of the two terms together has created a long list of exegetical and theological possibilities down the centuries. Nor shall I try to summarize here what is available in good commentaries. Let us only say this.

Firstly, the two different prepositions ahead of each word do not warrant any extra weight to the distinction between the terms, for the prepositions themselves are lexically interchangeable. Rather, secondly,

---

45. Soskice, *Kindness*, 45. See too esp. her later chapters 6 and 7, 100–156, "Trinity and the 'Feminine Other'" and "The Kindness of God: Trinity and Image of God in Julian of Norwich and Augustine."

46. The solution to this possible quandary is to refer to the archetype of the Trinity (as we shall see soon enough). As has been said before, while Jesus is wholly God and wholly human, as the Incarnate One, there is more to God than the Son, for no one Person alone is God in the divine fulness; there are the identities of both the Father and the Holy Spirit. Analogously therefore, re individual men and women, and the Image itself.

any distinction only comes from the use of the first word generally to depict physical images, notably of kings or gods in their due realms, to act as a form of representation. From this has arisen the view that humanity is God's vice-regent upon earth, his physical representative, ruling creation on God's behalf. This certainly makes sense when the consequences of this creature's being made in God's image and likeness are spelled out, twice, once in association with the decision to create, and then after the fact. All of which has led thirdly, historically, to trying to locate the significance of the image/likeness in some quality or disposition of humanity, like rationality or free will, as a key expression or means of that rulership; or even in some cases in locating certain qualities in the image and others in the likeness, as with Irenaeus's natural personal traits re the former and redeemed supernatural endowment through the Spirit re the latter.[47]

Whatever final conclusions we might draw, and those briefly mentioned have a broad consensus nowadays, the final aspect to highlight is the language form at the start, "Let us make . . ." followed by "and God created . . ." Here we might rightly allude to the equivalent command-execution pattern, "God said . . . and it was so." These both perform the same introductory function—with this one proviso. In the case of v. 26, the emphasis is upon the divine *decision* to create *uniquely* this very particular creature, *adam*, who is distinct from the rest even as *adam* is too a creature like the rest. Hence the slightly different introductory formula (even if we shy away from drawing too much from the plural "us" here, as one might). All of which underlines once more the role this creature is to play: before God, and before the rest of creation. *Adam*, male-and-female, are to rule on God's behalf as they authentically reflect the divine image, which is to say, as they faithfully relate to the One in Whose Image they are created. But this last way of putting it also anticipates the next phase of the story, Genesis chapters 2–3.

Here we would only point out the following. *Adam* is *homo faber*. Once God has "breathed into [the man] the breath of life" (Gen 2:7) after the common understanding of the times when priests ritually established representative images of their gods in newly built temples (the story of Gen 1 is just so God's building his own cosmic temple), so Adam is put into the garden to keep it and to till it/to work it and to keep it (2:15); he thus exercises some "dominion" again. (The business of "naming" makes another essential point, re language and culture and human being; but we

---

47. See Barth, *CD* III/1, 191–206 for an exploration of answers over the years; and Smail, *Like Father, Like Son*, for a more in depth analysis over a number of chapters.

shall not be making much of that here and now.) Next, *adam* is essentially a social creature: it is not good for him to be alone (2:18). Yet, only when there is the profound poetical response of the man (*ish*) to the woman (*ishshah*) is this truly satisfied and a due "helping companion opposite/corresponding to him" found:

> This one at last
> Is bone of my bones
> And flesh of my flesh.
> This one shall be called Woman,
> For from Man was she taken (Gen 2:23 NJPS).

Here the true *likeness* of the woman to the man—"bone of my bones / And flesh of my flesh"—is to the fore on the one hand, and yet the *differentiation* between them is also present on the other—"opposite/corresponding," *ish* and *ishshah*.

Much as a proper exegesis of these texts should continue into chapter 3—especially with the literary structure of chapters 2–3 with its dialogues almost demanding it, our probing the probationary command of the Lord God's not to eat of the tree of the knowledge of good and evil and the entry on scene of a *third* party in the form of the snake, which invades the otherwise covenantal relationship between the-man-and-the-woman and the Lord God, and so delineating the breakdown of all the harmonious relationships among God's good creation when this Creator God's authority is flouted, as humans arrogate to themselves "all knowledge"/authority[48]—we can only examine here the question of the gendered Image, and this vis-à-vis the doctrine of the Trinity.

> The first and typical sphere of fellow-humanity, the first and typical differentiation and relationship between man and man, is that between male and female. In theological ethics it deserves special consideration if only because, in its crucial expression called marriage, it is shown in the Old Testament to correspond to the relationship between Yahweh and His people and in the New to that between Jesus Christ and His community. Furthermore, the description of the first man in the two creation stories

---

48. The only other place where the expression "knowledge of good and evil" is found is in the story of David and the woman from Tekoa, 2 Sam 14. Here 14:17 is parallel to 14:20, so that textually at least "knowledge of good and evil" equates with "knowing all"; and if one "knows all" then one need not defer to anyone else, one is one's own authority.

points decisively to this differentiation and relationship. By the divine likeness of man in Gen. 1:27f. there is understood the fact that God created them male and female, corresponding to the fact that God Himself exists in relationship and not in isolation . . . the God who is no *Deus solitarius* but *Deus triunus*.[49]

So summarizes Barth of the textual evidence gathered so far, and more: *ish/ishshah*; male–and–female he created them; a helping companion matching him; let *us* make. All these expressions compound to ask, in the fullness of the Christian scriptural canon, Old and New Testaments together, whether the idea is not at all far fetched that the human ectype finds its due prototype in *trinitarian* deity. For even as Word and Spirit are the means of God's good creation, so Ps 33:6; and furthermore, with the entire cosmos cohering in the Image of the Invisible God, so Col 1:15–20; it is not only Incarnation but creation itself that probes the question, establishing a full anthropology that runs from Genesis to Revelation, via even such notions as Yahweh's betrothal to Israel and the church as Jesus' Bride.[50] Even apart from Karl Barth's understanding that with the *imago Dei* we have here a creature who is a "counterpart" to God, who is in "reciprocity" with God[51]—for "in God's own being and sphere there is a counterpart"[52] *already*, namely the Son of the Father—these Genesis texts we have assembled, in the light of the NT pressure of the trinitarian understanding of God's nature, press themselves the issue: human nature is relationally gendered and uniquely so, such that male and female uniquely and necessarily *complement* one another, each being irreplaceable vis-à-vis the other. And such too, as we have seen, are the respective identities of the Trinity. The Son is the Incarnate One; the Holy Spirit is God's own future and as such may be our ἀρραβών (*arrabōn*) guaranteeing that redemptive future. The personal and relational identi-

---

49. Barth, *CD* III/4, 117; the entire section, 116–240, "Freedom in Fellowship, Man and Woman," is seminal.

50. See Scola, *Nuptial Mystery* for a thorough examination of these latter themes, as well as John Paul II, *Man and Woman*.

51. Barth, *CD* III/1, 183–95.

52. Ibid., 184; and see 195: "The relationship between the summoning I in God's being and the summoned divine Thou is reflected both in the relationship of God to the man whom He has created, and also in the relationship between the I and the Thou, between male and female, in human existence itself. *There can be no question of anything more than an analogy.* The differentiation and relationship between the I and the Thou in the divine being, in the sphere of the *Elohim*, are not identical with the differentiation and relationship between male and female" (emphasis added).

ties of the triune Godhead are not to be confused or interchanged, being irreducible; each is uniquely complementary to the others, so that each mutually constitutes and is constituted by the others' particular identities. Just so, the human "counterpart" analogous to the triune divine reality is concretely and specifically in that relationship we term "male and female"—which two complementary identities *in marriage furthermore* may become "one flesh" (Gen 2:24, where *echad* here is the same as Deut 6:4's *Shema*), and only so may these two together become this sacramental union who are to reflect especially the triune divine glory.[53] Nor should we miss the fact that the opening chapters of the canon, Gen 1–2, and the closing chapters, Rev 19–22, both in their respective ways spell out firstly the crucial *sacramentum* (or sign) of human marriage on the one hand, and then the *res* (the thing signified), the Heavenly Marriage of the Bride and the Lamb, on the other hand. In this way we have displayed a powerful pair of bookends to the entire Scriptures of Old and New Covenants.

And yet we must note, if only in passing, something of the language of "fruitfulness" precisely in this regard—not least as many human relationships are fruitful in multiple ways. These include the physical, in sexual reproduction, but they also exclude this particular form of expression—indeed, they might very well preclude such a form. The celibate life is clearly one such form, one lauded throughout Christian history. Yet this very form of Christian life, with its due "fruit for Christ," within the Household of God,[54] says nothing whatsoever to our present-day calls for same-sex relationships and even "marriage." Christian celibacy is the celebration of the *single* life *for the sake of the Kingdom of God*, which has drawn near in the completed earthly mission of the Son, who has poured out the Holy Spirit upon his church that he may fulfill across all places and times and peoples what the Son has begun, to the Glory of the Father. Human marriage naturally continues, and will precisely continue until the End (Matt 24:36–44). But both marriage and singleness are now *equally* charisms of the Spirit within the one Body of Christ—so 1 Cor 7 (and see chapters 12–14)—where both equally relish disciplines of "continent asceticism" (John Paul II). And they both in their unique and special ways signify marriage: husbands and wives mediate God's relationship with his people; single men and women, on account of their immediate

---

53. See Robinson, *Understanding the "Imago Dei"*; and Roberts, *Creation and Covenant*.

54. See esp. Bennett, *Water Is Thicker Than Blood*.

betrothal to the Bridegroom himself, awaiting the final consummation of "all things," embody and personify the church herself. Each vocation has their eschatological stamp; *both together*—and the church ever needs its complementary vocations and gifts—display the tension between what has already been completed in Christ Jesus and what is yet to come, for the church and for the world. Moreover, this very tension exhibits classically, via the institution of marriage, the heart of eschatology, the heart of the life of the church in all its ministerial fullness and fruitfulness *between the times*:

> The pattern of the resurrection determines the pattern of the Spirit's work. And the pattern of Christ's resurrection is one of both continuity and discontinuity together. Something new appears, which is nevertheless not novel, but the fulfilment of what was there before. The Jesus who rises is in identity and continuity with the Jesus who died . . . And yet, although everything in him passes through death, it is raised up into a radically different mode of being . . . so that on the one hand he is scarcely recognizable, and yet at the same time seeks to establish with his every action that he is the same.[55]

In which case it is a tragic irony, driven by a contemporary confusion, that would view human nature and notably the *imago Dei* in some androgynous form. By failing to distinguish adequately men and women, contemporary western culture ironically turns its back on the very trinitarian source that has granted humanity such profound appraisal of human personhood and human relationality (chapter 7 will substantiate this claim). To be sure; such has been the history of male–female relationships down the centuries, with their often severe sense of inequality, that the overreaction of the past decades is not surprising. For all that, such gains for both women and men as have been made are almost nullified when the supposed "logic" flips into mistaking male–male and female–female same-sex relationships as being capable of reflecting fully as well the authentic *imago Dei*. As we have been at some pains to point out, the *specific* identities of the triune God are *not* interchangeable: such is the *irreducible identity of each* that it is only due to the sum of their particular *idiotēs*[56] and their interrelationships that there is the Trinity at all. As a result, we must say, it is classically *tragic* that present West-

---

55. Smail, "Editorial," 3–4.

56. This Greek term is almost equivalent to the Latin *proprium*, expressing that which peculiarly belongs to each person in particular, human or divine.

ern culture presses towards a supposed "equality" between heterosexual and homosexual relationships. For such is the essential nature of things human that we shall ever fall short of true fulfillment—indeed, we are tragically "fated" to do so—should we try to image the oneness of the triune God in homosexual form, as opposed to genuine heterosexual form according to Genesis 1 and 2. Seeking such fulfillment by means of the homosexual is ironically a form of fallen desire, as indicated by Paul's exposition of the fallen nature of human being in Romans chapter 1. As much as "desire" is a key and legitimate component of the human (and St. Augustine has made much of it in his theology), its expression and *telos* similarly are markers equally of the true, the good, and the beautiful, and their opposites, given our fallen world. The problem occurs whenever there arises a desire such as the postmodern to homogenize essentially differentiated categories as human maleness and femaleness. A full doctrine of the Trinity and its concomitant anthropology would seek to address and redress such vital things as these in our day.

And in the Church, Etc.

Careful readers of the Creed would notice it does not end with the statements regarding the Holy Spirit; there's more: "and in one holy catholic and apostolic church, etc.," which form an essential part of the Third Article. Nor should the observant reader miss the way I put it earlier: "during the unfolding of the mission of Jesus *and its aftermath in the life of the church* through the Holy Spirit"; this tries precisely to catch this combination of the Holy Spirit and the Life of the Church and the Life to Come. We shall conclude our discussion of the creeds with some comments about this combination.

In contrast to the Apostles' Creed, Constantinople has "(belief) εἰς / *in* the ... church," as an object of faith. Does this very preposition thereby also ask the question: is the church object or agent of salvation—or both? In addition, when the *church* is included under the article on the *Spirit*, it implies *God's economy of self-communication* finds the terminus or *telos* of God's ways *right here among God's People*. The NT images of "temple" and "spouse" or "body" of Christ, who himself receives the Spirit "without measure," all convey this sense. Finally, we might emphasize Western Latin views of church over against Eastern Orthodoxy, who have themselves decried the former's lack of a due *pneumatology* of church, since there is too much stress paid, they say, upon institutional forms.

"One holy catholic and apostolic."[57] These marks (or notes, as they are technically called) or features of the community of God's People are (to be) its essential characteristics. Yet history has often denied them reality, mostly on account of a false dualism that replaces a due eschatology, one that would feature properly the *pilgrim* church of God. Two sets of questions are immediately raised for the church in history by mentioning eschatology. Firstly, we need to map the historical tensions among Scripture, tradition, and the traditions of churches within an eschatological context, as does Telford Work.[58] Doing so is both insightful and helpful. Although, it is helpful again, in disentangling the struggling relationships among these three, to stress as well another, related factor. This has to do with how the various ecclesiologies relate themselves to God's rule itself, how they envisage church and Kingdom to be related, since it is both Golgotha and Easter, and Ascension and Pentecost which together have founded the church:[59] humans do not construct church exactly! The more "realized" ecclesiologies sense the eschatology is, the more they "collapse" matters of the Head into the Body, and so the more is Tradition deemed to be normative. Contrariwise, the more Kingdom and church, Head and Body are distinguished, so the more is Tradition relativized and Scripture allowed to come to the fore, as *the* school of the Holy Spirit for *all* traditions. And while Augustine's vision of the *totus Christus* after the vision of the church in Ephesians and Colossians is surely correct,[60]

---

57. See Nichols, *Figuring out the Church*. While written from an avowedly Roman Catholic perspective, this little book usefully addresses both the four "marks" of the Church in Part I and summarizes in Part II the ecclesiologies of four "masters," who have greatly contributed to the modern discussion.

58. Work, "The End of Scripture," 215–314, untangles much of this complex dynamic very helpfully.

59. Re these pairs of salvific events, the one pair attributed to the Incarnate Son and the other pair to the Holy Spirit, see Wilken, "Is Pentecost the Peer of Easter?," 158–77. See too note 5, chapter three, re Sanders, *Triune God*, with his emphasis on the two communicative divine missions of Word and Spirit, as expressed in the Incarnation and Pentecost—yet with due qualification as well, as per figure 2 above.

60. These two letters present a vision of the church, grounded upon the rich NT understanding of baptism, which sees a fulsome picture of Jesus as Head + Body and which therefore embraces the fullness of Communion in the Cosmic Christ. Augustine powerfully took up this idea in his phrase *totus Christus*, the Whole Christ. See Mersch, *The Whole Christ*, and *Theology of the Mystical Body*. Jenson creatively exploits this entire notion in his own theology, to which we shall come in due course.

even as this *goal* of the church seeks to become embodied and enacted among us, we must still carefully distinguish matters of God's grace and matters of human reception and "interpretation," and so cooperation in faith, within the divine economy.[61] Just so, there remain creative tensions among Scripture, tradition, and the traditions in the pilgrim churches, which tensions are functions of the eschatological emphasis on the one hand *and* respective ecclesiological emphases on the other: an evident triangulation is at play here, with varying emphases to be discerned and mapped accordingly.

A second set of issues is raised by stressing the eschatological dimension of redemption as opposed to a false dualism. For we have tended (falsely) to remove the marks of the church to some "invisible, spiritual realm" to describe the so-called "mystical body" of Christ [*contra* the original application of this term to the *sacramental Eucharistic* body].[62] Contrariwise again, we need to strive towards realizing *in space and time*, in concrete human history, both *institutionally* and *charismatically*, what is already given as the gift of God to be marks indeed of God's People, of Christ's Body, of the Temple of the Holy Spirit—the Household of the triune God, the *totus Christus* among us.[63] In other words, these four marks are firstly *God's gift to* the church, his divine stamp *upon* the church, before they then become a vital part of God's *calling to* the church, characteristics to be sought by the People of God as they enact their pilgrimage towards God's kingdom rule on earth as it is in heaven.

---

61. Chapter 8, "Deconstruction," below will directly address this matter.

62. So de Lubac: see *Corpus Mysticum*, with its painstaking detailing of the history over a number of key centuries, climaxing in the switch re the threefold body of Christ (the historical, the Eucharistic, and the ecclesial), reducing the term "mystical" solely to the church, as the Eucharistic body became solely the "real" (*verum*) body (see esp. chapter 9, 'Truth and Truth', 187–220). See too Boersma, *Return to Mystery*, and esp. *Heavenly Participation*, which is "a somewhat more popular account" (xi) of the former. However, as we shall see in chapter 8, his important thesis re a "sacramental ontology" might have to be reconfigured in light of a fulsome *operational* theology of the Trinity and its practice, which was denied us due to the Arian controversy—the thesis of chapter 8 below.

63. We should note the Westminster Confession's *trichotomous* distinction between "invisible/visible" church, *and* "visible/particular church organizations." And so, as a corollary, we might ask: why do certain church communions insist upon additional, non-creedal and non-canonical marks or notes of church, thereby dechristianizing, to a greater or lesser extent, other Christian communities? For often too these marks express *secular* means of achieving human community in contrast to the divine *modi operandi*.

One final and vital point: what might be the relationship between this creed and its confession, and the church appropriately so "marked"? For the fourth century context saw this creed as a canon promulgated among many other canons, mostly to do with church order and discipline. These latter were deliberately viewed as canonical means for the well being (*bene esse*) of the church, whose essential nature (*esse*) requires just that form of self-ordering to be reflected in its own structures and ethos *of which the creed speaks*. For the creed declares God's *ordo salutis* (order of salvation) to be that awesome and gracious self-offering of the triune God for the redemption of humanity, which is then to be humbly "imitated" (N.B. this word in Paul's two letters, 1 and 2 Cor, especially; and see again Phil 2) precisely in the church's *own* order, thus establishing "one, holy, catholic, and apostolic" community. What chance therefore have we, in our fragmented and "autonomous," "emancipated" West, of confessing truly this Apostolic faith, in the context especially of our denominational divisions that we so take for granted as being "normal"?

- *One*. In the first place, the church is One on account of there being One Head, Jesus, whose One Body the church is, establishing "One New Humanity" (Eph 2:11–22), as she seeks "the unity of the Spirit in the bond of peace", to the glory of the "one God and Father of all" (Eph 4:3–6). Moreover, within the unfolding of a trinitarian creed, a chief characteristic of the church is unity in diversity and diversity in unity (1 Cor 12–14). Yet surely this does *not* mean mere historic, denominational pluralism, predicated on *division*—let alone on consumer *choice* or *preferences*! There is too a contemporary, global problem at exactly this point. For the *contextualization* of local theologies tends to relativize all versions of Christian faith, rendering a ribald pluralism which knows only one universal—that there is *no* universal. However, it is also precisely at this fragmentary postmodern juncture that the Nicene Creed offers a unique solution, as a canonical means of "reading" that other canon, the Holy Scriptures of Old and New Testaments. To be sure; this ever embarks us on a hermeneutical journey (as suggested above). But one that insists upon genuine "mutual regard/love" and "openness" (as per the Trinity itself), ensuring the status of that *primordial* Christian *text* in any interpretative "conversation" or context. Just so may *the One God address* us all recognizably in our *various* localities, as we all aspire to see the one universal church manifest in the local. This then is the contextual pole. The textual pole, however, remains just as problematic. For *whose* "voice," amidst the fragmented Body, speaks/may speak for God? The Roman Magisterium? Westminster's Confession? Or Augsburg's? Or Lambeth? To say nothing of Copts (and other Asians) versus Constantinople, etc! The very number of possible claimants explodes the myth: *extra* hermeneutical sanction(s), trying to arbitrate among the dissonance, cannot assuage the basic, essential brokenness of the church today. Yet the ecumenical vision, of a restored and reconciled humanity in full communion with God, remains, and remains as an essential goal of the gospel itself. Given then this mission of *full visible fellowship* among believing Christians and their churches, a divided church is a contemporary consumer luxury none may afford.[64]

- *Holy*. Given the status of the creed as one canonical means of grace amongst others within the early church, it may be viewed more authentically as a form of *sanctification* by the Spirit of truth than reductively as a means of regulatory control, of separating the "believing sheep" from the "disbelieving goats," discerning the "wheat" from the "tares." For the confessionary nature of the Creed implies more than mere intellectual assent. Among a body of available church practices, all of which are gifts of the Holy Spirit in general, the creed *vocalises* a specific aspect of the wider business of evangelization at the heart of the church's mission: to (re)claim the world as *truly God's alone*, as holy indeed, and humanity as God's glorious Image, prompting our *due confessional eucharistic response*, corresponding in character and nature to the holy triune God by means of a most particular social, communal project, i.e., the church, whose Creed Nicaea is.

- *Catholic*. Literally, this alludes to the whole embrace of the gospel message, of which the church is the first fruits (e.g., Jas 1:18). Two implications may involve us here. There is an *ecological* and *cosmological* dimension to the concept of the "Oecumene," since the church inhabits quite literally a world of which it is a part. In a trinitarian setting, this means that humanity's dwelling in the world is a form of *coinherence*, not dominance—let alone pillage and plunder.

---

64. See Braaten and Jenson, *In One Body through the Cross*, e.g. 37–42, re division, church shopping, and the tribalization of church communities; and Braaten and Jenson, *Ecumenical Future*.

Once again, features of "mutual regard/love" are to the fore. Secondly, whatever institutional forms of catholicity might arise to try to embody the church across time and space (such as bishops-in-communion), neither the periphery or the margins must fall from view nor the center become the dominant voice, as the tradition lives and grows. To this end, the "catholic" seeks to integrate necessary *collegial and conciliar* traits within church structures, as well as finding expressions of church that are appropriately "organic."

- *Apostolic*. We might pursue two elements of the final mark of the church here—but from within a single stance, for, essentially, the church's apostolicity is a participation in the *Missio Dei* itself. Thereafter, on the one hand, adherence to the apostolic witness to this mission gives us the first element, while on the other hand faithfulness to the divine community (*communio Dei*), which the apostles founded offers the second. Yet there is always a tendency by the church to foreclose prematurely on what might constitute "faithful adherence" as it seeks her "apostolicity"; and this is due mostly to the sense that it is located historically in the past, as a function of that past. This is not exactly true however—once we relocate the apostolic source of the church firmly in God's own *eschatological promise* which is the premise for God's own mission. In its turn, this promise ensures a richer openness towards the *future* by the church, since it is only in that future that God himself will bear the fruit of his own mission through the Son and in the Spirit. Consequently, this fourth mark of the church finds its authentic fulfillment in a humble and respectful "reserve" on the part of the church, as she *both* actively works towards that fulfillment *and* passively awaits its completion under God. Institutionally speaking, therefore, a certain *caution*—a *penitential* attitude even—is better warranted by forms of church government that would seek to formalize the People of God's "essential characteristics or marks" in this world *too soon*, ahead of her appropriate time. All of which has awesome relevance among a *divided* Body, whose vocation after 2000 years seems more driven by the need for fellowship with Christ's crucifixion and conformation with his death, before we may ever witness renewal of forms of church that may better embody and therefore convey his resurrected Life.[65]

---

65. See here especially Radner, *End of the Church*, e.g., 339: "The adumbrating of

The "one baptism" which the church "confesses" "for the forgiveness of sins" is *firstly* that of Jesus *actively* in his incarnation and its climax in death and resurrection/ascension. Thereafter, *derivatively* and *passively*, she, among her individual members, receives, via the gift of this baptismal Spirit who effects the church's very incorporation and participation, nothing less than the triune divine communal life and mission. (Historically, "one" probably also meant unrepeatable.) Yet what was once a single, albeit complex package—a tightly woven cord of Christian initiation involving conscious assent, rites of water (and oil), and the Holy Spirit (so e.g., Acts 2:38-39)—has become over time frayed and sundered along separated lines of theology and practice (e.g., the evangelical, the sacramental, and the Pentecostal, in the Latin West). And this ironically of that foundational, initiatory reality of the church's membership—so 1 Cor 12 and Eph 4:1-6. Once more we need actively to strive towards a fuller incorporation of the church's inheritance, enacting that very "conversion" of which baptism speaks, a renewal of character and being that passes through death, burial and resurrection, climaxing in that ascended human being before God "in heaven" (Eph 2:6).

"We look for the resurrection of the dead, and the life of the (world) age to come. Amen." Firstly, "man (*sic*) is not saved *from* his body but *in* it; not saved *from* the material world but *with* it."[66] In saying this, Kallistos is only following the patristic principle, extolled by the Greek East, that "the unassumed is the unredeemed."[67] Then secondly, because "Jesus is risen into the future that God has for his creatures,"[68] so life

---

these elements, of course, presupposes the validity of the penitential impulse with respect to ecclesial division in the first place. And as a "theory," a penitential history of division was given over, in much of this book, to a process of testing: does the impulse itself makes sense; and are alternative reactions to division, many of them still controlling our ecclesial and theological practice, in anyway compelling? Simply listing the elements of the systematic question as we have done [during the course of the flow of the chapters: on Scripture's reading and interpretation; on holiness; on ministerial vocation; on the Eucharist—all within a divided church that seeks by and large to avoid this basic affront and so any sense of a need for an essential change of heart/mind] expresses the answer to this test: Christian division gives necessary rise to penitence *because* the Church derives its form from Christ's incarnate body and remains bound to this body in time, and hence cannot escape, even in its sin, the controlling love of God" (emphasis original).

66. Kallistos Ware, cited in Guroian, "And I Look," 206, emphasis original.

67. See Torrance, *Trinitarian Faith*, 163-64, subsequently elaborated, 179-90. For the maxim itself, see Gregory of Nazianzus, Letter CI, in *NPNF VII*, 440.

68. Jenson, *ST 1*, 198.

in the Spirit, who raised Jesus, is life lived in hopeful anticipation and confidence—and if necessary, courageously, even "unto death"—in the love of God declared unashamedly in the gospel of Jesus: e.g., Romans 8 most fulsomely! For "when creedal articles for the Spirit end with resurrection and life everlasting, they merely specify what the Spirit in himself as person is. . . . The Spirit is God as the Power of God's *own* and our future. . . . He is the eschatological reality of God, the Power as which God is the active Goal of all things, as which God is for himself and us those 'things not yet seen', that with us call for faith and with him are his infinity."[69] All of which calls for due embodiment now among God's people in the church and before the world for whom Jesus Christ came, and comes again—and again!

Perichoresis

We are done with the creeds. Yet not quite done with the vocabulary and insights conveyed by the terminology of the early church fathers. There remains one final word to introduce to the reader, which is περιχώρησις (*perichōrēsis*).[70] We may do this by summarising an insightful feature of the work of Tom Torrance, whom we have met before, and which may serve as a suitable summary of this entire chapter with its brief history of the early church's theology.

He has been describing the church's doctrinal development during the opening centuries as a progressive movement through various levels. We start with "our basic level of experience and worship, in which we encounter God's revealing and reconciling activity in the Gospel, all of which takes place, not privately, but within the context of the life and mission of the church—*the evangelical and doxological level*."[71] We then next:

> Feel our way forward [from an *incipient theology*] to a deeper and more precise knowledge of what God has revealed of himself, even to the extent of reaching a reverent and humble insight into the inner personal relations of God's Being. Our concern at this secondary level, however, while distinctly theological, is

---

69. Ibid., *ST 1*, 160, emphasis original.

70. See for example, John of Damascus, "Exposition of the Orthodox Faith," 1.8 and 14, in *NPNF IX*, 11, (esp. footnote 8) and 17.

71. Torrance, *Ground and Grammar*, 156–57, emphasis original. These three levels are treated more fully in *Doctrine of God*, 88–111, from which future extracts will also come.

not primarily with the organic body of theological knowledge, but with *penetrating through* it to *apprehend* more fully the economic and ontological and Trinitarian structure of God's revealing and saving acts in Jesus Christ as they are presented to us in the Gospel.[72]

> It is at this level that the inchoate form of the doctrine of the Holy Trinity *latent* in the triadic structure of God's redemptive revelation of himself through himself, and in the Trinitarian understanding of God *implicit* in the mind and worship of the God's people, evident in the various New Testament formulae which bring the Father, the Son and the Holy Spirit together in the Name of God, is given *explicit formulation* as the doctrine of the Holy Trinity that underlies and gives coherent structure to all Christian dogmatics. This, then, is the first definitely *theological* level in which we are concerned with expressing doctrinal knowledge of the Holy Trinity, in which our thought moves on from the intuitive incipient form of an understanding of the Trinity to conceptions of what is called the economic Trinity, the level in which the dynamic reality of God's triune Being is being brought into clearer and more explicit formulation in terms of his differentiated yet unitary personal self-presentations and acts as Father, Son and Holy Spirit.[73]

Finally, we may move from the economic Trinity to the meta-theological level of our knowing and understanding the triune God in himself. This means both a deepening and a simplifying of the organization of our basic concepts and relations we have discerned at the secondary level. It is a quite legitimate and even necessary move owing to one basic step made initially and summarized in the Nicene Creed. As Torrance avers:

> The *homoousion* is thus seen to have immense significance, for it enables us to deepen and refine our grasp of the self-revealing and self-communicating of God to us as Father, Son and Holy Spirit, in such a way that our thought has to move from the secondary level in which we have to do with the economic Trinity to the tertiary or higher theological level where we have to do with the ontological Trinity, that is, in patristic language, the move from οἰκονομία (*oikonomia*/economy) to θεολογία (*theologia*/theology proper).[74]

---

72. Torrance, *Doctrine of God*, 91, emphasis added.
73. Ibid., 92, emphasis added.
74. Ibid., 95.

> We come [then] to a higher theological and scientific level, in which we penetrate more deeply into the self-communication of God in the saving and revealing activity of Christ and in his Spirit. At this level we are explicitly concerned with the epistemological and ontological structure of our knowledge of God, moving from the level of economic Trinitarian relations in all that God is toward us in his self-revealing and self-giving activity to the level in which we discern the Trinitarian relations immanent in God himself which lie behind, and are the ground of, the relations of the Economic Trinity—that is, we are lifted up in thought to the level of "the Ontological Trinity" or "the Immanent Trinity," as it is variously called. This is the movement of thought in which we are compelled, under pressure from God's self-communication, to acknowledge that what God is toward us in the threefold economic activity of his revelation and redemption, as Father, Son, and Holy Spirit, he is antecedently and eternally in his own Being in the Godhead. This is the passage of thought from the Trinity *ad extra* [God in his works beyond himself] to the Trinity *ad intra* [God in himself], as theologians say.[75]

In this light, Torrance makes a pair of powerful parallel statements to portray the significance of God's very Being *ad intra*, which he derives from Athanasius' views on the ἐνούσιος λόγος (*en-ousian logos*) and the ἐνούσιος ἐνέργεια (*en-ousian energy*).[76]

1. That God's *Logos*, or Word, inheres in his Being means that God's Being is speaking Being, eloquent Being. He is not Being which also speaks, but Being which speaks precisely as Being, for his Being and his Word interpenetrate one another and are inseparably one. Hence, there can be no thought of knowing God in his mute Being, as it were, apart from his Word, behind the back of his eloquent Reality as God, for there is no such god.

2. That God's *energeia*, or Act, inheres in his Being, means that God's Being is in his Act and his Act is in his Being. He is not Being which also acts, but Being which acts precisely as Being, for his Being is intrinsically active, dynamic Being. Hence, there can be no thought of knowing God in his Being stripped of his Act, behind the back of

---

75. Torrance, *Ground and Grammar*, 157–58.

76. See Torrance, *Trinitarian Faith*, 72, and especially the references there to Torrance, *Theology in Reconciliation*, 222–23, 226–31, and 235–39, re the *implications* of these two notions of Athanasius.

his Act, or apart from his active Reality as God, for there is no such god.[77]

Such is the very nature of the fullness of God's "Reality" (*die Wirklichkeit*: so Karl Barth's German word for God's Life heading up *CD II/1*, chapter VI) that God is free to speak and act in his *self-communication* to us through the Son and in the Spirit; the trinitarian economy is grounded in and undergirded by Who God Is.

At this third level we are forced once more to *invent new language*, by means of which we humans may bring the God who has apprehended us to some kind of apprehension ourselves. The term *perichōrēsis* is derived from χώρα (*chōra*), the Greek word for "space" or "room"; it is associated also with χωρεῖν (*chōrein*), "to contain," "to make room," "to go forward." It suggests a mutual containing or enveloping of realities, giving rise to the notion of *coinherence* or *mutual indwelling*. We need to note especially here the Fourth Gospel's language regarding the relationship between the Father and the Son, and thereafter among believers and the Trinitarian Persons, of their "abiding/remaining/dwelling in" each other. This notion seeks to embrace the kind of *onto-relations* (the term is Torrance's) that subsist in the Triune Godhead, giving expression to the distinctive identities that mark off Father, Son, and Holy Spirit *from one another* in their unique, irreplaceable and irreducible *hypostases* on the one hand, and on the other hand to declare their *utterly inseparable and bonded* Communion one with the other, which flows into and out of each other, incessantly, in the form of an eternal dance, such that each *hypostasis* is formally constituted by and constitutes the others. Such indeed is the *perichoretic movement* that is the Life and Love of the eternally triune Deity, in the dynamic fullness and freedom of his ineffable Majesty and sublime Mystery, the Trinity's singular Glory. In all these ways we may, in Torrance's characteristic words, *genuinely* "apprehend" the triune God: our human *apprehension truly corresponds* to God's triune apprehension of us, even as it nonetheless may *never equate* with a *comprehension* of his divine nature, *his* Glory being ever infinitely beyond even our glorified human understanding in the world to come—such is the triune God's fulsome Life and Being in its transcendent ineffability.

77. Torrance, *Ground and Grammar*, 152–53.

Questions for Reflection

12. How have you found the new vocabulary? We often nowadays take for granted the emergence of new words in the realms of science and technology. And yet, when it comes to Christian things, sometimes our prejudice for what we deem to be the "old and familiar," the comfortable even, means we shy away from coming to grips with the grandeur of the tradition. Certainly, the profound struggles of the early church and their even more profound solutions are seldom on the agenda of any contemporary adult catechism class. Why do you think this is so? Should it be so?

13. The cultural and social context of late antiquity prompted for the most part the form(s) of debate surrounding Jesus' identity and thereafter the nature of God. What in your mind might be unique to their situation and what might be transferable nonetheless across the centuries? In other words, what can we learn from their struggles for our own struggles today? And not only in the matter of theology and intellectual and/or spiritual development?

14. "It would be more godly and more accurate or true to signify God from the Son and call Him Father, than to name God from his works only and call him Unoriginate." So says Athanasius. Yet there's a further, vital consequence as well, which he points out in another text, *De Decretis* or "In Defense of the Nicene Definition." Having repeated and elaborated upon his earlier saying, he draws this conclusion: "For the Spirit of the Word in us names through us his *own* Father *as ours*, which is the Apostle's meaning when he says, 'God has sent forth the Spirit of his Son into your hearts, crying, Abba, Father.'" *De Decretis*, ch. VII, 28–32, at 31, emphasis added—due to Anatolios' translation, *Athanasius*, 210: "The Spirit of the Word, in us and through us, names the Word's own Father as our Father, and this is the meaning of the apostle's saying . . ." What do you make of God's being not only your Creator, but notably, through Jesus and the Holy Spirit, your *Father*?

seven

CAD/CAM—2
Manufacture

Aurelius Augustinus

Countless people down the centuries, most of whom are professional scholars and monks, have sat at the feet of this giant of a human being, St. Augustine of Hippo.[1] Yet I am neither monk nor scholar! Nevertheless, we must attempt to draw from him two important insights with regards to the doctrine of the Trinity, in order to make it more serviceable again for us in the twenty-first century.

A proper job of even this smaller task would exegete at some length his *De Trinitate*,[2] placing it in the context of his developing trinitarian theology overall.[3] Yet we shall not even attempt this meager task. Rather, our focus will be upon only two things, Augustine's use of the term "relation" to give us some purchase upon understanding the nature of the

---

1. Probably the best English bio is still Brown, *Augustine of Hippo*; the best introduction to his intellectual achievement might be Rist, *Augustine*; overall, see Fitzgerald, *Augustine through the Ages*.

2. Again, the best English edition is probably, *The Trinity*, translated by Hill, accompanied by Hill's earlier *Mystery of the Trinity*, which places an exegesis of *De Trinitate* in a brief, summary context of OT, NT and the early church. Some readers may wish to consult Gioia, *Theological Epistemology*.

3. See Barnes, "Rereading," 145–76; Barnes, "Visible Christ," 329–55; and Ayres, "Fundamental Grammar," 51–76, being a prelude to Ayres, *Augustine and the Trinity*, the best summary available.

Trinity, and his search for analogies or vestiges of the Trinity, those natural signs within creation that seem to point towards the triune Creator, and so beyond this world to its source. With regards especially to the second, another temptation quite quickly then lurks. We could spend an inordinate amount of time discussing the traditional role of what are termed *vestigia trinitatis* (trinitarian vestiges), the link between this and analogy, and then the whole matter of appropriate speech of the divine, including both analogy and metaphor, and their interrelationships.[4] In a real sense, we are right back to where I began in the introduction and my talk of models! And I certainly do not want us just to go round in circles! So; with these clear qualifications of the task before us, let us begin our meager analysis of Augustine's trinitarian theology.

Relations

You will recall we began our last chapter with a brief foray into classical philosophy and metaphysics. We did this—had to do this—because the early church fathers had no other recourse themselves than to speak the technical language of their day when trying to formulate ways of bringing the God of the gospel to human speech. We now have before us such words as *substantia* in Latin, οὐσία/*ousia* in Greek (substance), *persona*, πρόσωπον/*prosōpon* (person/face/mask), *hypostasis*/ὑπόστασις (subsistence/essence/entity), ὁμοούσιος/*homoousios*, τρόπος ὑπάρξεως/*tropos hyparxeōs* (mode/manner of existence/subsistence), and *perichōrēsis*. We recall too that traditionally "substance" was set over against "accidents" among all the "categories," when we answer the question, What/How is this thing? Primary substance refers to a subject, who possesses secondary substance (e.g., tableness; that which is possessed, in order to be the thing it is, and not another), together with a string of accidents, those features which are variable and might have been otherwise. "Relation" was in Aristotle's list of accidental categories, describing how things/entities were in relationship with others: Bryden is Cathy's husband, and Mary's son-in-law, etc. Even as he might have never existed, and so never

---

4. All of which is prompted by Barth's necessary preamble in *CD* I/1, § 8.3, 333–47 re vestiges. The related literature is vast. Of special help are: Jüngel, *Mystery*, chapter IV §§ 17 and 18, "The Problem of Analogous Talk of God," and "The Gospel as Analogous Talk about God," 261–81 and 281–98; Lash, "Analogy," 105–19; Pannenberg, "Analogy and Doxology," 211–38; and White, *Analogy of Being*. This last is a formidable collection of essays and a *tour de force*, but well worth the effort.

been in relation, nonetheless he happened to become the son of Lewis and Margaret Black, who themselves established a family of five children in all. Thereafter, he might have also entered into an entirely different set of relationships; he might have married someone else for example. Nor should we forget our "fireside chat" of chapter 1, where it was described how Mary was first a spinster, then became a wife, married to Robert, and then again finally a widow, upon Robert's death. For the reality of marriage is such that "husband–and–wife," "wife–and–husband" constitute each other in the relationship of marriage, which relationship formally binds the two together "until death do us part." For once more, we need to recall the *essential difference* between Hellenistic "deity" and finite, temporal realities at this very point (even if the Greeks also created a host of intermediary levels of being between the Absolute Unoriginate One and all the rest of multiple reality, setting up a chain of graded beings or a *glacis* approach to reality, as we've seen).

Before we properly begin, a few brief words about *De Trinitate* as a whole might not go amiss at this point. As mentioned earlier, Augustine began this work around 399/400. While there are some initial polemical triggers to Augustine's enterprise (see books I–IV),[5] overall it seems rather an intensely personal pilgrimage by the author himself, a spiritual quest to satisfy his thirst to answer what it might mean to know "where and how the Trinity manifests itself/will be disclosed,"[6] and so to grasp the One who has grasped him and the rest of humanity through the missions of the Son and the Holy Spirit. It is a search for understanding the vision of this God—where to "see" is very much to "know" for Augustine, just as to "know" is furthermore to "love," where "love" too is inescapably our being drawn by the delight of Beauty itself. Such a quest, not unlike the *Confessions* earlier (written 397–400), where Augustine is in search of an adequate way of praising the eternal God who has found him, *despite himself*,[7] requires a profound exploration of the very way any human might be able to contemplate such a triune deity at all. It is this form of the quest that results in his probing the multiple operations of the hu-

---

5. See for example Barnes, "Visible Christ," 329–55.

6. Augustine, *Trinity*, book XV, 2.7, 400; and see too the conclusion of book I, 90.

7. See Kirby, "Praise," 333–50. And see esp. Stroup, "Narrative Structure," 170–98, where he explores the confessional role of faith in performing a new identity in Christ: the act of writing the *Confessions* is itself integral to the task of conversion and constructing a new identity for Augustine.

man mind, in whose Image God has created humanity, in the second part of *De Trinitate*, and to which we shall come in due course here. So, *De Trinitate* is not really a text book about the Trinity as such; and it is certainly not just a resource that might be plundered at will for helpful insights, to be quoted to prove a scholastic point or two. No, it is a Christian manual for spiritual pilgrimage along the Way of Christ, whose Sonship is his own joyous vision of the Father; it is a rational exploration in due humility into how we humans might aspire to climb in faith (or probe the depths; the metaphors are needfully mixed) eventually to meet God "face to face" "with a pure heart" at the End, upon eschatological fulfillment. It is little wonder he cites Ps 105 ("seek the Lord and be strengthened, seek his Face *always*," v. 4) at crucial stages: books 1 (again and again), 9, 15, and the concluding prayer (adding, "and with passionate ardour"). Such "seeking" naturally took up both Pss 24 and 27 as well. And how may all this be achieved, this seeking and "seeing God with a pure heart" after the sixth beatitude, where such "seeing" is ultimately to "love" truly, enraptured by Beauty? *De Trinitate* is his personal answer. All of which sets us up to appreciate the significance of St Augustine's trinitarian moves in books V–VII of *De Trinitate*, which is where we properly begin.

And so to business, to explore Augustine's critical move regarding "relation." From the outset, we must appreciate Augustine has received what has become by now a *bit of a tradition*. This was the very reason why we began this chapter with a résumé of the key terms hammered out over the preceding centuries. Standing at the start of the fifth century, his task, as he now sees it, is *to give added meaning to what he has received*, even as he also defends nascent Catholic, Nicene orthodoxy. (Curiously, our situation in the twenty-first century is not too dissimilar, although it is arguably more problematic and more urgent. There's this traditional trinitarian doctrine, with its summary symbols like the Nicene Creed; yet for all that, for most Christians and certainly for secular Westerners, it's a decided oddity, an impossible conundrum, with little effective use in the lives of would be Christians seeking a life of discipleship, following Jesus. To cite Rahner again: "Despite their orthodox confession of the Trinity, Christians are, in their practical life, almost mere monotheists." Can Augustine help us still today? I think so!)

And what he has received he is both sure about, and yet also unsure. He says candidly:

> By "being" I mean here what is called *ousia* in Greek, which we normally call substance. The Greeks also have another word, *hypostasis*, but they make a distinction that is rather obscure to me between *ousia* and *hypostasis*, so that most of our people (i.e. Catholics) who treat of these matters in Greek are accustomed to say *mia ousia, treis hypostaseis*, which in English [Latin originally] is literally "one being, three substances" [both *hypo-* and *sub-* are prefixes meaning "under," so that both words are etymologically identical it would seem]. But because we have grown accustomed in our usage to meaning the same thing by "being" as by "substance," we do not dare say "one being, three substances." Rather, "one being, three persons" is what many Latin authors, whose authority carries weight, have said when treating of these matters, being able to find no more suitable way of expressing in words what they understood without words.[8]

Compare this with Basil's insistence on distinguishing between *ousia* and *hypostasis*, and furthermore basing this on the meaning of *prosōpon*:

> It is not enough to count the differences in the Persons (*prosōpa*, plural). It is necessary also to confess that each Person (*prosōpon*) exists in a true *hypostasis*. Now even Sabellius did not deny the mirage of persons (*prosōpa*) without *hypostases*, who said that the same God, though he is one subject, was metamorphosed according to the need of the moment, and is thus spoken of now as Father, now as Son, and now as Holy Ghost.[9]

For Basil the conclusion was clear: "repudiating the *hypostases* [was to] deny the Name of the Son of God." Given *prosōpon* was itself derived from the world of the theatre and meant a face or mask, Basil's concern is to ward off *any* suspicion that the language of three "persons" might mean three such masks or mere appearances of God solely in the economy, succumbing to Sabellianism, while the language of three *hypostases* by contrast, to his mind, clearly insisted on three *distinct* entities, *all intrinsic* to the one being who is God.

However, Augustine was not alone in this linguistic difficulty. Jerome (c. 347–420), who was to pioneer the translation of the Bible into Latin, objected to the notion of three *hypostases* in the most forceful terms in a letter to Damasus I of Rome, written around 376/377. "And can anyone, I ask, be so profane as to speak of three essences or substances in the

---

8. Augustine, *Trinity*, book V, 2.10, 196.
9. Basil, "Letter CCX," 5.36, in *NPNF VIII*, 251.

Godhead? There is one nature of God and one only; and this, and this alone, truly *is*." He decries the language of *hypostasis*, declaring it to be an "unheard-of formula of three *hypostases* . . . [Rather] Let us be satisfied to speak of one substance and of three subsisting persons—perfect, equal, coeternal. Let us keep to one *hypostasis* . . . and say nothing of three."[10]

How then to escape these dilemmas of language—which threatened to be more than that, being also inadequate depictions of God's personal triunity? Augustine's solution is as simple (in one sense) as it is elegant. We recall Aristotle, in compiling the various categories, enumerated all but one, namely, substance, to be accidents, for these were all predications of a mutable kind, subject to modification under differing circumstances. Augustine however, in pursuing the sheer logic of the gospel's revelation of God to its conclusion, upped the category of "relation" from an accident to the same level as that of substance.

He builds slowly: "So there is no modification in God because there is nothing in him that can be changed or lost. . . . Nothing therefore is said of him modification-wise because nothing modifies him, but this does not mean that everything said of him is said substance-wise." Then he gets down to business, repeating the two premises.

> With God, though, nothing is said modification-wise, because there is nothing changeable with him. And yet not everything that is said of him is said substance-wise. Some things are said with reference to something else, like Father with reference to Son and Son with reference to Father; and this is not said modification-wise, because the one is always Father and the other always Son—not "always" in the sense that he is Son from the moment he is born or that the Father does not cease to be Father from the moment the Son does not cease to be Son, but in the sense that the Son is always born and never began to be Son. If he had some time begun or some time ceased to be Son, it would be predicated modification-wise. If on the other hand what is called Father were called so with reference to itself and not to the Son, and what is called Son were called so with reference to itself and not to the Father, the one would be called Father and the other Son substance-wise. But since the Father is only called so because he has a Son, and the Son is only called so because he has a Father, these things are not said substance-wise, as neither is said with reference to itself but only with reference to the other. Nor are they said modification-wise, because what

---

10. Jerome, "Letter XV," in *NPNF VI*, 19.

is signified by calling them Father and Son belongs to them eternally and unchangeably. Therefore, although being Father is different from being Son, there is no difference of substance, because they are not called these things substance-wise but relationship-wise; and yet this relationship is not a modification, because it is not changeable.[11]

A divine person is therefore classically a subsistent relation.[12] That is the linguistic coup and thereafter the metaphysical revolution Augustine precipitates. As Walter Kasper sums it up: "The need was to reflect upon the data of Scripture and tradition and to break away from the one-sidedly essentialist thinking of Greek philosophy and into a personalist thinking . . . laying the foundation of a new type of thought."[13]

The consequences have been utterly far reaching, even if they have taken centuries to flower fully. And even as Augustine's depiction of the personal triune God of the gospel has flowered these past few centuries, in matters like democracy and human rights, so it has also become soured, as the source of this personalist thinking and behavior has become cut off.[14] The twentieth and twenty-first centuries have tragically witnessed this profound ambivalence: the richness of the gospel's fruit in acknowledging human reality made in the Image of the triune God, whose personhood is stamped into this human creature, coupled however with a deliberate severance, historically and culturally, of the fruit from the root, as Western society turns its back upon its chief source, and turns in upon its autonomous, self-positing identity—*incurvatus in se*, as Martin Luther would say. In which light, the revival of interest in the Christian doctrine of the Trinity these past fifty years or so,[15] is no mere academic game. If

11. Augustine, *Trinity*, book V, 1.5 and 6, 191–2.

12. See Aquinas, *Summa Theologiae* 1.29.4: "Therefore a divine person signifies a relation as subsisting. And this is to signify relation by way of substance, and such a relation is a hypostasis subsisting in the divine nature . . . Thus it is true to say that the name *person* signifies relation directly, and the essence indirectly; not, however, the relation as such, but as expressed by way of a hypostasis." This is the final fruit of Augustine's own seminal move.

13. Kasper, *God*, 260. One might also mention the likes of Bloom, *Shakespeare*, xvii: "In Shakespeare, characters develop rather than unfold, and they develop because they reconceive themselves." This is abundantly true as well of Augustine's *Confessions*, viewed notably via Stroup's assessment (see note 7 above).

14. See Hanby, *Augustine and Modernity*, which contrasts the modern Cartesian self with that of humanity within Augustine's rich vision.

15. I date this revival from the publication of Jüngel's first edition of *Gottes Sein ist im Werden. Verantwortliche Rede vom Sein Gottes bei Karl Barth. Eine Paraphrase*,

handled properly, adequately, and apologetically, it may yet revive both the church (whose own memory of its true riches has dimmed: just so this small book!) and society. *On verra*; we shall see . . .

Returning now to Augustine. His observations are as simple as they are profound: there is ever and only and always the Father—of the Son, just as the Son is—of the Father. The identities of Father and of Son are utterly relational, constituting each other. Arising from these moves, we can say further that the Father possesses Godhead paternally and the Son possesses Godhead filially, the adverbs declaring each of the relations, paternity and filiation, to be an *act*. The triune Godhead comprises both substance or *ousia* and subsistent relations, in the actuality of divine Life. And what of the Holy Spirit; where does this third divine person fit in?

On the Holy Spirit

At this point in book V Augustine begins to address a thorny issue, the complete story of which we simply may not address in this book. Suffice to say, the entire church, East and West, still has not come to a common mind over the full identity of the Holy Spirit, even after 2000 years![16] The difficulty arises from the economy of salvation itself. For:

> . . . the Holy Spirit, in so far as he is properly or peculiarly called the Holy Spirit, is so called relationship-wise, being referred to both Father and Son, since the Holy Spirit is the Spirit of the Father and of the Son. This relationship, to be sure, is not apparent in this particular name, but it is apparent when he is called *the gift of God* (Acts 8:20, John 4:10). He is the gift of the Father and of the Son, because on the one hand he *proceeds from the Father* (John 15:26), as the Lord says; and on the other hand the apostle's words, *Whoever does not have the Spirit of Christ is not one of his* (Rom 8:9), are spoken of the Holy Spirit. So when we say "the gift of the giver" and "the giver of the gift," we say

---

1964. See ET by Webster, *God's Being is in Becoming: The Trinitarian Being of God in the Theology of Karl Barth*, which title only misses the element of *Verantwortliche Rede* = responsible/answering speech, which is the due task of any Christian theology, one that *follows/thinks after* (German: *Nachdenken*) the events and speech of the God of the gospel himself, and so *corresponds to* this triune God's own interpretation of himself, in speech and even nature.

16. Again the literature is vast: see only Vischer, *Spirit of God, Spirit of Christ*; Congar, *I Believe in the Holy Spirit*; Heron, *Holy Spirit*; Smail, *Giving Gift*; and supremely, Siecienski, *The Filioque*.

each with reference to the other. So the Holy Spirit is a kind of inexpressible communion or fellowship of Father and Son.[17]

Here Augustine combines both Scripture and interpretation arising from these Scriptures. We ourselves have already seen something of this tension in earlier chapters of this book. For example, Luke's pericope on the Lord's Prayer climaxes with the assured statement, "How much more shall *the heavenly Father give* the Holy Spirit to those who ask him" (Luke 11:13 NRSV). Then again we have Jesus describe the Holy Spirit both as "*the Father's* promise" in Luke 24:49 and Acts 1:4, and then with *Jesus himself* doing the actual "*sending*" in Luke 24, plus the composite picture emerging in Acts of *Jesus baptizing* people with the Holy Spirit (into himself, is the further goal derived from Paul, as we have seen). Acts 2:33 is the link in all this, with Jesus being described as the first one to receive the promised Holy Spirit, who is then shared with/poured out by Jesus upon his followers.

It is no less complex in John's gospel. Confining ourselves to the Upper Room Discourses, chapters 13–17, we've to note the following verses. 14:16 and 14:26 would appear to be parallel to one another. In both cases "*the Father gives*" or "*sends* the Holy Spirit/Paraclete," firstly at Jesus' "request of the Father," then secondly "in Jesus' name." In 15:26 (ESV modified) the situation is delightfully rich. "But when the Paraclete comes, *whom I will send* to you *from the Father*, the Spirit of truth, *who proceeds from the Father*, he will bear witness/testify about me." This witness is achieved both directly (16:13–15 ESV):

> When the Spirit of truth comes, he will guide you into all the truth, for he will not speak on his own authority, but whatever he hears he will speak, and he will declare to you the things that are to come. He will glorify me, for *he will take what is mine and declare it to you. All that the Father has is mine; therefore I said that he will take what is mine and declare it to you.*

It is also achieved indirectly via the witness of the disciples (15:27 NRSV): "And you also are to testify (about me) because you have been with me from the beginning." Lastly from the Upper Room, we might note 16:7 (ESV modified)—"Nevertheless I tell you the truth: it is to your advantage that I go away, for if I do not go away, the Paraclete will not come to you; but if I go, *I will send* him to you." This promise is realised on Easter evening, when Jesus stands among them to say again: "'Peace

---

17. Augustine, *Trinity*, book V, 3.12, 197.

be with you. As the Father has sent me, so I also send you.' And saying this, *he breathed* on them, and said to them, '*Receive* the Holy Spirit'" (John 20:21–22 NRSV modified, with abundant echoes of Gen 2).

The situation is similar in Paul's writings. We will recall only a sample here. Firstly, there's that celebrated creedal summary of Gal 4:4–6 (NRSV).

> But when the fullness of time had come, God sent his Son, born of a woman, born under the law, in order to redeem those who were under the law, so that we might receive adoption as children. And because you are children, *God has sent the Spirit* of his Son into our hearts, crying, "*Abba! Father!*"

Augustine has already alluded to the complexities of Rom 8:9–16, but we might take it even further than just vv. 9–10, to show how convoluted things might become.

> But you are not in the flesh; you are in the Spirit, since *the Spirit of God* dwells in you. Anyone who does not have *the Spirit of Christ* does not belong to him. But if *Christ* is in you, though the body is dead because of sin, *the Spirit* is life because of righteousness. If *the Spirit of him who* raised Jesus from the dead dwells in you, *he who raised Christ* from the dead will give life to your mortal bodies also through *his Spirit* that dwells in you.
>
> So then, brothers and sisters, we are debtors, not to the flesh, to live according to the flesh—for if you live according to the flesh, you will die; but if by the Spirit you put to death the deeds of the body, you will live. For all who are led by *the Spirit of God* are children of God. For you did not receive a spirit of slavery to fall back into fear, but you have received a spirit of adoption. When we cry, "Abba! Father!" it is that very Spirit bearing witness with our spirit that we are children of God (NRSV).

The difficulty Augustine (or anyone for that matter) is facing arises when we study the economic missions of both the Son and the Spirit, seeking to establish their immanent basis in God's own eternal triune Being, what are technically called the *intra-divine processions* of Son and Spirit, which he describes in some detail in book IV. That is to say, he maps the history of God's dealings with humanity, climaxing with the coming of Christ into the world and the subsequent gift of the Holy Spirit, as being due manifestations of how it is ever so in God's own Being, correlating the economic relations of the Trinity with the immanent trinitarian relations, the key Nicene idea we've seen before. In which case, the more simple dyadic pairing of Father and Son (where each term implies the other in their relatedness, where each person is to be viewed "relationship-wise") becomes inordinately complex when there is properly the *triadic set of relationships* of Father, Son and Holy Spirit among the triune Godhead—especially when it would appear there are further *dyadic* pairings between the Father and the Spirit, and between the Son and the Spirit; at least, so the texts we have assembled above would suggest. How do such suggestions establish suitable "subsistent relations," and how might *these* be viewed together with the *fullest, triadic* account possible?

To cut a long and complex story short, which crops up in key statements throughout *De Trinitate*, Augustine sums up the situation like this.

> So the Holy Spirit is something common to Father and Son, whatever it is, or *is* their very *commonness or communion*, consubstantial and coeternal. Call it friendship, if it helps, but a better word for it is *charity*. And this too is substance because God is substance, and "God is charity" (1 John 4:8,16), as it is written. . . . One loving him who is from him, and one loving him from whom he is, and love itself.[18]

This last sentence anticipates the fuller blown depiction from book VIII: "Now Love means someone loving and something loved with love. There you are with three, the Lover, What is being loved (the Beloved), and Love. And what is Love but a kind of life coupling or trying to couple together two things, namely Lover and What is being loved?"[19] While this last move anticipates in *De Trinitate* his explorations of *mens* or the soul's dialectics of self-love and self-knowledge, all of which give rise to the psychological analogy which we shall pursue soon, at this stage of our own analysis *the key* is to see the Holy Spirit as the *vinculum caritatis* or bond/chain of love, as the tradition famously terms it, between Father and Son.[20] This is Augustine's major contribution and resolution of the perceived dilemmas about the Holy Spirit's eternal identity. Well, not quite! For in book XV he will continue:

---

18. Ibid., book VI, 1.7, 209–10, emphases added. With regards to all this and that which follows, see notably Ayres, *Trinity*, 251–72, "Loving and Being".

19. Ibid., book VIII, 5.14, 255.

20. Augustine was influenced here primarily by Marius Victorinus, who speaks of the Spirit as "patris et filii *copula*" in one of his hymns (*Hymnus* 1.4).

> We have talked enough about the Father and the Son insofar as we have been able to see them through this mirror and in this puzzle [a reference to 1 Cor 13:12 and his psychological analogies]. Now we must discuss the Holy Spirit as far as it is granted us with God's help to see him. According to the Holy Scriptures this Holy Spirit is not just the Father's alone nor the Son's alone, but the Spirit of them both, and thus he suggests to us the common charity by which the Father and the Son love each other.... (And if the charity by which the Father loves the Son and the Son loves the Father inexpressibly shows forth the communion of them both, what more suitable than he who is the common Spirit of them both should be called charity? ... Because he is common to them both, he is called distinctively what they are called in common [i.e., love].)[21]

So far so good, and material with which we are now familiar. Yet he will also state necessarily, due to both Scripture and his assessment of how to interpret Scripture by a trinitarian hermeneutic:

> And yet it is not without point that in this triad only the Son is called the Word of God, and only the Holy Spirit is called the gift of God, and only the Father is called the one from whom the Word is born [begotten] and from whom the Holy Spirit principally proceeds. I added "principally," because we have found that the Holy Spirit also proceeds from the Son. But this too was given the Son by the Father—not given to him when he already existed and did not have it; but whatever the Father gave to his only-begotten Word he gave by begetting him. He so begot him then that their common gift would proceed from him too, and the Holy Spirit would be the Spirit of them both. This distinction then within the inseparable trinity must be diligently looked into and not casually taken for granted.[22]

One has to say that despite the caveat of the last sentence, as we said at the beginning of this section on the Holy Spirit in Augustine, after 2000 years of due Christian reflection the entire church is not satisfactorily settled on the question! Lukas Vischer's collection from the WCC shows only too well where there is common ground and where serious

---

21. Augustine, *Trinity*, book XV, 5.27, 418; with the (bracketed section) from 5.37, 424.

22. Ibid., 5.29, 419. The Latin word is *principaliter*, which may mean both principally and peculiarly, i.e., pertaining specifically/exclusively to. Augustine continues to discuss this original procession of the Spirit from the Father, which too is given to the Son in his begottenness, in XV, 6.47, 432.

caution is still needed and why, with Edward Siecienski's amplifying the "why" with great sophistication (see note 16 above). However, all of this is beyond the scope of this immediate introductory study. I wish only to conclude by offering the following, all of which arise from out of an Augustinian framework, as it were, presented as a series of theses.

Careful—diligent!—examination of the Holy Spirit's own person will show:

1. If "God is Spirit" (John 4:24), then we humans, even as those made in the Image of God (however we might construe that "image and likeness," i.e., Augustine has no monopoly on his own exegetical interpretations; there are other insights into the biblical text to be honored as well), are in a serious quandary, being at least the material creatures we are. Seeing God is essentially problematic for us.

2. The problem however is both moral as well as metaphysical. "Purification of heart" is a necessary aspect of any solution to the problem. For sin has meant our enjoyment of lesser things, as we become *incurvatus in se* (curved in upon ourselves/bent inwards), rather than our acknowledging duly the One who has himself created these things, who, when seen for Who He Is, enables both direct enjoyment of Himself, and the world's use and enjoyment as he has created it for us.

3. Insight therefore into "reading" the "signs" of God's presence in his world is a case of acknowledging those signs God has given, supremely in the Incarnation of the Word made flesh, in order that we might begin aright our journey back to God. Our ascent is never on our own (rational) terms however; rather, our understanding only follows as we seek in faith that Way granted us in Jesus, God's own mediator, and through the gift of the Holy Spirit, who sheds abroad in our hearts God's very own love, that we might dwell in God and he is us.

4. Our loving understanding of God who is Spirit may indeed legitimately involve the sorts of explorations Augustine offers through his psychological analogies. Yet the very images of the Holy Spirit's own activity as recorded in Scripture set up, in the first place, a simpler dynamic: wind is literally air in motion; fire's flames are ever moving; a spring issues in running water; a dove in flight. None of

these may be, as it were, freeze-framed and so put under the microscope for us to grasp.

5. On the contrary, such is the interactive dynamic of persons-in-relation, both human as well as divine, that when we seek to fulfill our created purpose of Love of God and Love of Neighbor, this may only be appropriately performed through an open ended approach of "mutual regard" (Aquinas of the persons of the Trinity), without any attempt at grasping or freeze-framing.

6. This means additionally, a form of kenoticism (the likes of which Phil 2 displays regarding the Son of God) among *all* participants. Firstly, among the Trinity itself, where each divine person seeks to glorify the Others (so John 17:1, 16:14)—yet also by means of a *specific* kenoticism *by each* towards each of the *Others*, given their principal and respective identities.[23] Then secondly, as Phil 2:1–5, 12–13 situates the hymn itself, as a collective human kenoticism which embodies the divine humility among all those "in Christ Jesus"; one where each human face-to-face encounter similarly enjoins upon the actors a quite specific and unique form, such is the particular dignity of each human being.

7. All of which now enables a fresh exploration into how it is the Holy Spirit is both the inspiration *subjectively* for us, with our exclaiming "Abba! Father!," and the inspiration of the *objective* acclamation "Jesus is Lord!" (1 Cor 12:3). For in each of these ways and peculiarly in these ways, the Holy Spirit glorifies first the Father in his *proprium* and then the Son in his *proprium*, since the Son is the objective Word-become-flesh as a creature in the middle of creation—indeed, as the crucial medium or source *and* crown of creation itself (John, Col, and Eph)—and since the Father himself, as the *archē*/root/source/"cause" of personal deity (as the Eastern Orthodox strongly aver), is ever and only the One Singular Subject.

---

23. No other theologian has expounded more fully the trinitarian divine nature along the lines of such a fulsome kenoticism than von Balthasar: see e.g., *Glory of the Lord*, 211–28; *Mysterium Paschale*, 23–36. Those readers who wish to explore further this essential feature of Balthasar's theology may go to either Leamy, *Holy Trinity*, or Martin, *Hans Urs von Balthasar*. The former pursues Sergei Bulgakov's influence in particular, and the latter all three members of the Russian School, including therefore Vladimir Soloviev and Nikolai Berdyaev—yet both by means of a creative engagement with the tradition itself, as was notably Balthasar's method also.

8. The Holy Spirit's own *faceless, kenotic* "relationship-wise" is then both of the Father and of the Son, but *asymmetrically, differently*: he indeed proceeds "principally" from the Father's subjectivity and rests upon the Son's objectivity, granting us humans to participate, via these two, *respective* "manners/modes of subsistence/existence," in nothing less than the triune God's common life and love. In which Way we humans may eventually come to behold the true vision of God.

The Psychological Analogies

It is interesting to note in passing, and we shall take it up again later, that already in the *Confessions* Augustine was exploring certain triads with respect to the Trinity: "Who can understand the omnipotent Trinity? . . . I wish that human disputants would reflect upon the triad within their own selves. . . . The three aspects I mean are being, knowing, willing [*esse, nosse, velle*]."[24]

Returning to *De Trinitate*, we will show by a series of brief extracted examples from book IX, how Augustine's mind works to reach his analogies, step by step. He begins by reminding his readers of the triad he has already mentioned in book VIII, which Ayres views as a kind of *exordium* or appetizer.[25]

> This being agreed, let us take another look at that trio which we seem to have found. We are not yet speaking of things above, of God the Father and the Son and the Holy Spirit, but about this disparate image, yet image nonetheless, which is man; it is likely to be easier, after all, and more familiar for our mind in its weakness to examine.
>
> Here you are then—when I who am engaged on this search love something, there are three: I myself, what I love, and love itself. For I do not love love unless I love it loving something, because there is no love where nothing is being loved. So then *there are three, the lover, and what is being loved, and love* . . .
>
> Now let us remove from our consideration of this matter all the many other things of which man consists, and to find what

---

24. Augustine, *Confessions*, 13.11.12, 279. Ayres, *Trinity*, 11–92, "Part I Origins," details Augustine's early explorations using to some degree Platonic notions of the day, adapting them for his own purposes.

25. Ayres, *Trinity*, 281–85.

we are looking for with as much clarity as is possible in these matters, let us only discuss *the mind* [*mens*]. So when the mind loves itself it reveals *two things, mind and love* [*amor*]. . . . [But] where then is a trinity? Let us look into the matter as closely as we can, and call upon the everlasting light to enlighten our darkness (Ps 18:28), and let us see in ourselves as far as we are permitted the image of God.

Now the mind cannot love itself unless it knows itself. How can it love what it does not know? . . . Just as you have two somethings, mind and its love, when it loves itself, so you have two somethings, mind and its knowledge [*notitia*], when it knows itself. *The mind therefore and its love and knowledge are three somethings*, and these three are one thing, and when they are complete they are equal . . .

At the same time we remind ourselves, if we are at all able to see it, that these things come to light in the soul . . . substantially, being-wise, if I may so put it, and not as in a subject like [a list of certain *accidents*]. . . . The comparison holds further: lover or knower is substance, knowledge is substance and love is substance; yet lover and love, knower and knowledge are said with reference to each other. . . .

As for our trio, though, I cannot see how they are not of the same being [*essence*], since mind is itself loving itself and itself knowing itself, and these three are such by our definition mind that is not being loved or known by any other thing. So these three must be of one and the same being. . . . *With these three, when mind knows and loves itself the trinity remains of mind, love and knowledge*. . . .

In a wonderful way therefore these three are inseparable from each other, and yet each one of them is substance, and all together are one substance or being, while they are also posited with reference to each other [i.e., "relationship-wise," as subsistent relations].[26]

This rather crude triad with its resemblance of a trinity is then refined in book X, along the lines of memory, understanding, and will (*memoria, intelligentia,* and *voluntas*), which captures more fully the dynamic aspect of each of the mind's operations. And then comes a decisive affirmation that these mental processes are one "life," one "substance":

---

26. Augustine, *Trinity*, book IX, 1.2–8, 271–75, emphases added.

> These three then, memory, understanding and will, are not three lives but one life, nor three minds but one mind. So it follows of course that they are not three substances but one substance.
>
> [Augustine further relates each operation to itself and to each other, resulting in:] each being contained by each, [and] all contained by each as well. . . . Therefore since they are each and all and wholly contained by each, they are each and all equal to each and all, and each and all equal to all of them together, and these three are one, one life, one mind, one being."[27]

The Analogies Emerge

It's not difficult to see what Augustine is suggesting, drawing key analogies between the mind's operations and the life of the Trinity: where the begetting of the Son parallels the mind's act of intellection, and the procession of the Spirit parallels the mind's act of the will.[28] However, we have not yet reached the real point of Augustine's explorations of these key vestiges of the Trinity re the human image. Edmund Hill describes it like this:

> We have been talking [in the summary of books VIII–X] about Augustine constructing rather than merely discovering a trinitarian image in the human mind or self. One good reason for this which I have not yet broached, but which is very dominant in his thought, is that it is our Christian calling as God-seekers (remember the whole *De Trinitate* is a sustained quest for God) to construct this image in ourselves. The only way to find God the Father, Son and Holy Spirit is to become truly like God the Father, Son and Holy Spirit—to realize in ourselves the divine image by constructing ourselves into the divine image. This is all the more necessary because individually and collectively we have already thoroughly deconstructed the divine image in us by sin.[29]

27. Ibid., book X, 4.18, 298–9. Again, for further commentary, see Ayres, *Trinity*, 297–305, 308–18.

28. There is an important qualification to make, however, lest this seeming simple conclusion be wrongly construed. For as with the extract at note 27 above and later in book XV, §§ 12 and 28, Augustine, *Trinity*, 403–4 and 419, we have: "All and each of them [the divine persons] has all three things [memory, understanding and love] each in his own nature (or personality)." I.e., the human mind's functions, viewed as analogies, may not be categorised and apportioned too neatly in the triune divine case.

29. Hill, *Mystery of the Trinity*, 134. Yet see note 43 below for the *divine source of*

Consequently, to achieve this, we've to acknowledge *the true role*, as Augustine envisages it, of this very Image in which humanity is made, which begins to emerge in book XII: "Man's true honour is God's image and likeness in him, but it can only be preserved *when facing him*[30] from whom its impression is received. And so the less love he has for what is his very own, the more closely can he cling to God."[31]

That is, for humans to image God properly is to *image God relating to God*, whereby we discern the image's opening up of itself to its source, to enable *God* to shine afresh *into* the human image and fully *return* to himself according to the triune God's own trinitarian dynamic, which is one of mutual glorification among the three (at least, this is my own gloss on Augustine's presentation!).[32]

Thereafter, Augustine makes a key distinction between knowledge and wisdom, between *scientia* and *sapientia*—that is, between functional knowledge related to finite material things, and contemplative knowledge related to eternal reality. For it is *sapientia* that perfects the image in us, as book XIV will explain more fully: the image of God only truly comes to itself when it is turned in contemplation to God's eternal reality, as opposed to the mind's addressing finite objects through its ability to know.[33]

Book XIII then makes use of this distinction between *scientia* and *sapientia* as Augustine addresses the significance of the Incarnation. At one level, we can know the material facts of the life of Christ: "But all these things that the Word made flesh did and suffered for us in time and space belong, according to the distinction we have undertaken to illustrate, to knowledge and not to wisdom."[34] But what really counts is that "wisdom is attributed to divine things and knowledge to human,

---

this reconstruction of the image.

30. Latin: *ad ipsum*: this honor as per the Image is reflected light, and the reflector (as per 1 Cor 13:12's "mirror," Augustine's founding metaphor) must be itself turned towards the source of light, God himself.

31. Augustine, *Trinity*, book XII, 3.16, 331.

32. For a wonderful because very profound elaboration of how the human self, as image of God, duly relates to the triune God, see Marion, *In The Self's Place*.

33. See the important summary of Gioia, *Theological Epistemology*, 219–31; and Hanby, *Augustine*, 27–71, where he elaborates "the unity of the one Christ—head of the body, who is both *exemplum* and *sacramentum*, *scientia* and *sapientia*, eternal and temporal, creature and creator." Just so, a fulsome Christology (which is Chalcedonian before Chalcedon) is the lynch pin of where and how the Trinity is disclosed/manifests itself.

34. Augustine, *Trinity*, book XIII, 6.24, 362.

[as we] acknowledge each of them in Christ,"[35] the eternal **Word** made *flesh*. For as we are "able to behold the invisible things of God, being understood through the things that have been made" (Rom 1:20, which Augustine quotes tellingly)—that is, as we discern the *true meaning* of the **Son of God's** mission in his assumption of *human flesh*—so we come to behold *with the eyes of faith* the role of Christ the mediator, whose undeserved yet obedient and humble death reconciles us sinners to God through this "divine justice," so that we may become God's children. It's not the mere sight of a Jew on a Roman gibbet that is significant; it's for those who "have the faith which must purify the heart if happiness is to be reached,"[36] who see beyond such a piece of historical knowledge to acknowledge rather the **Word of God's** conquering sin *in the flesh* by this form of death and resurrection.

This then is the first stage of reconstructing the image of God, through the humiliation of faith that sees, that *perceives*, the truths of the Word-become-flesh on our behalf, for in this way especially is the key sin of pride overcome. This parallels notably the Word of God's own humility, who though in the *form* of *God*, has taken upon himself the *form* of a *slave*, even to the point of death on a cross (so Phil 2:6–8 again, which is vital to Augustine's soteriology and spiritual epistemology).[37]

A second stage of purification is then reached by further internal reflection and exploration, to conclude with another triad:

> We must now bring this book to an end with the admonition that *the just man lives on faith* (Rom 1:17), and this *faith works through love* (Gal 5:6). . . . Whatever notions this faith and such a life produce in the consciousness of the believing man, when they are contained in the memory, and looked at in recollection [that is, when they are knowingly paid attention to], and please the will, they yield a trinity of its own kind. But the image of God . . . is not yet to be found in this trinity.[38]

---

35. Ibid., 363.
36. Ibid., 6.25, 364.
37. See ibid., 6.22, 361: "Another point about the Incarnation . . . is that man's pride, which is the greatest obstacle to his cleaving to God, could be confuted and cured by such humility on the part of God. . . . What greater example of obedience could be given to us, us who had been ruined by disobedience, than God the Son obeying God the Father *even to death on the cross* (Phil 2:8)? Where could the reward of obedience be shown to better advantage than in the flesh of such a mediator when it rose to eternal life?"
38. Ibid., 6.26, 365.

Augustine is surely "climbing up," so to say, step by step, "searching" as he goes, and not too hurriedly at that! Yet for all that, we are almost at his conclusion. For in book XIV he continues to probe away at the mind's interiority until he reaches this point: "So as regards something present, which is what the mind is to itself, one may talk without absurdity of *memory* as that by which mind is available to itself, ready to be *understood* by its thought about itself, and for both to be conjoined by its *love* of itself."[39]

For now the mind is no longer immediately attached to any exterior sensory perception, as in ordinary knowledge, nor even focused especially upon wisdom's first success, on account of knowing both the historical Jesus *and the significance* of the eternal Son's mission. Instead, it has begun to reach such a depth (or climbed to such a height, again to mix the necessary metaphors to depict "purity of heart/mind") that it is on the edge of encountering the One to whom Augustine once cried out in the *Confessions*: "*tu autem eras interior intimo meo et superior summo meo* = But you were more inward than my most inward part/closer to me than I am to myself and higher than the highest element within me."[40] With this, Augustine is now ready to describe the necessary and wonderful *final step*:

> This trinity of the mind is not really the image of God because the mind remembers and understands and loves itself, but because it is also able to remember and understand and love him by whom it was made. And when it does this it becomes wise. If it does not do it, then even though it remembers and understands and loves itself, it is foolish. Let it then remember its God to whose image it was made, and understand and love him. To put it in a word, let it worship the uncreated God (it is after all written: *Behold the worship of God is wisdom,* Job 28:28), by whom it was created with a capacity for him and able to share in him. In this way it will be wise not with its own light but by sharing in that supreme light, and it will reign in happiness where it reigns eternal. For this is called man's wisdom in such a way that it is also God's. Only then is it true wisdom.[41]

---

39. Ibid., book XIV, 3.14, 382, emphases added. And see again Ayres, *Trinity*, 305–18, for additional commentary and insight.

40. Augustine, *Confessions*, 3.6.11, 43.

41. Augustine, *Trinity*, book XIV, 4.15, 383.

As this step is undertaken, so we begin to learn truly to fulfill the commandment, "To love the Lord your God" (Matt 22:37; Deut 6:5); and the more one loves, so the more one understands and remembers truly one's intended nature, and the more one reflects back to God his intended image as his image bearer—"'*being renewed in the recognition of God according to the image of him who created*' (Col 3:10) man in his own image."[42] Just so:

> Those who do, on being reminded, turn to the Lord from the deformity which had conformed them by worldly lusts to this world are reformed by him; they listen to the apostle Paul saying, *Do not conform to this world, but be reformed in the newness of your minds* (Rom 12:2); and thus the image begins to be reformed by him who formed it in the first place. It cannot reform itself in the way it was able to deform itself.[43]

Thus the Christian life of discipleship is viewed by Augustine as a lifelong process, one of refashioning and refurbishment into the image of God once more, all of which climaxes at life's end, at the End itself. "For only when it comes to the perfect vision of God will this image bear God's perfect likeness.... The image of God will achieve its full likeness of him when it attains to the full vision of him."[44] Such has this disciple, Augustine of Hippo, sought to seek the Lord. "Let the heart of those who seek the Lord rejoice; seek the Lord and be strengthened; seek his face always"—so Ps 105:3 once more, cited at the start of book XV. And as "faith seeks," so "understanding finds"—yet also finds out "how incomprehensible what he is looking for [actually, truly] is"![45] For such is the triune God's *own* true and immortal life that:

> Shall we suppose that with such feebleness of mental capacity we can comprehend how God's foresight is the same as his memory and his understanding, and how he does not observe things by thinking of them one by one, but embraces everything he knows in one eternal, unchangeable, and inexpressible vision? It is a relief in this kind of difficulty and frustration to cry out to the living God, *"Your knowledge is too wonderful for me; it is mighty and I cannot attain it"* (Ps 139:6). From myself indeed I understand how wonderful and incomprehensible is

---

42. Ibid., book XV, 1.5, 399.
43. Ibid., book XIV, 5.22, 388.
44. Ibid., 5.23, 390.
45. Ibid., book XV, prologue.3, 396.

your knowledge with which you have made me, seeing that I am not even able to comprehend myself whom you have made; and yet *a fire burns up in my mediation* (Ps 39:3), causing me to seek your face always.[46]

So Augustine worms his way still—has to continue to worm his way yet more along the Way of Purity, working upon this "enigmatic mirror" that is his key text from 1 Cor 13:12. As he does so, page after page, *finally* he is *forced to yield* under the *brightness* of God's *own light*; for so great is the "*dissimilarity*" between the trinitarian Creator of the image and the "mirror" that Augustine finds within himself, that he "brings [his] book to a close at last with a prayer in preference to an argument".[47] Repeating Ps 105 one last time—"with ardour"—he cries out still: "Let me remember you, let me understand you, let me love you. Increase these things in me until you refashion me entirely."[48]

It is an absolute *tour de force*: there is no doubt about it! I hope as well to have conveyed something of the flavor of Augustine's argument through the selection of texts, coupled with reinforcing the results of his quest through such texts. Overall, it has certainly yielded "much [prayerful] fruit," "fruit that will indeed endure" (John 15:8, 16). But what *kind* of fruit exactly has been produced here? The question is prompted firstly by at least three key twentieth-century practitioners of the revival of the doctrine of the Trinity, even if some elements of their own positions are themselves open to qualification. Then secondly, we have those contemporary theologians who would stress the so-called "social analogy" of the Trinity to counter the "psychological" approach. Among the first group are Karl Rahner, Robert Jenson, and Colin Gunton.[49] I shall however confine myself only to Jenson's response to Augustine in this book, as it's the most direct. As for those who commend the "social analogy," we shall be

---

46. Ibid., 2.13, 405.

47. Ibid., 7.39, 426, and epilogue, 435.

48. Ibid., 436. And recall Augustine, *Trinity*, book XIV, 4.15, 383: "Let it [*mens*] then remember its God to whose Image it was made, and understand and love him. To put it in a word, let it worship the uncreated God, by whom it was created with a capacity for him and able to share in him. In this way it will be wise not in its own light but by sharing in that supreme light . . . It is after all written, *Behold the worship of God is Wisdom* (Job 28:28)."

49. Rahner, *Trinity*, 10–21, 46–48, 115–20; Gunton, "The History." However, for a concise and important "qualification" see Green, *Colin Gunton*; and especially Ayres, *Augustine and the Trinity*.

omitting them altogether at this point of our limited enquiry, having just noted them.[50]

The Question: Analogous to What?

At this point we have to highlight the history of a dilemma.

> Modern subjectivity and the modern concept of person which it has produced... is no longer understood in ontological terms but is defined as a self-conscious free center of action and as individual personality.[51]

So begins Walter Kasper in reviewing this fundamental topic, given the actual course of human thought in Western culture. In contrast, when comparing this contemporary Western notion with the fruits of the recent revival of trinitarian thinking—which after all spawned this very notion of "personhood"!—he concludes:

> Neither the substance of the ancients nor the person of the moderns is ultimate, but rather relation as the primordial category of reality.[52]

As we've seen earlier, it is to Augustine that we owe this basic insight concerning relationality at this ontological level. Yet paradoxically, it is also Augustine, who on account of his divine simplicity axiom, failed to view the *very being* of God as *constituted by these very relations* among Father, Son, and Holy Spirit—or so claims Robert Jenson.[53]

Nonetheless, the way Augustine went about trying to establish some meaning to the trinitarian language he inherited does have a major positive result overall. When he sets out in books IX–XIV to establish his famous "psychological analogy" of the Trinity, we need to note what he is trying to achieve, and what not. In the first place, Augustine is not so much interested in the nature of the mind (*mens*) as its *functioning*—which then gives rise to the sundry options he outlines, a set of structures

---

50. The literature, as one might expect, is vast, from Hodgson, *Doctrine of the Trinity*, through Moltmann, *Trinity*, to Boff, *Trinity and Society*, as key exemplars.

51. Kasper, *God*, 285.

52. Ibid., 290.

53. See Jenson, *ST 1*, 110–14, for a brief summary of this problem as he sees it; and compare Ayres, "Fundamental Grammar," esp. 67–70, where he presents the case for the divine simplicity.

of cognitive functions related to a set of affects. These notions, *volitional* and *affective* as well as *cognitive*, all try to grant *purchase* upon the *language* we use of the Trinity. However, they do not *explain* the triune God, nor his nature. Books IX through XI, which mainly address these psychological functions, parallel books V–VII, which are mainly logical and linguistic.[54] For the human mind's consciousness of both the exterior world and its interior "motions" is *rather* the workings of the *personal*, viewed it is true as the image of God, whose "mirror" is the soul/mind, as it undergoes increasing degrees of purification. As Jenson points out:

> what the analogies discover is my *personhood*, not triunity; they do not, as Augustine thought, reveal God's triunity or [even] give meaning to trinitarian language about him. The analogies do not mean that I am *triune* or even analogously triune, only that I am personal. God is a triune and therefore eschatologically independent person. I am a merely singular, though complex, and therefore eschatologically dependent person.[55]

"That personal being is an ontological kind of its own, and that God is personal, are deeply Christian notions, and an abiding contribution of Western theology."[56] This reality, then, of conscious being becomes "the great theme of all subsequent Western philosophy":

> If we line up Augustine's main soul analyses in columns, so:
>
> | being | knowledge | will |
> |---|---|---|
> | lover | loved | love |
> | mind | knowledge | love |
> | memory | knowledge | will |
>
> the asserted equivalence of the terms in the first column gives this proposition: the being of mind as subject is immediate self-consciousness. And there is future Western philosophy in a nutshell.[57]

In which case, we have to laud this staggering achievement of Augustine's, even as we express some reservation also about the way it was

---

54. See Hill's foreword to books IX–XIV, 258–69.

55. Jenson, *TI*, 179, emphases original. What Jenson means by independence vs. dependence we shall see shortly when we discuss his understanding of *temporality*.

56. Ibid., 130–31.

57. Ibid., 130, and 155 n. 136.

taken up as a depiction of the *trinitarian* being of God. For even as we search for the "true" and the "good" (exactly parallelled by knowing and willing/loving, and so necessarily the key elements indeed of our search for "faith seeking understanding," and on into the Scholastic Tradition[58]), so we will need to look further if God's *triune* personhood is to become genuinely thematic.

All the foregoing, as full of promise and ambiguity as it is, given the history of Western philosophy, paves the way for what Jenson terms "The Patrological Problem."[59] We will discuss two related topics at this point, and so close off this chapter: firstly, the question of person, especially in relation to identity; and secondly, the issue of deity and temporality, since it is the latter which allows us to formulate triunity.

Person and Identity

Rather than delve as we might into the full rationale of Jenson's arguments, which themselves have to cover much of the debate between the Latin West and the Greek East, for our purposes I shall rest content with a brief overview. We may begin by pointing out an implication of what we have seen already in the biblical material gathered earlier. When Jesus prays, he is praying to the God of Israel, whom he calls "Abba! Father!" Just so:

> The Father is the God of Israel; [yet] the Father is one among three identities of the God of Israel. How can both of these propositions be true? The problem has a converse form, in which it is perhaps more historically familiar: Wherein is the one triune God one? The Trinity as such is the one God, and therefore the God of Israel [recall the *Shema*]; but also one person of the Trinity, the Father, is the God of Israel and therefore the one God. . . . The oneness of God is constituted *both* in the singleness of the divine *ousia and*—using standard patristic language—in the "monarchy" of the Father, that is, in his role as sole *archē*, sole originating principle or source [re the processions of the Son and the Spirit].[60]

---

58. See esp. Hankey, "Psychological Image," 99–110.
59. Jenson, *ST 1*, 115–24.
60. Ibid., 115, emphases added.

The problem has been to fit together these two historical expressions of God's oneness.

> The East has located the oneness of God in the Father's monarchy, interpreting the oneness of God's being as constituted by the Father's sheer givenness as a person who is just as such the single source of all being, the being of Son and Spirit first and foundationally. The West has located the oneness of God in a posited utter simplicity of the divine *ousia*, reading also the relations by which the Father is *archē* of the Son and the Spirit as constituted in that simplicity. Neither solution has been satisfactory by itself.[61]

When we focus attention on the business of Jesus at prayer, we see starkly the Greek position: here is the very origin of the identification of "the Father," whose personal identity then (relationship-wise) is to have no *archē* and to be the *archē* of Son and of Spirit.[62] Yet the strength of the West is to view the simplicity which sees the *Trinity* to be the one God, *because* Father, Son and Holy Spirit are fully and mutually *homoousios*, fully operating as one, as the fourth-century Arian controversy strenuously concluded. (This was subsequently enshrined in the theological principle, *opera trinitatis ad extra sunt indivisa*, "the works of the Trinity *ad extra* are indivisible.")[63] Perhaps, surmises Jenson, we might approach these two valid enough positions and try to integrate them by putting a slightly different set of questions: is the Trinity itself/himself a *personal* reality? And if so, how then is *this* personal reality related to the *three* identities of Father, Son, and Holy Spirit?

A considerable amount depends upon how we define "person." For a start, the Western tradition opted for one derived from Boethius: "an individual substance of a rational nature" (*naturae rationalis individua substantia*). Given some criticism of this down the centuries, coupled with Aquinas's qualifications, Jenson opts for another approach: "a person is one with whom other persons—the circularity is constitutive—can

---

61. Ibid., 115–16. "Monarchy" is derived from two words: *mon* = single/sole, and *archē* = source. We are only derivatively then in the world of "kings and queens"!

62. See the work of Zizioulas, a key contemporary exponent of this Eastern position: e.g., *Being as Communion*; *Communion and Otherness*; and *Lectures in Christian Dogmatics*.

63. See Barth, *CD* I/1, 375: Barth attributes Augustine with using this rule first by means of slightly different wording.

converse, whom they can *address*."⁶⁴ This allows us some startling conclusions.

In the first place, the kerygmatic and doxological grammar of God-talk⁶⁵ views our being *enveloped by the triune God*,⁶⁶ whereby we *hear* the Father's address through the Son in the Spirit, and thereafter *respond* by acclaiming the Father with the Son in the Spirit. This is a formal way of putting what we concluded in an earlier chapter re Luke 11, in the context now of our present concerns. But what *personal agency/agencies* are in operation here? Might we be able to "stand outside" such envelopment and reflect upon what is otherwise only a confessional stance? This question delivers Jenson's conclusions, permitting us to declare, firstly, that each of the three identities of the Trinity is personal, has personality, according to their own respective *proprium*, or as the Cappadocians would say, τρόπος ὑπάρξεως/*tropos hyparxeōs* (manner/mode of subsistence/existence), as we've seen earlier. But, and this is the second move, we may *also* posit a personality of the Holy Trinity *as such*. For even if the Trinity as such may not be viewed as an "identity" (this just confuses all the hard work of the fourth century distinguishing *ousia* from *hypostasis*), in the proper sense we may *address* the *community* of the Trinity, where we address "the Father" in his role as *archē* of Son and of Spirit. This raises a final question and thereafter a final move: "Can we interpret the differing personalities of the Father as the Father, and of the Father as the Trinity, ontologically? Is this duality imposed by the reality of God or is it merely our device?"⁶⁷

To answer these questions, we need to remind ourselves (again briefly) of the three columns above and the end result to which they lead in Western philosophy, with Kant's triad of consciousness, ego/"I," and freedom.⁶⁸ Human selfhood is self enclosure according to this schema;

---

64. Jenson, *ST 1*, 117, emphasis original.

65. See Jennings, *Beyond Theism*, 162-208, "God in Kerygmatic Discourse" and "God in Doxological Discourse," where the first chapter sees God's approaching/addressing us humans, and the second chapter our response/return address in worship and giving glory, etc. In other words, these two movements, of "descent" and "ascent," are the entire sum of the gospel. Our chapter 8 below will take up the significance of these movements and more.

66. See notably Jenson, *On Thinking the Human*.

67. Jenson, *ST 1*, 122

68. See ibid., 120 — Kant's "transcendental unity of apperception" involves three phenomena of selfhood: the sheer *focus* of consciousness that constitutes consciousness as *a* consciousness; the "I" or me, that identifiable individual through time; then

and personality is ontologically the *possession* of an individual, the "I." But is this the only way to perceive matters? Suffice to point out that once postmodernity enters on stage, with its *bricolage* compilation of *multiple* discourses, any of which and all of which may constitute the self at any one time, the *finale* of Augustine's legacy which is Kantian self-consciousness is *undone*. For, typically, we see this human self for what it truly is—incapable of possessing itself—once it has no ability of focussing its consciousness upon the "I," and thereby no inherent stability. Within postmodernity's "critical theory" and secular ethos, the consequences are simply nihilistic. Yet is this the only conclusion?

We have just been reminded that each of the three trinitarian identities "could not be personal in quite the same way," as we follow the gospel's narrative.[69] Next; if we break out of an understanding of the "psychological analogy" as depicting the *Trinity*, coupled with this Kantian view of the person and now its postmodern collapse, and *rather* acknowledge the triune God as *personae dramatis Dei*, whose narrative coherence just *is* God's self-identity.[70] And if we further break with "the doctrine that distinct personality is correlate to distinct identity,"[71] as notably is the case with "the Father." Then; we may conclude: "the Trinity is regarded as in *one way* personal, and Father, Son and Spirit as in variously *other ways* personal, then Father, Son and Spirit can be fully acknowledged as persons and also interpreted as poles in the Trinity's personal life."[72] Thereafter too, and especially, as we map the various and complex dynamics of possible triune personal interactions: the Holy Spirit is none other than the Father's sovereign freedom as such; for it is singularly by means of the Holy Spirit, who is the other divine "pole" in relation to the Father, that the Father, as the one divine "pole," is granted *his* due freedom.[73] And here precisely the gospel's announcement of *hope* may

---

freedom, the mysterious relation between these two, in which focussed consciousness finds itself in the "I" whose consciousness it is. In finding its "I," transcendental consciousness does not achieve anything it was not all along. Freedom in this schema is rather a relation *internal* to a fundamentally *closed* single entity, a *possessed* faculty, "free will."

69. Ibid., 121, enforcing the Cappadocian line.

70. Ibid., 42–89, chapters 3–5, "The Identification of God," "The Way of God's Identity," and "The Persons of God's Identity," present the details.

71. Ibid., 121.

72. Ibid., 123, emphasis original.

73. This depiction classically incorporates Jenson, *TI*, 142–48, as well as *ST 1*, 122–24, for which see notably below.

enter our twenty-first-century human condition, with the triune God's freedom to address us humans and solicit a due response through the gospel as we humans "call upon the Lord's Name for our salvation" (Rom 10:13). Yet, what is the nature/are the natures of the poles of this intersubjective dynamic? This question propels us down the road of having to investigate now the triune God and temporality. For the "way" (*tropos*) in which each divine identity is personal is partially a function of temporality; each person of the Trinity performs the fullness of eternal time according to their respective identity or *proprium*, as we shall see.

Temporality

At this juncture the unsuspecting reader should be warned we are about to enter possibly choppy waters. The cause of the choppiness has to do with the classic Christian tradition's decided view of an atemporal eternity which simply is the deity. Two things however prompt at least a more serious attempt at construing the opposite. The first we shall soon see is best displayed by Robert Jenson's theological project.[74] This attends to one immediate proposition, encapsulated in Jüngel's tenet learned from Barth—*Verantwortliche Rede*. Jenson, also following Barth at this point, would agree, concluding our sense of Christian deity remains inadequately baptized into the gospel's due revelation, with Christian theology properly and responsibly answering the historic eventfulness of that divine speech. The second reason turns upon the emergence of a basic trait of the eighteenth century, itself a fruit of the Christian gospel, which now saturates the Western social imagination. For ever since the time of the Enlightenment, Western thought and culture has been preoccupied with issues arising from an intense awareness of the historical. Alister McGrath expresses the theological consequences in this way: "The central Christological problem of the present day is not the ontological problem which dominated the patristic period, but the question of the relationship between revelation and history."[75] That these questions are far from

---

74. The best single presentation of these two opposing views I have encountered is David Bentley Hart's delightfully ambivalent assessment of "the theology of Robert Jenson." See Hart, "Angel," 156–69. For further general views on Jenson's theological enterprise, see the *Festschrift*, Gunton, *Trinity, Time, and Church*. See too Farrow et al., Review of *Systematic Theology*, 89–104.

75. McGrath, *Making*, 2. Chapter 1 "The Cognitive Crisis of the *Aufklärung*: From Reimarus to Schleiermacher," traces the development well. A superb lengthy

settled is only too apparent in today's theological scene, with the last century seeing a number of different approaches to the question emerge. Names like A. N. Whitehead and Charles Hartshorne are well known for their "process theology," which attempts a particular answer.[76] This in its turn has given rise to a similar, more recent movement, "Open Theism." However, my own view is that neither of these really addresses either the rich tradition of trinitarian Christian theology or the complexities of time adequately.[77] But the way forward is at least clear. James Bradley, in an essay on the relevance of Feuerbach to modern thought—after one has rejected his presupposed naturalism, that is, of which Bradley is rightly critical—summarizes: "Metaphysics cannot illegitimately be dispensed with, but must attempt *a fundamental re-thinking of its categories in terms of the 'dramatic' nature of the world.*"[78] Applying thereafter his conclusions to our own concerns: "the point is, to interpret [in a theological, that is, trinitarian way] the changing world."[79]

In this respect, Jenson's trinitarian theology is of the utmost importance, due to its sustained crusade *for* the Christian gospel and *against* the "god" of the Greeks—at least, as far as that deity is perceived as a transcendental "refuge from time."[80] It is best summed up by the title, *Unbaptized God*, where he remarks:

> Our shared *false* construal of temporality also reflects a God. This is the God in whom there can be no time because timelessness is what makes he or she or it be God. Our shared false construal of temporality reflects the culture-deity of Western civilization, the Goddess once revealed to Parmenides of Elea. She revealed to him "the unshakable heart of . . . truth." That

---

essay addressing "the question of the relationship between revelation and history" is Kuschel, *Born Before All Time?*, which addresses both systematic theology and NT exegesis, from Harnack through Barth and Bultmann, and onwards to the present day. Lastly, see the tour de force of MacDonald's, *Karl Barth and the Strange New World within the Bible*, which seeks to establish Barth's appreciation of a sui generis form of "historicality" in the context of post-Enlightenment thought.

76. See Gunton, *Becoming and Being*, which compares Hartshorne and Barth.

77. DeWeese, *God and the Nature of Time*, would be quite the book but for one thing. His "deity" is merely of the generally theistic kind. If he'd only striven for a resolutely trinitarian understanding, in the manner of say Barth or Jüngel or Pannenberg or Jenson or von Balthasar, then his conclusions might have been spectacular.

78. Bradley, "Across the River," 139–61, at 156, emphasis added.

79. Ibid., 158.

80. See Jenson, *TI*, 4.

truth was that all that changes or can change, all for which time provides the horizon, is less than being.[81]

Therefore, "the first step is to free trinitarian doctrine from captivity to antecedent interpretation of deity as timelessness."[82] More specifically, this will affect the way in which the identity of the Economic and the Immanent "Trinities" is formulated. Two basic rules of trinitarian theology need to be affirmed, and affirmed together. On the one hand, Rahner's *Grundaxiom*, which we encountered in an earlier chapter, formally states there is only one God: God *in se* is God *pro nobis* (and vice versa)—and yet how is this concretely so? For on the other hand, the sovereign freedom of God must be affirmed also: God is who he is even apart from creation and its trinitarian history of redemption; the distinction between the "economic" and the "immanent" God has a certain and vital legitimacy— to preserve God's *aseity*. But how to reconcile these two rules apart from the "antecedent interpretation of deity as timelessness"—that is the question. Jenson proposes that "only if the identity of the 'economic' and the 'immanent' Trinity is *eschatological*"[83] can we resolve the predicament. In which case, "the Trinity is simply the Father and the man Jesus and their Spirit as the Spirit of the believing community. This 'economic' Trinity is *eschatologically* God "himself," an 'immanent' Trinity."[84] For the very God of the gospel would demur from any notions of timelessness! In other words, rather than conceiving "eternity as the Persistence of the first past that causes all," we may understand it as "Faithfulness to the last future."[85] Poignantly, Jenson declares:

> Gods whose identity lies in the persistence of a beginning are cultivated because in them we are secure against the threatening future. The gods of the nations are guarantors of continuity and return, against the daily threat to fragile established order; indeed, they *are* Continuity and Return. The Lord's meaning for Israel is the opposite: the archetypically established order of

---

81. Jenson, *Unbaptized God*, 118, emphasis original.
82. Jenson, *TI*, 138.
83. Ibid., 140, emphasis original.
84. Ibid., 141, emphasis original. It is extraordinary how persistent is Eliade's *The Myth of the Eternal Return* as the sole view of eternity. Significantly, Olson, "Trinity and Eschatology," esp. 222–24, 226–27, shows how such a future orientated being of God is not unique to Jenson: in Pannenberg's case it reaches a high degree of sophistication with his metaphysics of anticipation.
85. Ibid.

Egypt was the very damnation from which the Lord released her into being, and what she thereby entered was the insecurity of the desert. Her God is not salvific because he defends against the future but because he poses it.[86]

We may say therefore, the God of the gospel identifies himself across the dramatic panoply that is the gospel story in all its fullness; that is, the triune God *is dramatis Dei personae*.[87] God is the coherent "*following of the three arrows of time without mitigating their difference*"[88] during the entire drama which the Christian Scriptures unfold from Genesis to Revelation. That is, "nothing in God *recedes* into the past or *approaches* from the future."[89] "There is future in God, but not so as to transcend God: God *anticipates* his future and so possesses it . . ."[90] These last sentences set us up for an examination of Jenson's overall trinitarian proposals, notably with respect to temporality.

"'The doctrine of the Trinity' is less a homogeneous body of propositions than it is a task: that of the church's continuing effort to recognize and adhere to the biblical God's hypostatic being."[91] The results of such a task which Jenson has set before us in his writings over many years is immeasurably rich.[92] We can only attempt a brief summary here, one which furthermore will help us on our way to construct an operational theology of the Trinity in our Christian lives of faith and worship. Please note again that word "construct." We've already noted Tom Torrance's remarks on the creation of new language; and now I myself am only too aware that this task will involve second order reflection upon the first order gospel material itself. As with even Augustine, a particular set of questions in a given context will be driving the results of such constructive work.

Firstly, we need to note:

> All such language as "God" or "the one God" is the mutual life of Father, Son and Holy Spirit. Where the form divinity would be if "God" were a word for a form, there is instead a triunely

---

86. Jenson, *ST 1*, 67, emphasis original.
87. Ibid., 64 and 75.
88. Jenson, *TI*, 25, emphasis added.
89. Jenson, *ST 2*, 35, emphases original.
90. Ibid., 121, emphasis original.
91. Jenson, *ST 1*, 90.
92. As well as those texts already cited, we should mention "Second Locus," 79–191, and "Eighth Locus," 101–78.

personal perichoresis, a communal life. *This* being of God is not a something, however rarified or immaterial, but a *going-on*, a sequentially palpable event, like a kiss or a train wreck. The being of God, said Thomas [Aquinas], is not something actualized but the event of actualization.[93]

Then secondly, following Karl Barth:

> God's being is *life*. Only the Living is God. ... More precisely, ... God is the One who is event, act and life *in His own way—actus purus et singularis*. [For] God is not merely differentiated from all other actuality as actuality generally and as such, or as its essence and principle. ... [For] without prejudice to and yet without dependence upon His relationship to what is event, act and life *outside* Him [in creation and redemption for example], God is Himself free event, free act and free life.[94]

Then thirdly, with regards to "God's own singular way," and in accordance with the very structure of his eventfulness as revealed in the drama of Holy Scripture, we may "map" the triune deity's being like this. But we need to build the *full* picture slowly. In the first place, God the Father is fount, root and source (*archē*) as we've seen; he is the Unoriginate One. Then Jesus is the Begotten Son. This sets up the first personal "relationship-wise" we have already encountered, between Father and Son. The second "relationship-wise" of the Father's establishes the Holy Spirit as the One who "proceeds"—"through the Son," we may legitimately add, if we pay close attention to the details of the economy of salvation, as we've seen as well. However, this classical trinitarian theology has essentially depicted the persons and their relationships of distinction with reference only to their relationships of *origin*. In other words, these relationships are seen to all "run one way,"[95] with protological emphasis rather than eschatological significance—*despite the biblical narrative's distinctive character*[96]

This figure below represents the traditional outline of these relations:[97]

---

93. Jenson, *ST 1*, 214, emphases original.
94. Barth, *CD* II/1, 263–64, emphasis original, **bold** emphasis added.
95. Jenson, *Unbaptized God*, 139.
96. The language echoes Jenson, *ST 1*, 157.
97. Jenson, *TI*, 122, 138–48, present the following figures and their commentary; "Second Locus," 146–157, detail only figures 1 and 2.

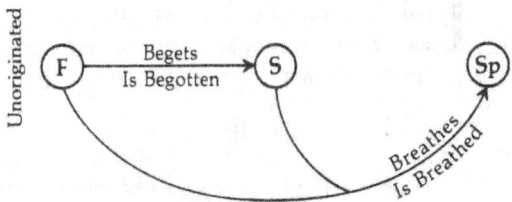

Figure 6: Traditional trinitarian relations—of origin only

So what might happen if, next, we "run" the relationships *also* the "other way," making them *fully reciprocal*? Not only does this better reflect the distinctive character of the biblical narrative with its essentially *future* orientation; it also addresses what Pannenberg sees as "a defect which plagues the trinitarian theological language of both East and West."[98]

> When Scripture bears witness to the *active* relations of the Son and Spirit *to the Father*, it is not good enough to treat these as not constitutive for their identity and in this respect to look only at the relations of begetting and proceeding (or breathing), viewing solely the relations of origin . . . as applicable to the constitution of persons . . . The nexus of relations among them is more complex than would appear from the older doctrine of relations of origin.[99]

Diagrammatically, we may therefore posit *two further pairs* of divine relationships: the Spirit, as the other pole of deity (God's "Whither," to anticipate our final comment in this regard), *"frees"* the Father from his inexorable "past" (and/or "transcendent Whence"), who thereby *"is freed"*; the Spirit similarly actively relates to the Son via an authentic witnessing, so that "witnesses/is witnessed" unto becomes the pair.

---

98. Pannenberg, *Systematic Theology 1*, 319. And see too *Jesus—God and Man*, 181–82, re the "reciprocal self-dedication" of the divine Persons.

99. Ibid., 320, emphasis added. And see too Jenson, *ST 1*, 156–60. Gunton, *Act and Being*, in his final chapter 8 on "Hypostasis and Attribute", 134–47, will also pursue this vital Pannenberg insight and its consequences..

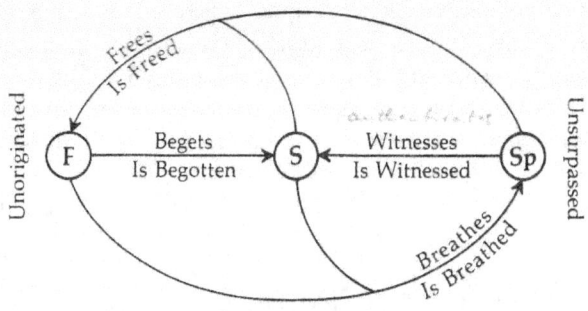

Figure 7: Reciprocal trinitarian relations

Lastly now, following Augustine's insights into the operations of personhood, as per the three columns of the soul's analysis above, and applying *these* to the triune Godhead's *reciprocal* relations, we get yet further clarification on the rich complexity of the "nexus of relations" that constitutes the unity of Personal Life that is the gospel's God. Not only does the Father *beget* the Son, who therefore *is begotten*; the Father *Intends* the Son as his Own: he knows and wills/loves this One, in whom he both knows and wills/loves himself (Jesus *is* God's "*Intended object*" even, in the Father's personal self-consciousness, as it were), and by whom we too may know him, since "Jesus [is] an item of and a subject in our history." Then, the Holy Spirit, still viewed as the twin pole of deity in parallel to the Father's Unoriginate Being, may be less "metaphorically" depicted (in contrast to the formal notion of "procession") as *being given* by the Father, who thereby *gives* the Holy Spirit. And so our last diagram finally becomes:

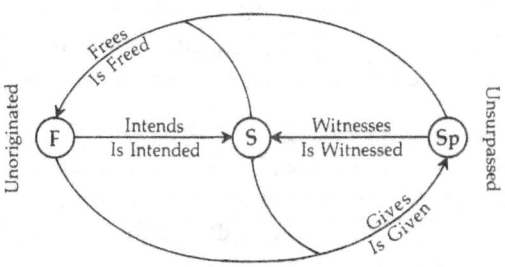

Figure 8: Revised reciprocal trinitarian relations

> We are now also able to make a choice earlier postponed. The life of God is constituted in a structure of relations, whose referents are narrative. This narrative structure is enabled by a difference between whence and whither, which one cannot finally refrain from calling "past" and "future," and which is identical with the distinction between the Father and the Spirit. This difference is not measurable; nothing in God *recedes* into the past or *approaches* from the future.[100] But the difference is also absolute: there are whence and whither in God that are not like right and left or up and down, that do not reverse with the point of view. Since now we find that what we know as time is located within and enabled by this structure, the last inhibition is surely removed. It indeed better suits the gospel's God to speak of "God's time" and "created time," taking "time" as an analogous concept, than to think of God as not having time and then resort to such circumlocutions as Barth's "sheer duration."
>
> God takes time in his time for us. That is his act of creation.[101]

This long paragraph of Jenson's is full of implications; we may only pursue some of them for our own purposes. Firstly, we are now in a position to appreciate what was said towards the beginning of this section: God is the coherent "*following* of the three arrows of time *without mitigating their difference*," etc. As we "map" the complex nexus of relations who *are* the triune God, there is a true "flow" from Unoriginate pole to Unsurpassed pole, as per the three diagrams above, a real Whence and Whither. Next, we need to unpack more of what this actually conveys about the Christian God, especially using the language of the fourth century, that is, with reference to *ousia*, *hypostasis*, and *perichoresis*.

Gregory of Nyssa states in his debates against Eunomius: "Now the Divine Nature is without extension, and, being without extension, it has no limit; and that which is limitless is infinite, and is spoken of accordingly. Thus it is idle to try to circumscribe the infinite by "beginning" and "ending"—for what is circumscribed cannot be infinite."[102] Or again:

> The Divine Nature, being limited in no respect, but passing all limitations on every side in its infinity, is far removed from those marks which we find in creation. For that power which is without interval, without quantity, without circumscription,

---

100. See notably Marion again, *In the Self's Place*, 226, re *Confessions*, 12.11.12.
101. Jenson, *ST 2*, 35, emphases original.
102. Gregory of Nyssa, "Against Eunomius. Book IX," §3, in *NPNF V*, 215.

having in itself all the ages and all the creation that has taken place in them, and over-passing at all points, by virtue of the infinity of its own nature, the unmeasured extent of the ages, either has no mark which indicates its nature, or has one of an entirely different sort, and not that which the creation has.[103]

Jenson takes these insights up directly when he considers "The Being of the One God" or "Triune Infinity." "In Hellenistic tradition, that something was 'infinite' meant it *lacks* definition. Gregory's God, on the contrary, is infinite in that it *overcomes* all definitions, in that he has irresistible Possibility.... Hellenistic deity is eternal in that in it circling time has its motionless center; Gregory's God is eternal in that it envelops time, is ahead of and so before it. The Greeks' God stands still, so that we may ground moving things in him; Gregory's God keeps things moving."[104] "God is not infinite because he extends indefinitely, but because no temporal activity can keep up with the activity that he is."[105]

The upshot of these moves is just this, as countercultural as they may have been—and may still be! If God's *ousia* is sheer infinity, having no limits whatsoever, being infinity-as-such, *of what* may we say such a thing? *Whose* predicate is such a thing, is the metaphysical way of asking the question. The answer Gregory gives, and which Jenson follows, is: "the mutual action of Father, Son and Holy Spirit."[106] More expansively, we can say, as we said earlier, but now continue further: "The one divine *ousia*, the *varied* sharing of which distinguishes Father, Son and Spirit, and the varied *sharing* of which qualifies their joint act as God, is *temporal unhinderedness,* the fact that the act of Father, Son and Holy Spirit overcomes all conditions."[107]

> What Father, Son, and Spirit have from each other to be three identities of *God*, and what characterizes their mutual action *as* God, is limitlessness. What happens among them accepts no boundaries; nothing can hinder what they enact. If we label the triune action "love," then we must say: the Father's love can embrace whatever the Spirit's coming brings; the Son's love can endure whatever his Father sends him to do; the Spirit's

---

103. Ibid., "Book VIII," §5, in *NPNF V*, 209.
104. Jenson, *TI*, 165, emphases original.
105. Jenson, *ST 1*, 216.
106. Ibid., 215.
107. Jenson, *TI*, 166, emphases original.

creativity of love is inexhaustible. Just so, this love is *God* and not creature.[108]

The three *hypostases together*, and together in their *mutual* nexus of complex relations, by which they *are* the very identities they are, each constituting one another—these are the Subject of the divine *ousia*. And finally, they are only such as they *mutually dwell within* each other, as they "posit" (Barth) themselves through that *perichoretic* temporal dance which is the triune life, as they live and move among each other with a *perichoretic* love that proves as intimate as it is also spacious, as uniquely complementary as it is also one,[109] each seeking the Others' "glory" "interminably,"[110] "end without end,"[111] "starting off from the Father, proceeding through the Son, and being completed by the Holy Spirit."

The One Who Has Room for Us

"God takes time in his time for us. That is his act of creation." This chapter must perform one last act of construction. Appropriately enough, it concerns God's act of creation, and especially of space-and-time. And appropriately again, Jenson begins in a counterintuitive manner: "God does not create a world that thereupon has a history; he creates a history that is a world, in that it is purposive and so makes a whole."[112] But how are we to appraise this history's notable feature, temporality? That's the question. Augustine may serve as our point of departure one more time.

> What is time? Who can explain this easily and briefly? Who can comprehend this even in thought so as to articulate the answer in words? Yet what do we speak of in our familiar everyday conversation, more than of time? We surely know what we mean when we speak of it. We also know what is meant when we hear someone else talking about it. What then is time? Provided that no one asks me, I know. If I want to explain it to an inquirer,

---

108. Jenson, *ST 1*, 216, emphases original.

109. For the ideas of intimacy/spaciousness and unity, see Barth, *CD* II/1, § 31.1, "The Unity and Omnipresence of God," 440–90.

110. For these attributes of "eternity's interminability" and "glory," climaxing in an extended essay on "beauty," see ibid., § 31.3, "The Eternity and Glory of God," 608–677; and recall our comments on the Fourth Gospel's Glory earlier.

111. This is Williams' expression from *Wound of Knowledge*, the title of chapter 3, majoring on the Cappadocian fathers.

112. Jenson, *ST 2*, 14.

I do not know. But I confidently affirm myself to know that if nothing passes away, there is no past time, and if nothing arrives, there is no future time, and if nothing existed there would be no present time. Take the two tenses, past and future. How can they "be" when the past is not now present and the future is not yet present? Yet if the present were always present, it would not pass into the past: it would not be time but eternity. If then, in order to be time at all, the present is so made that it passes into the past, how can we say that this present also "is"? The cause of its being is that it will cease to be. So indeed we cannot truly say that time exists except in the sense that it tends towards non-existence.[113]

While this may work as a reasonably good introduction to our problem, thereafter things get awkward, especially as we note this "passage of time." The reason for this is based yet again on those assumptions of classical culture we've met so often before. More specifically, they run like this.

If the soul is God's image, viewed as being the human ectype to the divine prototype, then the eternal God and his Presence to all time may be mirrored somehow in this soul. How? Via the twin notions of, firstly, *distentio animi*—a "distending of the soul/mind," by which it may embrace simultaneously the past's preservation in memory on the one hand and the future's anticipation as imagined on the other, beyond the ever elusive present's "now" (sc. *transience*)—and of, secondly, *praesens de praesentibus*, the soul's presenting this entire expanse of time *as it passes* to itself by *contuitus* (direct attention) in the present via the soul's/mind's own *sensed* consciousness.[114] Only so may eternity be located, it must be said, analogously, in creaturely apprehension. Of course, right here is the set of assumptions already referred to, that God by good Hellenistic definition is all that creaturely existence is not: that "if the present were always present, it would not pass into the past: it would not be time but eternity," and "Lord, eternity is yours."[115]

Q.E.D.: God is eternal Presence, the still point that is equidistant to all points of created time in the divine Mind. And this so-called conventional construction passes down into the tradition, viz. only Aquinas:

---

113. Augustine, *Confessions*, 11.14.17, 230–31.

114. For a wonderfully rich analysis of all this, see Marion, *In the Self's Place*, §§32–36, 202–29.

115. Augustine, *Confessions*, 11.1.1, 221.

Just as the notion of time starts from the notion of the present moment as passing, so the notion of eternity starts from the idea of an instant that abides. Eternity principally characterizes God who is utterly unchangeable. Indeed, because he is his own unvarying existence, God and eternity are the same thing. So God is not really measured by eternity; this notion of measurement is only our way of conceiving the matter. Verbs of different tenses are applied to God not because he varies from past to present to future, but to show that his eternity encompasses every phase of time. Truths exist in the mind; so necessary truths are eternal only because they exist in the eternal mind; nothing besides God is eternal.[116]

As to any alternative paradigm, we may start with Ps 131 (NRSV):

O Lord, my heart is not lifted up,
  my eyes are not raised too high;
I do not occupy myself with things
  too great and too marvelous for me.
But I have calmed and quieted my soul,
  like a weaned child with its mother;
  my soul within me is like a weaned child.
O Israel, hope in the Lord
  from this time on and forevermore.

Thereafter, other extensive accounts are offered by Robert Jenson and Wolfhart Pannenberg. Respectively, in *Systematic Theology*, vol. 2, *The Works of God*, chapter 17, sections I and II re time, moving on to matters of creation by the Trinity in sections III–VI, and space in VII, concluding with matter and consciousness in VIII. Then, a parallel account is Pannenberg's own *Systematic Theology*, vol. 2, chapter 7, "The Creation of the World" – II. The World of Creatures, §2 *The Spirit of God and the Dynamic of Natural Occurrence* . . . b. Force, Field and Spirit; and c. Space and Time as Aspects of the Spirit's Working.

1. The brilliance of the former assessment is that it combines two vital ingredients of the tradition:

Surely our primal intuition of time is that it must possess the characters of both Augustine's "time" and Aristotle's "time," of both "real" time and "imaginary" time. Time is precisely the

---

116. Aquinas, *Summa Theologiae*, 1a. 10.2 and 3, 23–24.

horizon of experience, with both nouns demanding full weight. A resolution suggests itself: that time is indeed, à la Augustine, the "distention" of a personal reality, and that just so it provides creatures with an external metric of created events. That is: the "stretching out" that makes time is an extension not of finite consciousness but of an infinite enveloping consciousness [which, as we have seen, is the triune God himself].

God makes narrative room in his triune life for others than himself; this act is the act of creation, and this accommodation is created time. Thus as we "live and move and have our being" in him, the "distention" within which we do this is an order external to us, which therefore can provide a metric that is objective for us. Yet we are within the divine life as *participants* and so experience this metric as a determining character also of our existence as persons.

Time is *both* the inner extension of a life, as for Augustine, *and* the external horizon and metric of all created events, as for Aristotle. For time is a "distention" in the life that is God and just so is the enveloping given horizon of all events that are not God.

It is in this matter as in others: Augustine's doctrine of divine simplicity[117] made it impossible for him to acknowledge in God himself the complexity of the biblical God, and he compensated by contemplating that complexity, which as an ardent student of Scripture he could not avoid, in the created images of God. But the triune God is not a sheer point of presence; he *is* a *life* among *persons*. And therefore creation's temporality is not awkwardly related to God's eternity, and its sequentiality imposes no strain on its participation in being [and so, to repeat . . .].

We are now also able to make a choice earlier postponed. The life of God is constituted in a structure of relations, whose referents are narrative. This narrative structure is enabled by a difference between whence and whither, which one cannot finally refrain from calling "past" and "future," and which is identical with the distinction between the Father and the Spirit. This difference is not measurable; nothing in God *recedes* into the past or *approaches* from the future. But the difference is also absolute: there are whence and whither in God that are not like right and left or up and down, that do not reverse with the point

---

117. For a succinct presentation of the Tradition's rendering of this conventional notion, especially re the metaphysics of form and matter, via Aquinas, see Davies, *Thought of Thomas Aquinas*, 40–57. See too Mazzocco, "Divine Simplicity," 434–443. An alternative metaphysic, unafraid of the thematic of potentiality and differentiation as these might pertain to the deity, would offer a rather different paradigm for understanding the gospel's triune God. Just so, Jenson, and also Jüngel's views in *Mystery*.

of view. Since now we find that what we know as time is located within and enabled by this structure, the last inhibition is surely removed. It indeed better suits the gospel's God to speak of "God's time" and "created time," taking "time" as an analogous concept, than to think of God as not having time and then resort to such circumlocutions as Barth's "sheer duration."

God takes time in his time for us. That is his act of creation.[118]

2. Then the latter has his own brilliant contribution to make, which is the theological application of key understandings taken from contemporary physics: firstly, that "bodies" may be termed "forces of energy"; and then "fields that occupy space" may be compared with the original Stoic notion of Spirit in the world. Yet there is a crucial *refinement* to this *theological* use of field theory. Rather than view the *world* as some divine *Plenum*, or *Nous* as Spirit, we may model the intra-divine field of personal trinitarian relations, the *perichoresis* of Father, Son, and Spirit, as just such a dynamic "space," with especially the Holy Spirit, in his specific identity or *proprium*, as the unique form of this notion (as per Basil of Caesarea's notion of χώρα (*chōra*) of the Spirit himself).[119] "The idea of the divine life as a dynamic field sees the divine Spirit who unites the three persons as proceeding from the Father, received by the Son, and common to both, so that precisely in this way he is that force field of their fellowship [χώρα] that is distinct from them both."[120]

---

118. Jenson, *ST* 2, 34–35, emphases original; and see again, *On Thinking the Human*. Furthermore, it is exactly at this point of Jenson's summary, and notably with his desire to bring Augustine's and Aristotle's intuitions together, that we must introduce Jeremy Begbie. See *Music*, 74: "both modernism's tyranny of clock-time and postmodernism's fragmentation and multiplicity of times" need a suitable "counteractive"; and 55: "One of music's distinctions would seem to be that its time-intensiveness is connected not only to socially and culturally contingent temporalities, and not only to the temporalities of intellectual construction, and not only to the temporalities of our bodies, but to the temporalities of the physical world at large in which all these temporalities participate." We shall have occasion to refer again to Begbie.

119. Basil, *De Spiritu Sancto*, XXVI, 62, in *NPNF VIII*. And N.B. Hanby's discussion contrasting Stoic immanentist cosmology and Augustinian creation *ex nihilo* (generally but particularly chapter 4), and the consequences for how one views the Trinity itself.

120. Pannenberg, *Systematic Theology* 1, 382–84. The idea of a "field of relationships" is typical also of Torrance; see e.g. *Space, Time and Incarnation*, chapter 3, "Incarnation and Space and Time," esp. 68–90, which will feature prominently in the next chapter.

Creation then is an act from the Father through the Son *in that Spirit*[121]—unto the Father as "the power of his future."

Likewise, in the view of contemporary physics, the "concept of time . . . is constitutive for that of space. The simultaneity of what is different constitutes space."[122] This means for Pannenberg his dealing with space first and then time. But when we come to his treatment of time and eternity, there is a parting of the ways between Pannenberg and Jenson.

> Eternity is the undivided present of life in its totality. We are not to think of this as a present separated from the past on the one hand or as the future on the other. Unlike our human experience of time, it is a present that comprehends all time, that has no future outside itself. . . . A present can be eternal only if is not separate from the future and if nothing sinks for it into the past. [So far so good perhaps . . .]
>
> We are not to think of eternity as the epitome of time. Rather, we are to think of time with its sequence of events—future, present, past—as proceeding from eternity and consonantly comprehended by it. Eternity is constitutive for the experience and concept of time. Only if time is basically a unit, i.e. as eternity, can we understand the nexus of that which is separated in its course. . . .
>
> Although eternity is constitutive for the nexus of time and of that which is separated by the sequence of moments in time, we cannot derive time from the concept of eternity. Any attempt to conceive time's origin presupposes time. . . . Augustine rightly taught that God created time [together] with all the creatures . . . as the temporal form of their existence.[123]

121. Basil Basil, *De Spiritu Sancto*, XXVI, 39, in *NPNF VIII*): "It is an extraordinary statement, but it is nonetheless true, that the Spirit is frequently spoken of as the *space/place* of them that are being sanctified, and it will become evident that even by this figure the Spirit, so far from being degraded, is rather glorified."

122. Pannenberg, *Systematic Theology* 2, 90.

123. Ibid., 92–95. He continues with a discussion of cosmic time and its eschatological consummation, notably with regards to finite creatures who require the duration of time's sequence to attain their (relative) individuation—which then presents their destiny as either "the fate of their dissolution" or the "possibility of the future" in God himself, in his eternity. See further Pannenberg, "Eternity, Time and the Trinitarian God," 62–70, where the differences clearly emerge. We may also gain additional perspective upon this "dispute" between Jenson and Pannenberg from Knight, "Jenson on Time," 71–79, due to his insistence on the biblical narrative's depiction of God's "availability" via Jesus, the God-Man, where "availability" is just Jenson's notion that "combines language and bodiliness"—and we would also add specifically "time"—among persons, human and divine.

Clearly there is a dispute between these giants. As an African proverb puts it, the grass suffers when elephants fight. But what if this blade of grass wishes to stand up tall? What if we conceive *our present* universe's space-time as but a *facet* of *eternity's singular temporality*, whose very fullness we may view according to a trinitarian understanding via Gregory of Nyssa's "unboundedness/limitlessness" (even if we may not of course exactly get our heads around such a notion!). Here our encounter with created time indeed "proceeds from eternity," and so is "constitutive of the nexus of [created] time"; and yet, as per Jenson, we may still allow the fullness of eternity's temporality to govern this precondition of created time. Just so, to repeat: "God makes narrative room in his triune life for others than himself; this act is the act of creation, and this accommodation is created time."

What this might look like and how we may articulate it is perhaps best seen in an essay by George Hunsinger, where "eternity is the unique time of the triune God."[124] For here he explicitly and formally deals with this divine attribute of eternity after the logic (one might even say the theo-logic, following von Balthasar) of Barth's own trinitarian doctrine. Something of this very logic was in the background of my own summary paragraph immediately before this new section, "The One Who Has Room for Us." This paragraph deliberately picks up echoes of this essay of Hunsinger's, via notably the three motifs of *ousia*, *hypostasis*, and *perichoresis*, all three of which govern not only trinitarian language but also the three forms of triune eternity discussed in the essay: the beginning of pretemporal divine life, the middle of supratemporal divine life, and the end of posttemporal divine life, in their totality, simultaneity, and interminability. But perhaps all this is getting too heady for an introductory book on the Trinity! And so I shall leave those readers who wish to pursue the matter further to chase up the relevant literature I have signaled—with one caveat. Our final two chapters will return to this issue of temporality via the trinitarian model I set in motion at the end of chapter 2. But before we may examine this model in any great detail, there's one further chapter to the history of the doctrine's formal emergence, its design and manufacture, we need to cover.

---

124. Hunsinger, "*Mysterium Trinitatis*," 199. And see notably Langdon, "Confessing Eternity," 125–44, which offers a most helpful summary of the discussion re eternity and time, climaxing with an assessment of Barth in this rich context.

Revisionary Metaphysics

While still bearing in mind the desire to make this book an introduction to things Trinitarian, nonetheless what this entire chapter has thrown up by way of "Manufacture" and so construction has proven to be vital for any way forward. On the one hand, we have felt the need to demonstrate Augustine's brilliance in elaborating the nature of the "personal" behind "all things" via his raising the concept of "relation" to the same categorical level as "substance" when viewing the nature of the Christian God. This begins to alter radically Hellenism's metaphysics, as we've seen. It impacts too our understanding of things human, as creatures made in the divine Image. Yet on the other hand, we've also seen that Jenson has exposed a further need. Already in chapter 6 with the church's challenge to Arianism (see especially note 25), we noted some serious consequences of the Nicene settlement on Hellenistic patterns of thinking, with notably the Gospel's "Evangelizing Metaphysics" (Leithart). Not least, we claimed the *homoousion* singularly addressed and undid the basic dualism of Hellenism. Now with Jenson's insistence, based on the sheer narrative of this Gospel story and its eschatological thrust, we've to highlight the impact of his observations on the nature of temporality itself in relation to divine nature, and notably Trinitarian identity. For it has been his ongoing contention that much of the Christian Tradition persists in accepting—accommodating itself to even—Greek notions of eternity as precisely that which is *atemporal*. Deity, by definition for the Greeks, is simply that which is not of this world, with its transience. But the Gospel would reveal such a "culture–deity" for what it is. This last section of chapter 7 would therefore briefly outline some consequences of Jenson's stance for ongoing work in the area of Trinitarian theology, and notably the metaphysical consequences. He puts it succinctly in his response to a review by George Hunsinger:

> As stated early in the book,[125] the whole of my systematics is in one aspect an effort of revisionary metaphysics, aimed at allowing one to say things about God that scripture seems to require but that inherited metaphysics inhibits. The attempt is to revise certain inherited deep patterns of thought, partly by explicit

---

125. I.e. *ST 1*, 20–21, section VIII, after delineating theology's task to be "a sort of grammar" 18, section VII, emphasis original.

proposal and partly by treating the material topics within the emerging new patterns.[126]

But why might metaphysics be important? Surely there's the possibility that such questions may undermine and so distort our understanding of the Christian faith. Such has been the claim over the years, and especially nowadays with the derision of "ontotheology".[127] Yet Robert Jenson would wish to construct his own metaphysical reappraisals differently from this contemporary movement, which is based more on a brand of philosophy derived from Heidegger (and subsequently Derrida), as well as interreligious dialogue, than perhaps the scriptural revelation of the Gospel, with the Word–become–flesh, with YHWH/"I am" in a material, human body within the theater of creation's space-time. What might be the metaphysical implications for any understanding of triune divine nature derived from Jenson's form of questioning?[128] How too might the hint from James Bradley, with which we started the section on Temporality above, be further pursued? Not for nothing does so great a theologian as von Balthasar say this:

> We have shown, however, that all of today's influential theological trends—aware of the inadequacies of systematics as practiced so far—converge toward a theological dramatic theory yet without being able to reach it; this is in part because they are not aware of their mutual convergence and often imagine that they can get along on their own, or in twos or threes. It is time, therefore, to attempt a synthesis: theology is pressing for it from within, and from outside—from drama—we have so much material at our disposal.[129]

Anticipating now (itself a double entendre) section 3 of chapter 9 below, "The Living God's Fullness of Loving Time—and GGR," after we have lain out the significance of the model of GGR in relation to God's being–in–becoming, let us say just this. The eschatological thrust of the Gospel precipitates a form of faith, hope, and love,[130] which drives

---

126. Jenson, "Response," 230.

127. For a general introduction and how it might impact theology, see the likes of O'Leary, *Questioning Back*.

128. This section is derived somewhat but not exclusively from Jenson, *Revisionary Metaphysics*, and Wright and Green, *The Promise*.

129. Von Balthasar, *Theo-Drama*, 1:125. See too therefore Nichols, *No Bloodless Myth*, who introduces the reader to this rich, five volume magnum opus.

130. Parsing these three theological virtues reveals an inherent temporality: faith

everything *from* the divine promise *into* the divine future. Just so indeed, the central Actor of the beginning, middle, and end of the biblical narrative of the economy of salvation is not merely to be appropriated to each of the triune identities respectively: these identities *are* respectively the beginning, the middle, and the end.[131] It was not insignificant we introduced the section above on Jenson's contribution with the quote from *ST* 1 as follows:

> Gods whose identity lies in the persistence of a beginning are cultivated because in them we are secure against the threatening future. The gods of the nations are guarantors of continuity and return, against the daily threat to fragile established order; indeed, they are Continuity and Return. The Lord's meaning for Israel is the opposite: the archetypically established order of Egypt was the very damnation from which the Lord released her into being, and what she thereby entered was the insecurity of the desert. Her God is not salvific because he defends against the future but because he poses it.[132]

Which leads us to formulate explicitly the anticipation: the sheer faithfulness of the triune God, whose chief characteristic is "fullness of grace and truth" (*hesed* and *'emet*), ensures the freedom of this God to *fulfill and complete* what God *initiates*. Yet what he fulfills in *himself, immanently,* is rather End without End. The divine *telos* itself is *never ending* among the perichoretic transcendent dynamic of the three identities of Father, Son, and Holy Spirit. The metaphysical implications of the Gospel for the divine nature are the *condition of possibility* whereby we humans created in the divine Image, and the creation itself, *may truly live in faith, hope, and love—both* now, *between* the times of Jesus' two Comings, *and eternally,* unto its and our true purposive wholeness. Just so, the triune God's metaphysical nature undergirds the drama of the economy of salvation, from *start* to *finish,* and *beyond.* The eschatological tension of the Gospel itself reveals and reflects something of the triune God's

---

in the past historic divine word/act of promise, hope in the divine future fulfilment, and the divine love that embraces past, present, and future. Just so, 1 Cor 13, as well as Rev 1:8.

131. For this summary depiction invoking this "temporal schema," see Watson, "America's Theologian," notably 219–23, and Jenson's "Response." In addition, I would venture too neither Watson nor Scott Swain (*God of the Gospel*, in what is an otherwise most helpful summary introduction to Jenson) have worked through enough the implications of the fully reciprocal nature of the divine relations.

132. *ST* 1, 67, emphasis original.

eternal temporal nature via the sense of God's own futurity, prompting an anticipatory metaphysic of some kind. The fullness of the Gospel's triune deity demands the traditional figure 6 above be extended and completed by those subsequent figures 7 and 8, taken from Jenson's early work (1982) on formulating the nature of the God of the Gospel. Nor should we miss the implications of the *fully reciprocal* nature of the divine relations these revised figures portray: we may *not* play off eschatology from protology either therefore. A much later work of Jenson's (2016) returns emphatically to summarize the matter.

> We have used that word "metaphysics" before, but let me remind you of something that I have been insisting in these lectures: when we begin doing metaphysics—that is, when we begin asking questions like "what is it 'to be'?"—we are not just playing empty word games. The questions we ask and the answers we give both express and shape the way we perceive and act in the world. The metaphysical challenge that Modernity has posed to the church and its message has proceeded on two lines.[133]

A summary of the metaphysical implications of Robert Jenson's Christian theology would itself insist on showing how "the strange new world within the Bible" (after Karl Barth)[134] "upends" not only classical Hellenistic assumptions around notions of time,[135] but also the consequences of contemporary nihilism's greatest challenges triggered by Modernity and Postmodernity, derived from an autonomous anthropology. That is, a more fulsome addressing of any revisionary exercise would need to engage with not only those vestiges of the cultural worlds of the Classical Tradition, but also our present cultural horizon—horizons, both western and even global, that potpourri of the emerging 21st century, which is the mission field of the Gospel today, with all its various "idols."

---

133. Jenson, *Theology in Outline*, 108. The rest of the chapter spells out some key consequences of Modernity for how Christian theology might proceed and so the consequences for metaphysics, 108–15.

134. See again Neil MacDonald's *Karl Barth and the Strange New World within the Bible*.

135. The word "upends" is taken directly from Jenson: "In . . . my Heidelberg dissertation, which was on 'The Election of Jesus Christ in the Theology of Karl Barth' . . . I argued, as bluntly as possible, that his doctrine of election in II/2 upended traditional understandings of the relation between time and eternity and thus inaugurated an innovative ontology, and that this complex was then—for better or worse—the ruling center of his subsequent theology." Jenson, "Saving Karl Barth," 132. See too Long's rejoinders, "Responses to Reviewers," 155–8.

One rebuttal of Jenson's schema has come from Francesca Aran Murphy's *God is Not a Story: Realism Revisited*. She distinguishes "monotheistic Trinitarianism", her own stance, from "descriptive Trinitarianisms" like Jenson's, with only the former being adequate methodologically in her view, since she claims it does not collapse the triune Being of God into a *mere melodrama*; rather, it expounds the full *Theodrama* of the God Who is Love. That is *her* claim.[136] A counter claim would come however from Fout,[137] via whom, I'd have to suggest, Jenson's approach has already constructed just such "a third way between philosophy and theology" (Fout). It is only not Murphy's (or Hunsinger's)! For in effect, Jenson has sought to baptize sufficiently both "philosophy" and "religion" by and with "Christian theology" *precisely in light of the triune Theodrama's revelation*. The (theo)logic of Jenson's entire programme drives us in this direction.

Yet how all these matters might be further unpacked will have to be delayed a little (another double entendre) until chapters 9 and 10. For we've to explore something of a vital consequence of the Nicene Settlement that church history threw up despite itself in our next chapter 8.

---

136. Placher, Review of *God is Not a Story*, 511–13, suitably begins the process of rebutting Murphy's claim. Notable is Jenson's proposal that "the identity of the 'economic' and the 'immanent' Trinity is eschatological," as we've seen earlier in this chapter, plus the clear metaphysical implications of this idea, which Murphy seems not to want to allow; Hunsinger's review of Jenson's Systematic Theology follows a similar prejudicial course. Chapters 9 & 10 below also show how many of these conclusions are not necessarily the case.

137. Fout, Review of *God is Not a Story*, 475–78.

Questions for Reflection

15. By now one suspects many a reader's head might be starting to spin giddily! To be sure, the topics raised by the debates of the fourth and fifth centuries are enormous, and their scope vast. For all that, there's an important difference between a simple faith and a simplistic one: any adult faith worth its salt will seek some measure of authentic understanding. The missionary context of the twenty-first century demands we have ready answers for those who ask us to give a reason for the hope that is within us (so crucially 1 Pet 3:15). This is especially the case when our "global village" now resembles the ancient Mediterranean world with its religious and cultural polyglot diversity, unlike the days of Christendom. There are lessons then to be learned from their context which are all too applicable to ours. A major one concerns the identity and nature of "God." And so the sorts of questions they had to deal with and the kinds of answers they proposed might after all have considerable relevance. "Those who have ears to hear, let them hear!"

16. One of our human instincts would seem to be to itemize and categorize individual things, learning and appreciating their differences. Yet one key lesson from Augustine's insights and the tradition he established is counter intuitive: *relation* is the essential category, the basic way of viewing the world, since this is the nature of its Creator. In addition, not just any form of relation is the case; rather, a rich view of interdependence is the case, of a complementarity and interweaving among things, and notably human persons. Certainly, any ecological view of reality confirms this. How might you appraise the world in which you find yourself/yourselves?

17. The human person: we Westerners take this notion for granted. And yet even as we do so, it is curious to note its very reality is most under threat like never before. Why is this so? And what might we, as Christians who believe in the Trinity, do to address this grave concern?

18. While the issue of temporality itself may appear somewhat speculative to some, what is most certainly not mere intellectual indulgence is the question of *hope*. We humans may not survive

without hope; the concentration camps of WW2 surely taught us that. Consequently, once again 1 Peter 3's bold instruction is relevant. "The God of hope" (Rom 15:13, and see 5:1–5 and 8:17–39) is none other than the kind of triune deity the likes of Jenson and Pannenberg, each in their own way, are presenting. And something like this understanding needs to underscore and undergird our Christian faith into the twenty-first century, if it is ever not just to survive but also to thrive.

19. Finally, related to this question is an entire set of questions that concern our appreciation of human *history*. Nor again is this mere intellectual indulgence. If our own personal stories and little histories are ever to have the *confessional depth* of the likes of a St. Augustine, then we need to work a bit more robustly upon trying to place ourselves *within* the Grand Story or Drama that is in fact God's very own triune Life and Love revealed in the Economy—for *this* is the God of the gospel! Or rather, we need to learn to appreciate that God himself has placed us within his very own Life and Love, in Christ Jesus: and so, what does *this* mean? How aware are you of *this* God's placing *you* into his very own triune Being via the Incarnation? Echoes of Phil 3, the whole chapter; and see especially note 16, chapter four, for consider this, taking our cue from a man called Auerbach, who is contrasting the likes of Homer's *Odyssey* and Old Testament narrative:

> Far from seeking, like Homer, merely to make us forget our own reality for a few hours, the OT seeks to overcome our reality: we are to fit our own life into its world, feel ourselves to be elements in its structure of universal history. . . . Into it everything that is known about the world must be fitted as an ingredient of the divine plan.[138]

---

138. Auerbach, *Mimesis*, 15.

eight

Deconstruction

THE STRUGGLE OF THE early church to reach due acknowledgment of Who the God of the gospel is was truly epic. We've tried to tell something of this story in the two previous chapters, emphasizing the emergence of some of the new forms of language this required, as well as noting some of the key actors and events in the drama, all of which gave rise to the creeds of 325 and 381. However, enough has also been suggested, and notably by the likes of Robert Jenson, to hint the task of trinitarian doctrine is not complete; there's more that may be done. The issue of "timelessness" formed the last part of the last chapter. This chapter will focus our attention on another matter, which still haunts the church deep within its basic assumptions. And more than in its intellectual assumptions, as we shall see; its very organizational structures reflect the theological conundrum this brief chapter will expose. I begin by approaching the very heart of the gospel through some comments on the atonement, given some of the less than helpful yet oft used ways this key doctrine has been formulated in the Christian tradition.

Personal Atonement

We start by referring to Tom Torrance's continual insistence that God's revelation and reconciliation "takes place" *within* the very Being of the triune God, for it occurs *within* the very reciprocity that is the Father–Son relationship, as this is embodied in the Person of the Incarnate Word-made-flesh. Atonement, in other words, is no *external* affair between

God and humanity which may be expressed sufficiently in either forensic or instrumental terms. Rather, we need to "consider the redemptive and renewing . . . vicarious life, death and resurrection of Jesus in terms of the way Jesus drew the covenant partnership between God and Israel, and between God and humanity as a whole in Israel, into his own relation as Incarnate Son to the Father, thereby *anchoring it for ever* in his own Person as the Mediator."[1]

> He does not mediate a revelation or a reconciliation that is other than what he is, as though he were only the agent or instrument of that mediation to mankind. He embodies what he mediates in himself, for what he mediates and what he is are one and the same. He constitutes in his own incarnate Person the content and the reality of what he mediates in both revelation and reconciliation.[2]

"It is this identity between Mediation and Mediator in Jesus Christ who is God and man in his one indivisible Person that is so supremely important for us to hold on to, for the very essence of the Gospel is bound up with it."[3] The history of the church is littered with examples of the consequences when this indissoluble link is fractured in any way. Torrance lists some of them in the pages that follow the last quote (pages 67–72), just as he details some of the realities of what is indeed the case in pages 73–82. While we may not delve into all these details here,[4] there is one key feature of how muddled and muddied things have become in the history of the church that does bear some teasing out. For it is so embedded and appears so "natural and obvious" to many of us. Yet it is actually a classic example of "putting the cart before the horse," and so of weakening the fullness of the life and reality of the gospel.

In a word, the problem has to do with "the mediation of Christ in our human response"[5] to God. For as Torrance says, quoting Athanasius, the Incarnate Son as Jesus "ministered the things of God to man and the things of man to God."[6] It is to the latter movement especially that we

1. Torrance, *Mediation*, 51, emphasis added.
2. Ibid., 67.
3. Ibid.
4. These themes of the Didsbury Lectures are amplified extensively in Torrance's Edinburgh lectures now published posthumously in two volumes as *Incarnation* and *Atonement*.
5. Torrance, *Mediation*, 83, the title of chapter 4 of *The Mediation of Christ*.
6. Athanasius, "Against the Arians: Discourse 4.6" in *NPNF IV*, 435. And see

must now attend in some detail, albeit also briefly, for the story is long and complicated.[7] Yet it is a most important story, since it impacts directly upon any ecclesiology (doctrine of church), and the consequential questions of church order, ministry, and sacraments which inevitably arise.

Like John Calvin,[8] Tom Torrance directs our attention to people's union with Christ Jesus and therefore their communion, their participation, their sharing in all that he is and does as mediator. Nor are these links surprising, as both derive much of their thinking from the Greek fathers of the church and their theology of "exchange." "The 'wonderful exchange' embedded in the incarnation . . . was the redemptive translation of man *from* one state *into* another brought about by Christ who in his self-abnegating love took our place that we might have his place, becoming what we are that we might become what he is."[9]

Yet these consequences of the hypostatic union need themselves to be placed within a quite specific field of understanding. Nor is this metaphor of a "field" to be underestimated: *everything hinges upon our due appreciation of what it conveys.* (The final sections of the last chapter introduced us to this vital metaphor, which derives from contemporary gravitational theory and theories of electromagnetic radiation.)[10]

> The saving reality with which we are concerned here is the twofold but indivisible activity of God: of God as God upon man and of God **as man** back towards himself, the movement of saving love which is at once *from* the Father, **through** the Son and **in** the Spirit, and *to* the Father, **through** the Son and **in** the Spirit. This has already taken place once for all in the self-giving of God to us through the incarnation of his Son and the self-offering of

---

especially Torrance, "Athanasius," 228.

7. The story is lain out in some detail by Torrance in "Mind of Christ" and "Athanasius." He takes his cue notably from Jungmann's seminal study, *Place of Christ in Liturgical Prayer*: "seminal," since it is he who outlines the serious consequences of the ant-Arian backlash with regards to Jesus' *ongoing* Mediatorial work. Finally, in this respect, attention is drawn to Gunton, "Mediation," 41–64.

8. See *IJST* 11/4 (2009), which is devoted to commemorating Calvin. Articles by Horton, "Union and Communion," Garcia, "Imputation as Attribution," and Billings, "John Calvin's Soteriology," are especially noteworthy with respect to our present concern—as is the last writer's *Union with Christ*.

9. Torrance, *Trinitarian Faith*, 179, emphases original; 179–190 fill out the significance of this "exchange," climaxing in the concept of *theopoiesis*—for which see esp. Habets, *Theosis*.

10. For further details, see again Torrance, *Space, Time and Incarnation*, and *Space, Time and Resurrection*.

Jesus Christ through his ascension to the Father. To that objective movement of redemptive descent and ascent, *katabasis* and *anabasis* [as the church fathers were wont to say], in Jesus Christ himself, [all churchly, human activity thereafter] corresponds, as, through the Spirit mediated to us by the glorified Christ, we participate in the self-giving of God in the incarnate Son which is consummated in his passion and resurrection, and participate in the self-offering of the ascended Son which is grounded in his passion and resurrection.[11]

Now; it is this dynamic, trinitarian field, set up by "the economic condescension and ascension of the Son of God"[12]—the Trinitarian movement of *katabasis* and *anabasis*, one more time—that *is* Jesus' life, death, resurrection and ascension as the One divine–human Mediator between God and humanity, between heaven and earth, that has *slipped* from being *absolute center stage*. How so?

The Anti-Arian Backlash

In a word, through what Josef A. Jungmann terms the *anti-Arian backlash*.[13] We can see this most poignantly in the disputes over the doxology, which acts as a litmus test. Hitherto, Jesus' High Priesthood was clearly seen as a function of his *vicarious humanity*, so that formal Christian worship was *with* him and *through* him and *in* him in the power of the Holy Spirit. Our all too human prayer and worship is *caught up into* Christ's

---

11. Torrance, "Paschal Mystery," 118; **bold** emphasis added, *others* original, some punctuation slightly altered. And see too the wonderful summary, Torrance, *Theology in Reconciliation*, 82.

12. Torrance, "Mind of Christ," 212.

13. Jungmann, *Place of Christ*. Chapter 10 traces developments up to the fourth century, while chapter 11 tells the story of reaction to the Arian struggles upon liturgical prayer. Chapter 13 details finally the emergence of formal prayer *to* Christ: "The particular cultivation of the Trinitarian theme in connexion with the Anti-Arian attitude automatically implies a closer attention to the divinity of Christ, while the position of Mediator, appropriate to him in his humanity, was *in practice allowed to fall more and more into the background*, since it was constantly *misinterpreted* by the Arians" (220, emphases added). A more comprehensive and subtle assessment of Jungmann's thesis is provided by Spinks, *Place of Christ*. However, the overall thesis of this chapter 8 remains, despite the necessary qualifications justly provided by this valuable collection of essays derived from the Yale Institute of Sacred Music conference held in 2005. Furthermore, Hurtado's contribution, "Binitarian Pattern," 23–50, is a suitable addition to note 3, chapter three above.

own worship and prayer *on our behalf* before the Father in the heavenly Sanctuary, an ongoing, present activity still: just so, the letter to the Hebrews in all its forcefulness.[14] The prepositions in all the liturgical prayers from the second to the fourth centuries are the real clue here: through whom, in whom, and with whom predominate. However, from the 330s onwards, the change is remarkable. For "glory" is now offered not only to the Father, but also *to* the Son and *to* the Holy Spirit, in formulae of praise and those applying to creation. Moreover, what was previously a *dynamic* "through whom," Jesus Christ/the Son, as our great High Priest—διά + genitive, Χριστοῦ (*dia christou*), in Greek grammar, became instead διά + accusative, that is, *on account of/because of/for the sake of* Jesus Christ the Son, as if it were some spiritual principle that happens to govern things.

Against the backcloth of the intense Arian struggles, the old order and formulae of Christian prayer fell into bad odor, and a certain sentiment arose: *never again is Jesus going to be allowed to be viewed as anything less than fully divine.* We may no longer stress his weaknesses and his humiliation—and this despite, for example, Athanasius' great emphasis precisely upon the Word's economic condescension. Therefore, as the identity of Jesus gets *pushed up* into the full grandeur of the Godhead, as it were, so his human, and especially his mediatorial human identity and capacity—his vicarious humanity, no less—*slips*. It is as if Christ's once great mediatorial role, the Jesus who is Mediator and Mediation in Person, as we have had him so clearly presented by Torrance, is pushed aside. And thereafter too, consequently, surreptitiously, a vacuum begins to appear—ever so slowly but surely. All in all, it is a paradoxical conclusion, let alone an ironical state of affairs, given where and how we started in chapters 4 and 5.

The Solution of the Church

Just as nature abhors a vacuum, so too does the supernatural world even more—and this way of expressing the issue is itself important. For a solution creeps in that is decidedly ambivalent, since it is based on that old problem we have met before, Hellenistic dualism, via Neo-Platonism, the *lingua franca* of the world of late antiquity. Once again to cut a long and

---

14 For a superb examination of this letter, see Bauckham et al., *Epistle to the Hebrews*, being a collection of papers given at the St. Andrews Conference on Scripture and Theology, 2006.

complicated story all too short, we may only present the offered solution.[15] We find it notably in the Book of Common Prayer interestingly enough. For in good Augustinian style, the catechism there defines a sacrament as "an outward and visible sign of an inward and spiritual grace given unto us . . . as a means whereby we receive the same, and a pledge to assure us thereof"; but of course, we'd say! Yet we must note the essential assumption of this post-Augustinian, (early) medieval period. For on the one hand, there are heavenly, spiritual, noetic, and intelligible realities, while on the other hand there are earthly, visible, material, and sensible things. And *grace it is that bridges* now Heaven and earth. And with such a view of grace goes a theology of the church as the *container and dispenser of grace,* where grace itself is viewed as a *supernatural* substance, and so by definition requires some *visible, natural* expression, in order to *so bridge* Heaven and earth. This grace is seen to be *infused* into the church's *structures and institutions,* and is under its *control* through *legal definitions,* especially those that pertain to its *personnel* and *subjects* and *key holy objects.* That is, the church's human priest is now seen as *sacerdos,* who has the *sacra potestas* or divine power to uniquely administer the sacraments *par excellence.* Christ has founded the Mass and has instituted its commemoration; the church's priests receive this sacramental, even sacrificial, command, and so perform it—on behalf of the church and in the presence of those who behold this drama of Christ's merits set before them.[16] Moreover, such an earthly performance is necessarily enhanced when the merits of those who have gone before, the saints, are added to it, and notably when Mary, the Mother of the Church, is increasingly invoked as "mediatrix," since she is surely *gratia plena,* "full of grace," as the now canonical Vulgate translates the Greek appellation of Luke 1. Christendom by this stage is nothing if not a marriage between Heaven and earth, the desire to see and institute the kingdom of heaven on earth—yet at what cost?

All this is a far cry indeed from the patristic world of for example Cyril of Alexandria. I let Torrance, commenting on Cyril, have the last word:

---

15. Jaroslav Pelikan may be our guide. See *Christian Tradition,* 3:158–214, chapter 4, "The Communication of Grace," and *Christian Tradition,* vol. 4, esp. 10–68, chapter 1, "Doctrinal Pluralism in the Later Middle Ages," which summarily extends much of the earlier volume's main chapters.

16. The long complex history of ministry from NT times to today is well told by Schillebeeckx, *Church with a Human Face.*

This worship, which characterized the whole life and obedience of the Incarnate Son in the form of a servant, and fulfilled in a heavenly mode in which Christ continues to exercise his priesthood as man, or according to the form of man (κατά τό σχμα τό ἀνθρώπινον/*kata to schēma to anthrōpinon*), is essentially spiritual. As Jesus himself taught, while pointing to himself as a human worshiper of God among us, it is worship in spirit and in truth (ἐν πνεύματι καὶ ἀληθείᾳ/*en pneumati kai alētheia*, John 4:23–4). Cyril interprets that to mean that it is worship appropriate to the nature of God who is Spirit, and thus worship that transcends the legal and carnal worship of the Jews in Old Testament times. It is worship belonging to the whole sphere of life in Christ, in which we are justified in the Spirit through union with Christ, and not by the works of the law or of the flesh. . . . Cyril goes out of his way to stress the *noetic* or *spiritual* nature of Christian worship in sacrifice and sacrament, contrasted with the external and physical rites of the Old Covenant. That does not import the rejection of physical acts in liturgical worship, or of the need to embody devotion in deeds and good works, but rather the rejection of *institutional substitutes* for worship of God in spirit and in truth. **After the glorification of Christ and the coming of the Spirit liturgical acts have essentially** *a typical and indicative function,* **for they direct us to the actual** *leitourgia* **and** *latreia* **which Christ fulfilled on our behalf**—and in which all the prayers and devotions of the faithful are gathered up and vicariously mediated through the self-consecration and self-presentation of Christ to the Father.[17]

One has to say the entire medieval edifice was a classic case of putting the cart before the horse. True, they sought to address the valid enough question of how grace might be communicated among us humans. And yet this very question was *also posed* from within a framework that was tragically crippled or hobbled from the start. For *without* a fully adequate sense of an *operational* theology of the Trinity, with its notable movement of *katabasis* and *anabasis* of the God-man in Person, the One in whom Mediator and Mediation are singularly combined, the institutional features of the gospel are almost inevitably truncated and weakened, and

---

17. Torrance, "Mind of Christ," 179–80, emphasis of the last sentence **added**, *other emphases* original. We may translate *leitourgia* and *latreia* as "ministry" and "worship" respectively. See too the important conclusions of Alan Torrance, *Persons in Communion*, 310–25, re his Doxological Model of both Christian theology and life itself.

our ecclesiology compromised, even corrupted. For Jesus Christ the Giver who gives *himself* as the supreme Gift, and Jesus Christ the Offerer who offers supremely *himself* as the Offering,[18] are overshadowed and overtaken by those others who are meant *to bear witness* to God's singular trinitarian drama, as *they/we* become caught up into *God's own* dynamic triune field. Only when we come with the antidote to this "Roman Doctrine of Grace from the point of view of Reformed Theology"[19]—that emphasizes the *Personal* nature of Jesus' *vicarious* humanity—and integrate it once more with a vibrant Nicene Trinitarianism, may we harness the church "cart" authentically to the triune God's *own* "horse."[20]

In which case, we repeat below the earlier diagram to reinforce the point. (To emphasize the geometry of the diagram: the lines αO and CA indicate the economic descent and ascent, the *katabasis* and *anabasis*, of the God–man, the divine–human Mediator, who embodies his own singular, vicarious Mediation. And then, AB/E parallels αO, with the entire triangle AB/ECA pointing to the movement of our immersion into God's own personal mediation provided in the Incarnate One, who pours out the Holy Spirit upon the church.) For only if we renew our sense of church by means of its *trinitarian* theological premise, as does Torrance

---

18. The language of Giver and Gift, Offerer and Offering being "identical" in the Incarnate One is taken from Torrance, "Paschal Mystery," 131–38. Further elaboration is given by James Torrance, *Worship*, esp. 1–83. See too Smith, "Sacraments," 185–203, for a reasonably helpful but limited attempt at situating the two dominical sacraments in a trinitarian setting—"limited" on account of his stance having not quite the necessary sense of "depth" provided by both T. F. and J. B. Torrance (suggested by figure 9 as well); and so less than a fuller understanding of the rich participation in the fulsome trinitarian "field" presented in this chapter. See too again the important thesis of Boersma (note 62, chapter six), which this chapter 8 seeks itself to reconfigure.

19. The expression is taken from the title of chapter 10 of Torrance's *Theology in Reconstruction*, where he emphasizes the Personal nature of Jesus' vicarious humanity who thus *is* the Gracious One.

20. See esp. Ziegler, *Trinitarian Grace*, for a beautiful analysis of God's personal gracious Presence through the Son and in the Holy Spirit. This importantly underscores and elaborates the position of this whole chapter—not least the summary figure 9 below, which itself stresses the needed sense of "depth" via the lines AB/E and B/ECA (see note 18 again). "Torrance's concept of grace ruthlessly refers to the personal self-giving movement of the triune God and the personal communion such a movement creates," xv, n.15. "The source of the Church determines the form of the Church. Because the Church is grounded 'in the self-communication of the Holy Trinity,' Torrance argues that any legitimate ecclesiology must make the trinitarian movement, 'from the Father, through the Son and in the Spirit, and to the Father, through the Son and in the Spirit,' the regulative center of all its worship, faith and mission," 188 (citing also *Trinitarian Faith*, 263).

so brilliantly I venture (following after Karl Barth but also working beyond him),[21] may we sufficiently proclaim and live the gospel of the Lord Jesus Christ for the twenty-first century in a way that is fulsomely evangelical, catholic, and pneumatological. And only then may we truly confess, as we said in chapter 6 under an exposition of the Creed, that "when the *church* is included under the Article on the *Spirit*, it implies *God's economy of self-communication* finds the terminus or *telos* of God's ways *right here among God's People*." Just so and only so is the church the Household of the triune God.

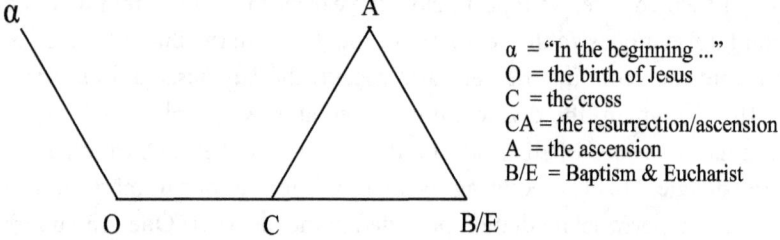

Figure 9: Luke–Acts revised displaying both dominical sacraments

---

21. See too Badcock, *House Where God Lives*, which is suitably broad and deep in its analysis of church. For those who desire a general introduction to Torrance's life and work, see McGrath, *T. F. Torrance*, Colyer, *How to Read*, and Molnar, *Thomas F.*

Questions for Reflection

20. "Wonderful exchange" and "Union with Christ": when we are put into/immersed in Christ Jesus, by the grace and power of the Holy Spirit, Jesus comes and lives his life with us and through us and in us and for us. Realizing this divine–human reality in our midst is the heart of Christian discipleship, with our being transformed (back) into the Image of Christ. What practices and so habits of mind might encourage this realization and transformation, do you think?

21. While I do not wish us to get too involved in the huge debates surrounding the divisions of the churches, the main thrust of this chapter does *reframe* many a debate about these divisions. When Jenson subtitled his *Unbaptized God* with "The Basic Flaw in Ecumenical Theology," we might just as well have referred to Jungmann's thesis re the "Anti-Arian Backlash" in addition. For while we continue to fail to address an operational theology of the Trinity and fail to see how to actually institutionalize such practices that reflect and embody such a theology, we shall always only address surface issues. The real cause for such symptoms will not itself be addressed. This book seeks in its own modest way the added goal of granting us some extra purchase upon this entire range of church difficulties, proposing something of a solution.

22. In which light, what is your own experience and understanding of things like water baptism and the Lord's Supper/Eucharist, those two sacraments our Lord formally commanded his church to perform? What is your experience and understanding too of the sheer freedom and boldness of the Holy Spirit in worship and the liturgical gathering of God's People? And finally, how does the ministry of the Word function in your own Christian experience and understanding?

23. "We may not face the world in mission unless we have first faced our God in worship; yet the authenticity of our worship is tested by the reality of our mission" (chapter 5 above). How might this maxim impact your experience and understanding of each, of worship and of mission, remembering that both are inextricably and fulsomely trinitarian?

nine

Reconstruction and Reconceiving for Renewal and Reappropriation

1

WITH ALL THE FOREGOING chapters before us, it is time to change gear once again. This chapter and the next, our final one, will take the notion of GGR and unpack it as much as we dare for our own project. In addition, this elaboration will explicitly interact with much of the contemporary literature on the revival of the doctrine of the Trinity. What this suggests is that my own ideas are part of an entire movement, one which has gone through quite a few rounds now, as each phase interacts with past ones. Nor is this movement anything like over; one can easily envisage further phases to come. Not least, there is now a renewal of interest in scholastic medieval theologies of the Trinity.[1] And yet, even as these theologies engage in the overall conversation and debate, what we still need is adequate translation of the doctrine into concrete enrichment of people's actual Christian lives of discipleship. I trust this aim has been at least broached for the reader as we've gone through these pages.

The Model of Giver–Gift–Recipient

We begin by formally stating the GGR model in its two key forms:

---

1. E.g. Coffey, *Deus Trinitas* (see esp. 46–65, notably, 63), Levering, *Scripture and Metaphysics*, Emery, *Trinity in Aquinas*, and idem., *Trinitarian Theology of St Thomas Aquinas*.

A. *God is that eternally reiterative event during which he gives himself to himself. Or, God eternally reiterates himself in giving himself to himself.*
B. *More "personally": God is the "history" of the Father from eternity giving the Holy Spirit to the Son unto eternity.*[2]

This translates directly into the life of the church and into the lives of Christian disciples on the analogy of St. Paul's notion of "adoption." Just as humans become adopted sons and daughters of the Living God, through and in *the* Son, Jesus, crying "Abba! Father!" in the Holy Spirit, so too do we humans become recipients in *the* Recipient, becoming participants in the triune life of GGR. We humans are caught up into/baptized into the very "reiterative event" that *is* the triune God, sharing in the eternal "movement" of the Father's giving the Holy Spirit to the Son, etc.[3] Nor is this understanding of Paul's unique. The conclusion we drew from our brief examination of the Fourth Gospel's prologue in chapter 4, "More Dots and Some Colors," follows a similar line of interpretation: the Glory of the Father is . . . the begetting of many additional sons and daughters (τέκνα/*tekna*/children) from among humanity, through *the* Son (υἱός/*huios*), Jesus, and the gift of the Holy Spirit. One last observation: just as individual men and women, girls and boys, together become members of the Household of God, together are members of God's family, so too are individuals recipients together in the *totus Christus*, the Whole Christ, *the* Recipient. And so extending this observation to combine Paul and John, we may say that Jesus is the Temple Recipient (John 1:14, 2:19–22), the abode of the immeasurable Gift of the Holy Spirit (John 3:34) from the Father, the Giver, who builds Christians together into the triune God's true dwelling place, the divine Home, through Jesus and in the Holy Spirit (1 Cor 3:16–17, Eph 1:15–23, 2:11–22, 4:7–16, 1 Pet 2:4–10).[4]

---

2. More properly, we should use the word "historicality" rather than "history" in this definition, since the former is the presupposition for the latter. But we shall leave such metaphysical concerns to one side for the moment.

3. We should note Myk Habets has now provided a complementary treatment of these themes to ours: see *The Anointed Son*; likewise Thomas Weinandy's earlier *The Father's Spirit of Sonship* parallels our own material nicely; lastly, see Del Colle, *Christ and the Spirit* for a probing résumé, biblical, historical, and systematic or dogmatic.

4. See notably Beale, *The Temple and the Church's Mission*, chapters 12 and 13, "Theological Conclusions: the physical temple as a foreshadowing of God's and Christ's presence as the true temple," and "Practical reflections on Eden and the temple for the church in the twenty–first century."

Elaborating the Model of GGR

With this summary clearly before us on the table, we may now plunge into our elaboration of the significance of the model of GGR.

1.0 The Living God of Love Whose Being Is in Becoming

1.1 In the first place, we have a "distinct blending of Nicene and Reformed theology," the characteristic concern, highlighted by Tom Torrance, of Karl Barth's to fully integrate the Nicene concept of God's Being-in-his-Act with the Reformation emphasis of his Act-in-his-Being.[5] "[This] inherent unity of Being and Act in God forces upon us an understanding of God in which movement belongs to his eternal Being. . . . the Being of God is essentially and eternally *dynamic*."[6] And secondly, because it ties in so closely with this first point, there is Eberhard Jüngel's appreciation of God's being as "*self–related* being":

> The modes of God's being, which are differentiated from one another, are so related to each other that each mode of God's being *becomes* what it *is* only together *with* the two other modes of being. The relational structuring in God's being is the expression of varying "original–relations" and "issues" of God's being. God's being as the being of God the Father, Son and Holy Spirit is thus a *being in becoming*.[7]

---

5. Torrance, "Legacy," 289–308, at 300 especially. Nor are Barth and Torrance alone in this judgment. Hart summarizes his opening paragraphs on the Trinity of his "minor dogmatics" like this: "Trinitarian thought uninformed by the gospel narrative results, inevitably, in an impoverishment of both that thought and that narrative; hence the importance of the affirmation that the Trinity as economic or as immanent is *the one God as he truly is, whose every action is proper to and expressive of his divinity*" (*Beauty of the Infinite*, 156, emphasis added).

6. Torrance, *Christian Doctrine of God*, 149, emphasis original. See also 120, which artfully details the situation, and 242 which summarizes the implications: "This does not mean that God ever becomes other than he eternally is or that he passes over from becoming into being something else, but rather that he continues unceasingly to be what he always is and ever will be in the living movement of his eternal Being. His Becoming is not a becoming on the way toward being or toward a fullness of being, but is the eternal fullness and the overflowing of his eternal unlimited Being. Becoming expresses the dynamic nature of his Being. His Becoming is, as it were, the other side of his Being, and his Being is the other side of his Becoming."

7. Jüngel, *God's Being* (Harris), 63, emphasis original. As we have already seen, Pannenberg, *Systematic Theology 1*, 308–27, goes further, insisting upon the "The *Reciprocal* Self–distinction of Father, Son and Spirit as the Concrete Form of Trinitarian

With regards to our model therefore: the Father who *is* the Giver/being the Giver *becomes* the Giver in or during the Act of giving the Holy Spirit to the Son; the Holy Spirit who *is* the Gift/being the Gift *becomes* the Gift in/during the Act of being given by the Father *and* received by the Son (*both* are necessary); the Son who *is* the Recipient/being the Recipient *becomes* the Recipient in/during the Act of receiving the Holy Spirit from the Father. Just so, in Jüngel's words again:

> "Becoming" thus indicates the manner *in* which God's being exists, and in this respect can be understood as the ontological place of God's being, . . . the place which God chooses. However, when God is understood as the one who chooses, his being is already thought of as a being in becoming.[8]

The GGR model thus provides for an understanding of the historicality of the divine triune being, which, as a foundational concept, permits the elaboration of a material dogmatics or narrative theology (taking up some basic themes of Jüngel).[9] Two consequences immediately arise.

Within the model, neither *substance* nor *event* has the metaphysical priority; we need not debate further which is "primary" in the divine case.[10] Similarly, there is no priority vis-à-vis *person* or *event/substance*. For example, the Father, in his own identity and essence, instantiates his divine life, which singularly *is* the divine life, during the very movement and exchange that happens with the giving of the gift to the recipient, the receiving of the gift by the recipient, and the gift's being given and being received: such is the plentitude of "divine donation" that its depiction *requires simultaneously* the categories of event, being, and person. The GGR model conveys how we may encapsulate all three categories immediately.[11]

1.2 A third feature of the model is the way it complements Jüngel's formal summary of the Trinity from his magisterial *God as the Mystery of the World*: God comes from God, God comes to God, God comes as

---

Relations," stressing not only relations of "*origin*." This Jenson does as well, as we've seen.

8. Jüngel, *God's Being* (Webster), xxv, emphasis original.

9. See Jüngel, *God as the Mystery*, e.g. 304–14, 346–47.

10. For a quintessential presentation of this quandary, see MacKinnon, "'Substance' in Christology," 279–300.

11. See again the summary by Hunsinger of Barth's trinitarianism in "*Mysterium Trinitatis*," 190.

God.¹² It is true that Jüngel is directly relating such a trinitarian doctrine to his "analogy of advent," where, to paraphrase, "gospel talk is understood as the event of correspondence in which God himself is said to arrive." He is further presupposing the twin notions of God's "address" and thereby the "interruption" caused by that address, coupled with the notion of human being as "fundamentally addressable being."¹³ The GGR model on the other hand does not necessarily operate out of such a framework, with the result that something is possibly lost. And yet, there are gains too when we consider this "analogy of *donation*," and construe the event of the analogy [x is to a (God is to the world) as b is to c] as primarily "the donation of God himself," which is the essence of love. Summarizing: God receives from God, God gives to God, God is the One who is given and received. We then escape from that over-concentration on *language* to which Jüngel is prone and to which critics such as John Webster have rightly objected.¹⁴ A further advantage in the alteration is the fact that we can avoid the alleged weakness of both Barth's and Jüngel's trinitarianism, namely, their depicting the mode of being of the Holy Spirit as the event or act of love itself. There is considerable gain in allocating this essential divine activity to the *entire* being of God, among *all* the persons and not only to one mode. Each person acts, lovingly, in their own appropriate manner, according to each one's *proprium* or their specific irreducible identity. Consequently, we are able to use the model of GGR to construe this essential trinitarian activity among the three persons by means of the idea again of Pannenberg's: "The idea of the divine life as a dynamic *field* sees the divine Spirit who unites the three persons as proceeding from the Father, received by the Son, and common to both, so that precisely in this way he is that force field of their fellowship [or χώρα/*chōra*; so Basil of Caesarea again] that is distinct from them both."¹⁵

1.3 A fourth consideration emerges therefore from the nature of God as love, the loving One who lives in freedom. (Once again we combine both Barth and Jüngel, reinforced by Jenson and Pannenberg, to say nothing of von Balthasar; yet also notice the way in which the analysis is extended by each subsequent theologian.) To love is to give—oneself.

---

12. Jüngel, *God as the Mystery*, §25, 376–96.

13. See briefly Jüngel, *God as the Mystery*, 285–86, 155–161, 164–65.

14. See Webster, *Eberhard Jüngel*, 50–51; noting especially: "What is demanded of Christian faith is not only language which 'brings God to speech' but also patterns of thought and strategies of action, both ritual and ethical."

15. Pannenberg, *Systematic Theology 1*, 382–84, emphasis added.

But "God *is* love," (1 John 4:8). Thus God *is* the very fullness of the event of love *itself*—giving, being given, receiving, being received. This *action* which God *is* furthermore "*takes place* as God *corresponds* to himself, says 'Yes' to himself, and so comes to himself," to use the language of Jüngel.¹⁶ God's being as self-movement is thus one of total self-determination and self-affirmation in the fullness and the freedom of the Godhead's perichoretic co-response. Just so, *God intends himself* (Jenson).

> Thus divine love constitutes the concrete unity of the divine life in the distinction of its personal manifestations and relations. The personal distinctions among Father, Son and Spirit cannot be derived from an abstract concept of love. We may know them only in the historical revelation of God in Jesus Christ. But on this basis, they and their unity in the divine essence make sense as the concrete reality of the divine love which pulses through all things and which consummates the monarchy of the Father through the Son in the Holy Spirit.¹⁷

We may justly relate this summary with the one of Lewis Ayres, where he says, "[While Augustine] insists that the divine three are irreducible . . . he consistently founds the unity of God in the Father's eternal act of giving rise to a communion in which the mutual love of the three constitutes their unity of substance."¹⁸

And yet such a vision of God's aseity does not preclude his coming to humanity, for he *determines* to come to himself *only with* the human: there is ever "the humanity of God."¹⁹ Nor again, and crucially, does it preclude the possibility that this sovereign God can precisely *be himself*

---

16. See e.g. Jüngel, *God's Being* (Harris), 73–74, 96; Jüngel, *God as the Mystery*, §§20–21, 314–43. We should note too the double wordplay of "takes place": both deliberately occurs/happens, and requires space. Just so, see again Barth, *CD* II/1, "The Unity and Omnipresence of God," 440–90.

17. Pannenberg, *Systematic Theology 1*, 432.

18. Ayres, *Augustine*, 319.

19. See Jüngel, *God as the Mystery*, e.g. 37–38, 191, 195, 280, 299–302, 304–14, 343, which of course follows the later Barth, "Humanity of God," 33–64. More specifically, we should say: God determines to come to himself *together with* his human creature. Not only as Father, Son and Holy Spirit does God determine to be God; God chooses to be both himself and the electing God in Jesus Christ, such that simultaneously ("one and the same," Chalcedon) Jesus Christ is both the electing God and the elected man, both subject and object of the decree of election. See e.g. *CD* IV/1, 66, which climaxes a long discussion on the covenant as the presupposition of atonement in Jesus Christ. N.B. also note 51, chapter ten.

in giving himself *away*: he "can *die* as a human being."[20] God comes to *himself* in the bringing together of perishability–and–nothingness *and* his very own being. Thus God *is* in the struggle between being and non-being and its resolution.[21] In determining himself to be *this* God, as he intends himself *thus*, God reveals himself as "the original unity of life and death for the sake of life," who in this way "ex–ists out of himself into nothingness."[22] All of this is another way of saying that God *is* love, covenant/election–affirming, steadfast love—and moreover, "the *fire* of love,"[23] in which death is extinguished, for in this is love "the event of a still greater selflessness within a very great self-relatedness."[24]

1.4 The model of GGR has been specifically formulated to articulate this whole complex set of ideas, wherein we are able to emphasise the trinitarian correspondence between God *in se* and God *pro nobis* (God in himself and God towards us), between God *ad intra* and God *ad extra* (God within/"inside" and God beyond/"outside"). For something of the dynamics of both the Cross itself and the Way to the cross becomes expressible as the Way of God's very being. The crucifixion, viewed as the surrender/giving up of the Son by the Father for the sake of God's love for the world, becomes the "moment" when the Father as the Giver precisely "withdraws" what has been hitherto the unique divine Gift from the Son. And yet this is not a unilateral move; there is *full reciprocity* and affirmation among the divine persons. The Son as Recipient deliberately "yields up the Spirit" to his Father, not wishing "to cling to" this Gift.[25] Hence Gal

20. Jüngel, *God's Being* (Harris), vii; and note Webster's introduction, *God's Being*, xvii: "what makes [Jüngel's] work distinctive is something learned from Barth, namely, an insistence that God's passion as the incarnate and crucified one is not an alien fate, somehow the occasion of God's renunciation of divinity, but the chosen mode of God's sovereign capacity: God *can* die. Thus, part of the force of the term 'becoming' is to provide a theological account of the being of God in which the trinitarian God can *be* in self-surrender" (emphases original).

21. See Jüngel, *God as the Mystery*, 213–20.

22. Ibid., e.g., x, 217–25. The notion of God's being as "a Going–Out–Of–Himself into nothingness," literally *ek–sistere*, should be highlighted, as the noun, *ekstasis*, will feature prominently below.

23. Ibid, 326: "The unity of life and death in favour of life, as we have understood love, is expressed with one word and pregnantly in the old metaphor which speaks of the *fire of love*" (emphasis original); and ibid., 329.

24. Ibid., 317–18; and see further 324, 358, 369, and 391 re the combination of divine selflessness and self-relatedness.

25. See Luke 23:46, John 19:30, Phil 2:5–8. But see also the commentaries for the various interpretations on these verses relating to Golgotha.

2:20, "the Son of God who loved me and gave himself up for me." The resurrection likewise becomes the supreme "moment" when the Father bestows the Gift of the Holy Spirit afresh upon the Son. Just so, we should notice how the model ties up with the Lutheran notion of God's "hiddenness," the divine presence-in-absence, which forms such an important part of Jüngel's inquiry into a trinitarian theology of the Crucified One.[26] For God the Recipient "remains" precisely at the very moment when the Giver with his Gift "appear" "wanting." For in the *silence* and *stillness* that is Holy Saturday, the Word Incarnate and Author of Life situates himself within the sheer emptiness that is *das Nichtige*.[27]

While the GGR model complies with Jüngel's quoted maxims and themes well enough, we can also reformulate his language a little and say, "God so is, in the dialectic of loss and gain for the sake of love and life's ever greater increase." (The full significance of this statement will be seen when we add Jenson's contribution below.) Additionally, the GGR model firmly provides a role for the Holy Spirit in Jesus' crucifixion, a weakness that can be raised against Moltmann's otherwise very insightful approach.[28] Perhaps too it sheds some light on that otherwise enigmatic verse from the letter to the Hebrews, 9:14, "how much more will the blood of Christ, who through the eternal Spirit offered himself without blemish to God . . ." (NRSV).

1.5 These initial observations concern the model's ability to articulate God's historicality; but, "historicality is not history," only its presupposition. A general reference to the "humanity of God" has also been made, together with the possibility of "perishability" in considering God as love. Yet a major feature of the contemporary trinitarian discussion has been the concern for the specific integration of being-and-time: this is humankind's concrete experience, our actual involvement. What therefore of God's?

---

26. See again McGrath, *Luther's Theology*, 201–32, chapter 5, "*Crux sola est nostra theologia*: The Emergence of the Theology of the Cross, 1514–1519."

27. See Barth's discussion of the *nihil, das Nichtige*, in CD III/3, §50, 289–368, which is usefully parallelled by von Balthasar's *Theo-Drama*, 5:300–21, and idem., *Mysterium Paschale*.

28. See e.g. Moltmann, *Crucified God*, esp.112–290, and idem., *Way of Jesus Christ*, 151–273.

2.0 The Ecstatic, Epektatic God of Life and Love

2.1 As we've seen in chapter 7, Robert Jenson's trinitarian theology is a sustained crusade for the Christian gospel against the "god" of the Greeks, at least, as far as that deity is only a transcendental "refuge from time."[29] And so to repeat: "the first step is to free trinitarian doctrine from captivity to antecedent interpretation of deity as timelessness."[30] More specifically again, this will affect the way in which the identity of the Economic and the Immanent "Trinities" is formulated. But, as both he and Jüngel, and Barth before them, avow, the sovereign freedom of God *in se* is ever to be affirmed; God's aseity is cardinal. The trick is to reconcile these two points. This may only be done when "the identity of the economic and the immanent Trinity is *eschatological*, if the immanent Trinity is simply the eschatological reality of the economic,"[31] as we've seen. "[Therefore] instead of interpreting Christ's deity as a separate entity that always *was*—and preceding analogously with the Spirit—we should interpret it as the final *outcome*, and just *so* as eternal, just so as the bracket around all beginnings and endings."[32]

2.2 The GGR model draws together these concerns with utmost brevity. Dispensing altogether with the notion of *logos asarkos*—but *not* in any Barthian protological manner that would merely posit *Jesus*-with-God "in the beginning";[33] rather, viewing the "antecedent" nature of the Son as the triune divine determination of ever coming-to-be, as Jesus, who then eventuates historically in Mary's womb and under Pontius Pilate[34]—we stress now the definition of the Christian God as being the history of the Father *from eternity* giving the Holy Spirit to the Son *unto eternity*.

Essential to this depiction is Gregory of Nyssa's notion of *epektasis*, which Jenson exploits so fruitfully in his last chapter of *The Triune*

---

29. See e.g. Jenson, *TI*, 4.

30. Ibid., 138.

31. Ibid., 140, emphasis original. See also again Olson, "Trinity and Eschatology," 213–27, esp. 222–24, 226–27.

32. Ibid., emphasis original. An entire discussion is found in Jenson, *ST 1*, chapter 8, "The Christological Problem," notably re pre-existence, §IV, 138–44.

33. See Barth, *CD* II/2, 94–106; and N.B. Roberts, "Barth's Doctrine of Time," 88–146.

34. See Hector, "God's Triunity," 246–61; and see further note 51, chapter ten.

Identity, "Triune Infinity."[35] We recall some of his conclusions. Οὐσία in the divine case is sheer infinitude, one of "Unboundedness/Unsurpassability." The event of which this is the case is the love enacted by the Father, the Son, and the Holy Spirit, whose "varied sharing" (it depends on which word one is emphasizing)[36] of this trinitarian history "ensures the overcoming of all conditions." Accordingly, the ultimate profession: "Resurrection is this God's *ousia*."[37] For only if there is truly that "end without end"[38] which is love, may we say, as was said above, "God so is, in the dialectic of loss and gain for the sake of love and life's ever greater increase." Just so, God *ever more fully* gives himself to himself in love and freedom. More formally, *God is that **eternally** reiterative event during which he gives himself to himself*. The triune being of God is indeed "overflowing being"[39]—which expression leads directly to the next step of our analysis.

2.3 If on the one hand Gregory of Nyssa speaks of the *terminus ad quem* of God's life and love in freedom, another Christian mystic of the early church supplies us with the *terminus a quo*.

> We must dare to affirm (for 'tis the truth) that the Creator of the Universe Himself, in His Beautiful and Good *Yearning* towards the Universe, is through the *excessive* yearning of His Goodness, *transported outside of Himself* in His providential activities towards all things that have being, and is touched by the sweet spell of Goodness, Love and Yearning, and so is *drawn from*

---

35. Jenson, *TI*, 161–84; summarized, Jenson, *ST 1*, 215–21. For a summary of Gregory's idea itself, see Gregory of Nyssa, *From Glory to Glory*, 51–71. See also Ferguson, "Progress," 307–14, and Macleod, "Allegory," 362–79, esp. 372–78. Similarly, note Basil's notion of *prokopē* (*De Sp.S.*, VIII,18), which should be linked to the Spirit's being "the perfecting cause" in God's economy of salvation (*De Sp.S.*, XVI,38), esp. in the life of Christ, and so the agent of such an "advance," XVI,39, in *NPNF VIII*, 12, 23–25. In other words, there are some very real affinities between the two notions of *epektasis* and *prokopē*, although we would want to modify the latter somewhat, since the "state of perfection" in Gregory is more exactly "end without end." See again Coakley, *ModTh* 18/4 (2002) for an entire discussion on Gregory of Nyssa.

36. Jenson, *TI*, 166: "The 'one divine *ousia*', the *varied* sharing of which distinguishes Father, Son and Spirit, and the varied *sharing* of which qualifies their joint act as God, is *temporal unhinderedness*, the fact that the act of Father, Son and Spirit overcomes all conditions" (emphases original).

37. Ibid, 168.

38. See again Williams, *Wound of Knowledge*, chapter 3's title, of which we shall be making much soon.

39. See Jüngel, *God as the Mystery*, 222–25 once more re *ek-stasis*.

His transcendent throne above all things, to dwell within the heart of all things, through a superessential and *ecstatic* power whereby He yet stays within Himself.

So writes Dionysius, the Areopagite.[40] Granted the different purpose to which "ecstasy" is put in the original context, it nevertheless serves our purposes very well once an appropriate change in the frame of reference is made. For this is a vision of the Christian God whose "history" of eventful love is constituted by the Father *overflowing beyond* himself and primordially *bestowing* the Holy Spirit, the Gift of love and desire, upon the Son—for it is in the *eternal* Spirit that the Father "generates" the eternal Son, we might say.

2.4 We would take up these two terms, *the ecstatic* and *the epektatic*, and fashion them into a coherent picture of God via the use of GGR. But first a little foray into the tradition to better set the scene. We find, for example in Athanasius, the oft-repeated expressions of οἰκονομία (*oikonomia*, the economy of salvation) and τάξις (*taxis*, or order/the tracing of a pattern) together with the formulae "*from* the Father *through* the Son and *in* the Holy Spirit" and/or "*to* the Father *through* (and *with*) the Son and *in* the Spirit."[41] These are ways of describing and coordinating the descent (*katabasis*) and ascent (*anabasis*) of the triune God in the Incarnation and its aftermath, the mission of the Holy Spirit to/in the church (we encountered these ideas in the previous chapter). Naturally, such devices for depicting the Trinity were conceived from within the ethos and worldview of classical culture, albeit greatly Christianized. But they have something to teach us still, even if and when one wants to alter things fairly radically, as in our own proposals. A similar sense of the trinitarian activity of God is provided by the contemporary notion of the *Missio Dei*.[42] While mission is made up of sundry dimensions—the evangelistic, the communal, the diaconal, the search for justice and peace, the environmental/ecological—each and all are expressions of the Trinity's

---

40. Dionysius, *Divine Names*, 106, emphasis added. See also Louth, *Origins*, chapter 8, on Denys, esp. 175–77; see also 89–90 for a discussion on the similarities between "ecstasy" and "epektasis," and the development in Gregory's writings from the former to the latter.

41. See again Torrance, "Athanasius," 251, emphasis original.

42. Re the dimensions of mission, see e.g., Bosch, *Witness*, 15–20; Verkuyl, "Ways and Means"; nowadays refined to the "Five Marks of Mission." For extensive elaboration, see Bosch, *Transforming Mission*, notably part 3, with "Mission as . . ." multiple times; and lastly, Wright, *Mission of God's People*. And N.B. again Flett, *Witness*.

"creating, sending, seeking love" together with the corresponding "redeeming, uniting, glorifying power" of the Trinity.[43]

2.5 With these traditional ideas now as a backcloth, we can similarly interpret the GGR model via the notions of "*ecstasy*" and "*epektasis*." The gain is to have boldly presented both "the Unoriginate *terminus a quo*" and "the Unsurpassable *terminus ad quem*,"[44] the "Whence and Whither in God," deity's "twin poles."[45] (We shall take up more of this "movement," especially with regards to temporality, in a moment.) Furthermore, in the very process of the divine actuality itself, there are two essential twin movements to the God whose being is in becoming; there is a vital double, double heartbeat to this trinitarian historicality of love. These we may term the "ecstatic-cum-epektatic" on the one hand, and on the other the dialectic of presence and absence—which itself is an expression of the profound and unique *kenoticism* of the divine persons and their *perichoresis*.[46]

Such a description marries remarkably well with the following statement of Jüngel's, which concerns God's self-identification in the death and resurrection of Jesus:

> The love, which began as the event of a still greater selflessness [viz. crucifixion] in the midst of such great self-relatedness [viz. divine love] perfects itself now as the event of a new self-relatedness [viz. resurrection] coming out of still greater selflessness which continues as such.[47] [Hence our phrase earlier: "ever greater increase."]

---

43. The phraseology is Moltmann's. See "Church," 50–65; and *Trinity*, chapter 3. See also Rosato, *Spirit as Lord*, 134–41.

44. See Jenson, *TI*, 141–48, esp. figs. 7 and 8 again.

45. Jenson, *ST 1*, again.

46. Together with Jüngel and Moltmann, I would want to emphasise the intra-divine dynamic of Good Friday's sheer "godforsakenness." Then there's von Balthasar's particular sense of *Holy Saturday*: see *Mysterium Paschale*, chapter 4, "Going to the Dead: Holy Saturday," 148–88; *Glory of the Lord*, "self–abandonment," 142–61, "Momentum of the Cross," 202–35 (e.g. the "face-to-face confrontation between the 'naked' God and 'naked' sin . . ." in Jesus' burial, 231); and finally, *Theo–Drama V*, 250–69, "Death/Life; Sorrow/Joy," "Separation as a Mode of Union," and "A Darkness Reserved to God Himself." All of which variously stress the *essential emptying of each divine Person on behalf of the Other(s)*, the Singular Divine Glory.

47. See Jüngel, *God as the Mystery*, 324, and see 318–19, 358, 369, and 391 re the combination of divine selflessness and self-relatedness

In a similar way, Moltmann speaks of "an inversion of God," "a *self-limitation* of the infinite, omnipresent God [that] precedes his creation, [which] . . . creation, as *opera ad extra*, then presupposes . . . [In sum] *outward incarnation* presupposes *inward self-humiliation*."[48] Such is the dialectic of the historicality of the God who, using the schema of GGR, withdraws and gives (viz. creation), gives and withdraws himself (viz. incarnation and crucifixion) to/from himself, etc, etc, over and over, ever establishing his presence-in-absence and his ever-greater fullness of presence, through "the whole Christ," ecstatically-cum-epektatically.

3.0 The Living God's Fullness of Loving Time—and GGR

With all the foregoing in place, we are able to come finally to that most problematic feature of all regarding the divine historicality, the business of *time*—at least, the history of Christian theology has seemed to make it so; but perhaps only due to its *lack* of totally "baptizing" its "God" by the gospel and fully immersing the resulting "deity" by God's trinitarian revelation in the story of Jesus.[49] Moreover, we venture to suggest too that the GGR model offers some assistance in clarifying these very problems. We may put it in its most lapidary form.

3.1 The Father is the Giver, and to give is thereby to initiate—among personal Subjects! And to initiate is to grant a future. Just so, the Gift of God is the Future itself.[50] Yet an unfulfilled future is no future at all. Hence there is the Recipient, whose identity is to grant likewise due fulfillment, the necessary *telos* for that which is given/offered initially. But to give *ecstatically*, to give again and again out of oneself, in a continuously overflowing manner, a sheer effulgence, as the Father does, for that is Who He *Is*—that means the Gift of the true Future is One of Unbounded Possibility. All of which also means that the Recipient is no mere terminus, no end—period/full-stop. Nor yet a mere infinite "deferral" (as some postmodern might say), on account of the *telos* remaining. Rather, they are (once more) true End without End. And just so is God that *epektatic* triune being, whose eternal life knows no limits whatsoever, whose

---

48. See Moltmann, *Trinity*, 109,119, emphases in the text.

49. This way of expressing the issue is taken of course from Jenson's *The Unbaptized God*, which we've cited already.

50. It is on this basis that Spirit is the αρραβών of our redemption in the economy of salvation, a "slice" of the Future, given the Holy Spirit's *proprium*, as we've seen above.

whence and whither are precisely pure infinitude during love's true "donation." And mentioning "love" offers us the final aspect of the *fullness of time's intention*: the offer of a due "space" wherein One may *care for* Another; time's possibilities are those during which Another seeks One's *attention*, via *desire*.[51] The resulting careful address among these *is* love's infinite future, eternal time's plenitude/pleroma of "mutual lively regard" (Aquinas). Just so is there the triune *faithfulness, of each One desirously attending to the Other* across all eternity. This *is* GGR![52]

3.2 Yet again, we may substantiate/elaborate via some quotes from Robert Jenson.

> The biblical God's eternity is his temporal infinity.... The true God is not eternal because he lacks time, but because he takes time. Yet... simply that source and goal are real in God would not make his eternity a "duration," a *temporal* infinity. He is *temporally* infinite because "source" and "goal" are present *and* asymmetrical in him, because he is primarily future to himself and only thereupon past and present for himself. It is in that he is Spirit that the true God avoids—so to speak—the timelessness of mere form or mere consciousness.... When all is said, the compendious interpretation of the triune God's eternity remains that of the Old Testament: Thus Ps 119 [vv. 89–90] has in one line, "Forever [*leolam*], O Lord, your word is firmly fixed in the heavens," and then, in strict parallel versification, "Your faithfulness endures to all generations..." The eternity of Israel's God is his faithfulness. He is not eternal in that he secures himself from time, but in that he is faithful to his commitments within time. At the great turning, Israel's God is eternal in that he is faithful to the death, and then yet again faithful.[53]

> What Father, Son and Spirit have from each other to be three identities of *God*, and what characterizes their mutual action

---

51. Mentioning "desire," as the authentic ethos of donation's mutual regard, might be said to rehabilitate Augustine's meditations on "time," at least, with regards to Marion's own appraisal of them: *Self's Place*, §36, 223–29, "Conversion of the *distentio*," where such *distraction* gives way to *attraction*, "the upward call," which thus *extracts* one—all of which, in a way, it has to be said, emulates "end without end."

52. In another setting one would have to elaborate greatly this subsection: e.g., re temporality and dramatic narrative—see Quash, *Drama of History*, re von Balthasar; and Vanhoozer, *Drama of Doctrine*; and see especially again, Begbie, *Music*, whose insights overall are seminal.

53. Jenson, *ST 1*, 217, emphasis original, which view of God's eternal faithfulness is vintage Jenson.

as God, is limitlessness. What happens among them accepts no boundaries; nothing can hinder what they enact [apart from God's own faithfulness and righteousness]. If we label the triune action "love," then we must say: the Father's love can embrace whatever the Spirit's coming brings; the Son's love can endure whatever his Father sends him to do; the Spirit's creativity of love is inexhaustible. Just so, this love is *God* and not creature.[54]

3.3 But what of the poor creature? For if the previous sections offer something of how we may express the nature of eternity, then what of ordinary time? Created time, as we currently know it, is an instantiation of God's own eternal time, within which we might posit our time. And since it is this, and not the whole, not the pure duration of the perichoretic fullness of the three persons in the lively divine being,[55] but only one facet of this eternal fullness of time, it is therefore a limitation. *As a limitation (peras)*, it is simply under the threat of transience, of perishability, of nonbeing—even as it is held faithfully in being by the One in Whom we live and move and have our being, until such a time as this God's purposes are fulfilled for it.

And what of the God of time, of historical time, *as we know it?* Awesomely, this God is not threatened by it at all—at least, the triune God is not. For under our proposed model of GGR, this God is precisely free to surrender the gift of this time, any time, with the Recipient's handing over the Spirit, with the Father's withdrawal of the Gift, with the Gift's own suspension. And just so, in this event of sovereign singular freedom, nonbeing and the threat of Nothingness may be found their one place or *topos*, to use the language of Jüngel, *in the Crucified One*.[56] It belongs to the very fullness of the triune God's own eternity, God's own self-determination, to grant *within deity's own* eternal trinitarian being that unique *topos* of all that would threaten God's good purposeful creation—even "the Judge judged in our place" (Barth). Such is the condition of possibility for the Gospel's narrative, of the Story of God *as* the Crucified One; such is God's own triune historicality that the history of Jesus finds too its place as the

---

54. Ibid., 216, emphasis original.

55. For an elaboration of how this last fulsome phrase might be, see again Hunsinger, *Mysterium Trinitatis*.

56. See Jüngel, *God as the Mystery*, 216–19, where Jüngel is being typically Barthian, establishing creation *christologically*, which is to say via the lens of the Crucified One. And N.B. again Webster's introduction, note 20 above. For details, see again Barth, *CD* III/3, 289–368, §50, "God and Nothingness."

trace or parable of the Vulnerable God,[57] who, precisely in not exploiting his deity, as such truly reveals the divine form: *forma Dei* as *forma servi*, *forma servi* as genuine *forma Dei*—so Phil 2:6–11, "even death on a cross. Therefore God has highly exalted him, and bestowed on him the Name above every name." Consequently and finally, it is precisely and only on this basis that in *faith* we may, during the course of the divine economy's unfolding, which is our human history too, genuinely know *peace* with this God and *rejoice* in whatever befalls us, as the overflowing *love* of God is poured into our hearts, and the Spirit's yearning and groaning for the final Future encourages our own faithful maturation in *hope* (so Rom 5:1–5 and 8:15–39), as we anticipate our sharing in the Son's own resurrection, knowing too the fellowship of his sufferings (Phil 3:10).

Interim Conclusion

All our model of GGR is attempting is some acknowledgment of the Name of the Trinity in God's revelation: "Father, Son and Holy Spirit." And given "God's being revealed" (Jüngel)[58] in such a way, such a manner, so may we enter into a way of articulating God's being, which permits its explication via such a model as GGR. For the τάξις (*taxis*/order) within the divine economy, of which this model is "a summary concept,"[59] of Father-Spirit-Son, corresponds to the differentiated being of God *in se*. And it is *this* God who thereby shows himself as ever the Living God—the God of life who loves in freedom—and who shares that life with his creatures, even his dying creatures, in the freedom of his holy love. Such a declaration of human dignity surely promotes a corresponding acknowledgment of the divine worth, in all its genuine fullness.[60] For "the point"

---

57. The expression is taken from Placher, *Narratives*. And see MacKinnon, *Themes in Theology*, 162: "Yet within the context of this totally uninhibited, but triadic aseity, we have to reckon with the actuality of limit, of *peras* or boundary. It is through this actuality that, for instance, the *idiotēs* of the Son *as eternal receptivity* is constituted, a receptivity that in the manner of the Incarnate life is expressed in his dependence, realized in the form of his human submission in respect of the hour of his agony and his glorification" (emphasis added).

58. Once more, we should note the *double* meaning wordplay of "God's being revealed": see esp. Jüngel, *God's Being* (Webster), xiii.

59. Jüngel, *God as the Mystery*, 346.

60. See Barth, *CD* IV/1, 41: "χάρις (*charis*) always demands the answer of εὐχαριστία (*eucharistia*). Grace and gratitude belong together like heaven and earth. Grace evokes gratitude like the voice an echo. Gratitude follows grace like thunder

(Jenson)[61] of trinitarianism *is* the divine address of the Father's Son, Jesus, in the Spirit, who himself then so solicits and gathers our Eucharistic response with and through and in Jesus unto the Father, that humanity joyously receives its share in that eternal triune Conversation in sheer integrity. The doctrine of the Trinity *is* doxological acknowledgment: "Glory to God, Father, Son, and Holy Spirit; as in the beginning, so now, and forever. Amen!" is the confessional cry of the whole of creation![62]

---

lightening."

61. Jenson, "What is the Point?," 31–43.

62. See esp. Marion, *In the Self's Place*, 11–55, for a magisterial treatment of this confessional theme. See too Sanders, *Triune God*, who delightfully commences his whole argument with "Attunement: *Gloria Patri*," as chapter 1, 25–35.

Questions for Reflection

24. "The doctrine of the Trinity *is* doxological acknowledgment": this suggests the same kind of thing we find in Exod 3:14–15; 34:5–7. See e.g., Pss 20:1; 45:17; 72:17; 102:12. For the OT Name, "Yahweh," has become in the NT, "Father, Son and Holy Spirit," into whose very Name Christians are baptized, to share the Life, the Reality of *this* God. How goes your confession of this Name/these Names?

25. Trinitarian spirituality according to GGR becomes in essence a question of cultivating "receptivity." What do you think this might mean for you? What sorts of spiritual disciplines might *enhance* receptivity and what sorts of things would *hinder* it?[63] Bear in mind one set of answers will appreciate each individual "recipient" is only such when they participate in the Reality of *the* Recipient, analogous to each child of God being a member of the Father's Household, each individual a member of the Body of Christ. All this derives from their union with Christ Jesus himself, establishing the Whole Christ, *totus Christus* (see note 60, chapter six).

26. With the Trinity being the kind of God who gives himself to himself, according to GGR, this means he is free to give himself to "another," and so to create, and even to become the Incarnate One. Furthermore, he is free to give himself away—free to die! How do

---

63. Kierkegaard "is from the very beginning setting his face against some of modernity's most cherished assumptions. In particular, he is taking issue with the modern aspiration to autonomy, an assumption that, from Kant to Sartre, sees only what we are able to think and do for ourselves as humanly valuable. As Sartre would put it, "You are the sum of your actions"—but for Kierkegaard we are never able to think or to do anything if we have not first been given and accepted the gift of being. We only "are" on the basis of life being given us in the first place. Of course, we must *accept* the gift and, as these discourses show, Kierkegaard was well aware of the many strategies by which people seek to evade the responsibility involved in such acceptance and how prone they are to indulge more or less disreputable fantasies about how much better life would be if they were somewhere else or someone else. In this Kierkegaardian perspective, then, acceptance is the first and most difficult of all the tasks with which life confronts us." And: "We don't want to be as nature intended us to be; instead, we want to choose the values and the projects in which we find fulfilment so as to be fulfilled only on our own terms." So Pattison in his introduction to Kierkegaard, *Spiritual Writings*, xix–xx, xxi.

you imagine this appreciation might affect, and even help to effect, your relationship with the triune God?

27. Once again, some of the moves in this chapter might appear to some people inordinately abstract. And yet, once we allow ourselves to become better "placed" *inside* the sorts of depictions of the triune divine Life being presented here, they should enhance our very own Christian identity, strengthening our Christian life of discipleship, as we see the Trinity envelop us. How aware are you of being so "placed" inside God's very own Life and Love and Being, of the triune God's Life being situated in and through you? It is helpful to recall Edmund Hill's description of how discipleship is a constructive task in Augustine's hands (note 29, chapter seven).

ten

Reconstruction and Reconceiving for Renewal and Reappropriation

2

OUR FINAL CHAPTER EXTENDS our elaboration by focusing on each phrase of our two trinitarian depictions. Then we finally close with another means again of engaging in the Life of the triune Godhead.

- A. *God is that eternally reiterative event during which he gives himself to himself.*
- B. *God is the "history" of the Father from eternity giving the Holy Spirit to the Son unto eternity.*

Elaborating Definition A

A.1 — That . . . Event

With regard to the being of God, [therefore] the word "event" or "act" is *final*, and cannot be surpassed or compromised. To its very deepest depths God's Godhead consists in the fact that it is an event—not any event, not events in general, but the event of His action, in which we have a share in God's revelation.[1]

In the characteristic words again of T. F. Torrance, we have a "distinct blending of Nicene and Reformed theology," which profoundly

---

1. Barth, *CD* II/1, 263, emphasis original.

integrates the Nicene concept of God's Being–in–his–Act with the Reformation concern for his Act–in–his–Being.² We may deduce (once more) from this that:

> God's being is *life*. Only the Living is God. . . . More precisely, . . . God is the One who is event, act and life . . . in His own way—*actus purus et singularis* . . . [for] God is not merely differentiated from all other actuality as actuality generally and as such, or as its essence and principle. . . . [Thus] without prejudice to and yet without dependence upon His relationship to what is event, act and life outside Him, God is Himself free event, free act and free life.³

It may appear a nice distinction between, say, "the" event and "that" event; but the latter, a demonstrative as opposed to the article, captures Barth's authentic concern for "*et singularis*," and so is not merely incidental. It also prepares us for the *kind* of event that God is *according to the GGR model*, i.e., "donation," which itself accords with God's own revelation.

A.2—Eternally Reiterative

A.2.1 Together with many other commentators, Barth notes the place of the threefold Name in the church's baptismal confession.⁴ He affirms that the object of faith in such a confession—the identifying Name of the God henceforth to be believed in, because the candidate desires *this* particular God's "salvation"—is not triple, but is named three times, as Father, Son, and Holy Spirit, in accordance with God's own repetition of himself in his self-revelation. Furthermore, because this revelation may not be interpreted in any modalistic fashion, "God is the one God in threefold repetition . . . in such a way that the repetition itself is grounded in His Godhead."⁵

---

2. See again Torrance, "Legacy." There is hardly a publication of Torrance's that does not mention this, "one of [Barth's] most important contributions to Christian theology."

3. Barth, *CD* II/1, 263–64, emphasis original, **bold** emphasis added.

4. See Jenson, *TI*, 7–20, Kasper, *God*, 212, 245–46, 276–77, and Vickers, *Invocation and Assent*, 1–28, all of whom spell out the important role of the rite of baptism as the *Sitz im Leben* or basic setting of the early church's naming and confessing the triune name of her God.

5. Barth, *CD* I/1, 348–350. Note also: "The so-called persons are a *repetitio*

When therefore we change our focus from the dynamics of biblical revelation (we may recall Barth's "Root of the Doctrine of the Trinity"[6] is his *interpretation* of the God who *so reveals himself as* attested in Scripture) and onto who/what that revelation does, his concrete act(s), the idea of repetition or *reiteration* fits remarkably well with the business of *donation*.[7] For God's being is in threefold differentiation (GGR) *as* the one who relates supremely to himself via that singular activity of giving: giving; being given; receiving; being received. God's complete correspondence via the intra-divine "Yes" is enacted by means of the full, mutual consent(s) of the divine perichoretic "donation." Moreover, precisely such a God—and *only* such a God—*is* the freedom "to give himself away."

A.2.2 One final theme might occupy us in this section: the ontological plus of being—the "ever new"—and the *topos* ("place") of Nothingness. At first blush, the notion of an eternally reiterative event may suggest endorsement of Mircea Eliade's "The Myth of the Eternal Return."[8] However, this is not the case; quite the opposite in fact. For we recall the earlier statement, "The Father is the Giver, and to give is thereby to initiate—among personal Subjects! And to initiate is to grant a future. Just so, the Gift of God is the Future itself. . . ." This echoes explicitly both Pannenberg and Jenson:

> The divine identity of the Father is conceived in terms of the power of his future, which is the very source of new events in history, including the incarnation of his Son and the consummation of all creation by the power of his Spirit. . . . The identity of God as the power of the future constitutes the "dramatic coherence of his eventful actuality" (Jenson).[9]

Such a view of the reiterative God who is ever new, given that "he is primarily future to himself" (Jenson), precisely endorses Jüngel's view that "possibility [and so the emergence of the new] is the ontological plus

---

aeternitatis in aeternitate, not then a threeness of eternity *extra se* but a threeness of eternity *in se*" (350).

6. Ibid., §8.2, 304–33.

7. The language of "reiteration" occurs not surprisingly also in Jüngel, *God's Being* (Webster), 110–11, of God's being as event uniquely capable of self-interpretation; and see again, 118–19, re God's being in becoming as that which is capable of self-relatedness and self-correspondence—the divine "Yes" which *is* the complete consent of "giving" and "receiving," I would furthermore add.

8. Eliade, *Myth of the Eternal Return*.

9. Pannenberg, "Eternity, Time and the Trinitarian God," 67.

of being."[10] Christian ontology, in the light of the eschatological story of Jesus, simply *shatters* much traditional Hellenistic views of reality and the actual (i.e., their metaphysics).[11] "The occurrence of something unsurpassably new which does not grow old, but rather remains *new for all time*, is completely out of joint with the popular understanding of time . . . Understood in this way as a renewing power, the new which endures is a *divine predicate*."[12]

And this predicate is exactly what "*that eternally reiterative event—during which God gives himself to himself*" is suggesting. The ecstatic-cum-epektatic act of donation that is God's being-in-act, his act-in-being, that is his being-in-becoming, establishes the eschatological surpassing of all things—even and especially nothingness and its undertow of annihilation. For God, through the death, burial, resurrection and ascension of Jesus, has granted even *this* its true *topos*—that is, within his very own reality and being. Just so, "God does not cease to be the one who begins. He remains the one who begins in freedom."[13] And begins again and again—and again, superabundantly. And if *beginning again and again*, just so GGR's apprehension of time (chapter 9, 3.1) grants the *faithful fulfillment* of all possible initiations/intentions—yet precisely as End without End.

A.3—During Which

One final comment is required. Just as it was a subtle but significant shift in meaning to have "that" rather than simply "the" in our summary description, so it is important to note the change from, say, "in which" to "during . . ." We recall the elaboration above, of God's being in becoming: "the Father who *is* the Giver/being the Giver *becomes* the Giver in the Act of giving the Holy Spirit to the Son;" and so on through . . . In other words, what may appear as less than fully dynamic, fully *alive*, due to the construction ". . . becomes the Giver *in* the Act of giving," becomes explicitly so, with deliberate connotations of eternal temporality, when

---

10. Jüngel, *God as the Mystery*, 214.

11. See Buckley, "Intimacy," 17–21, for such "revisionary metaphysics", as well as Leithart, *Athanasius*, 1–25 (though see too 140–45 for a subtle, point counterpoint discussion of divine impassibility and the "Word on the Cross").

12. Jüngel, "Emergence," 53, 55, emphases original.

13. Ibid., 57.

one says, "... becomes the Giver *during* the Act of giving." And it is this "interminably" *enduring* nature of the divine being,[14] whose being is in singular becoming via the actuality of the threefold divine personal donation, that we wish also to sense clearly via the model of GGR.

From this first section we may say that the Christian gospel announces the God of hope, who is love itself, in whom we humans may have faith eternally. For having indicated the divine being as the predicated phrase, "that eternally reiterative event during which ..." we need to establish the subject(s) of such an expression.[15] This paves the way for our more "personal" depiction of the triune deity in section B.

Elaborating Definition B

B.1—The History ... From Eternity ... Unto Eternity

Two complementary points are being made here. Firstly, together with Fergus Kerr, "the hypothetical Archimedean God's eye view" is being deliberately eschewed,[16] by stressing the concrete particularity of a specific story, by "tracing" a distinctive history—that of Jesus, the Jew, by whom and with whom it is claimed God has uniquely identified himself. But secondly, if this identification is not to "reduce" God entirely to the historical process, more needs to be said. The problem is what and how to "say" the "more" without spinning out into wisps of abstract mystification.

The language of protology and eschatology is an attempt to sit right on the very edge of the universe, as it were—an event horizon—to view from the limit of our time's end (which "time" though? "old" or "new"?)[17] the coherent sum of the whole story. The only reason this procedure can be said to work is because the substance of the story is that of *love*; that is, here is something present and actual which is both clearly knowable and specifiable, and yet is also by its very nature utterly open-ended from the depths of its (re)generative wellsprings. This presents an "end without end" indeed, which enables and ensures once more "the ontological plus

---

14. See once again Hunsinger's "*Mysterium Trinitatis.*"

15. When speaking of subject(s) and predicate, note again Jenson's use of such language following Gregory of Nyssa on page 125 above. What follows now merely echoes once more such a train of thought.

16. See Kerr, *Theology after Wittgenstein*, specifically of Rahner, but generally of the Cartesian self.

17. See Jüngel, "Emergence," again.

of being" (Jüngel), replete also with all love's possibilities right from its very Source. And what is finally to be noted is that such a dialectic derives itself from the heart of the story; namely, this One, who showed (past) his gracious love to the uttermost in the course of our concrete space-time universe, now stands (present continuous) "vindicated" beyond himself while nonetheless remaining still himself.[18] Consequently our Christian hope is not one of escape *from* this world but of *this* world's redemption and transformation, even—nay especially—of its problematic, limited historical and fallen processes.[19]

B.2—Giving

The word "God" in the Christian scheme of things is a verb rather than an abstract noun. When asked to specify the subject of this verb, one needs to refer to the threefold Name, "Father, Son, and Holy Spirit," which we shall pursue in a moment. This is another way of saying that God's being is event, a singular eventfulness which the trinitarian persons variously share, each constituting the life of the one God in their distinctive way (so the Barth–Jüngel–Jenson–Pannenberg tradition).[20]

To give is to love, to love is to give, particularly to the point of self-dispossession. But, where such a thing would overwhelm the likes of humankind, it is the trinitarian calculus of crucifixion–burial–and–resurrection that, in God's, case such annihilation only releases a superabundance, such a "distancing" a more intense "intimate nearness." The GGR model attempts to unfold something of the essential dynamic of

---

18. For an extensive elaboration of the significance of what this "beyond"—and so apparent "absence"—of Jesus's ascended humanity might mean, via sundry lines of interpretation down the centuries, see Farrow, *Ascension and Ecclesia*.

19. We need to note how Jüngel starts his essay, "Emergence," by contrasting "old" and "new," and so trying to establish their true *theological* interrelationship: the old is rendered old by the emergence/arrival of the new.

20. Whether this emerging common tradition itself—even if we may so call it—fully succeeds in subverting and/or converting the traditional substance ontology to an event (or dramatic) ontology (see Farrow, "Robert Jenson's *Systematic Theology*," 89–95, MacKinnon, "'Substance' in Christology" again, and especially Alston, "Substance and the Trinity," 179–201), I am not finally decided. This said, however, certainly the GGR model does accord Aristotle's concepts of both primary and secondary substance *equal* weight, the latter being precisely the infinite eventuality that is God's being and the former the three identities of GGR *per se*—hence 1.1's final paragraph in chapter 9 above.

this profound presence-in-absence, which leads to an even greater fruitful presence, this stepping into Nothingness, the archetype of Gehenna,[21] which then newly liberates Everything, into the divine Effulgence—the dramatic, coherent quality of eternal Love itself. In addition, we should note that during this divine surrender each person endures the loss according to their own particular identity, and each secures their identity, not merely upon "vindication" or resurrection, but precisely also through such (reciprocal) surrender and self-emptying, which von Balthasar emphasizes so well.

On the one hand, the death-and-resurrection of Jesus and its character illustrates a divine principle, a divine possibility, which after the event may be seen to operate throughout creation. But on the other hand, the atonement *achieved* by the mission of Jesus cannot be reduced to merely the level of the exemplary; *a truly novel situation* has been brought about. There is a very real tension here, a problem of theological approach that the GGR model on its own is incapable of solving.[22] Where the tradition has spoken of such things as Nature and Grace, or Creation and Redemption, and hotly debated their interrelation, our model rests content to indicate God's ecstatic, overflowing "donation," which then permits our speaking of a "withdrawal." Yet this, in its turn, does not lessen God's loving purposes, for divine "surrender" itself paves the way for that superlative gift who ever abides, epektatically. The "moments" of divine giving, givenness, and receptivity "become" ever more expansive by means of the "movement" of the triune God's historicality.

B.3.1—The Father as Giver

The model retains the idea of the Father being "fountain" or "root" of the Trinity: he is "*the* Author" indeed. And what of the other side of the coin, freedom itself?[23] One might tender the following definition. Freedom is

---

21. See again Barth's discussion of the *nihil, das Nichtige*, in CD III/3, §50, 289–368, and von Balthasar's *Theo-Drama, V: The Last Act*, "Approaching the Reality of Hell," 300–321 (and overall, *Theo-Drama, IV: The Action*, "Dramatic Soteriology," 317–423). See also Fiddes, "Overcoming Nothingness," 261–67.

22. See, e.g., Marshall, *Christology in Conflict*, re a general philosophical method versus the concrete particularity of Jesus as criterion. This contrasting dynamic echoes Hunsinger's Barthian "motifs": see *How to Read Karl Barth*.

23. Behind this opening move is an entire discussion regarding the interrelation of authority and freedom, both divine and human. Again, the literature is vast, but see

the integrated capacity of heart and mind, will and intellect that enables the person to be present to and so engage with another for their mutual Good, for, as concluded earlier, freedom is essentially a *relational* term.²⁴ It is that most specific characteristic of "persons," where the personal may be described (once more) in this way:

> In this work, we have from the beginning assumed a modification of Boethius' definition that need here only become explicit: a person is one with whom other persons—the circularity is constitutive—can *converse*, whom they can *address*. In this amendment of Boethius, the biblical logos as *communicated* sense replaces the Greek logos as merely *possessed* sense.²⁵

Where therefore any "other" is more than inanimate, and more again than the merely animate, and so is also *personal*, then *freedom* begins to realize its potential in subjective interaction and enhancement, the "space" that constitutes and enriches each subject. Thus the Father offers or gives; and gives furthermore in accordance with the Goodness which God is himself, for the mutual enrichment of All.

The notion of authority, and concomitantly authorship, raises another issue, that of divine *unity*. It need not imply, as it does in traditional Greek theology, that the Father is also "the principle of unity" within the Godhead.²⁶ The essentially *reciprocal* relational form of the respective divine identities in the model of GGR means that "each mode of God's being *becomes* what it *is* only *together with* the other two modes of being," as we've seen. This trinitarian nature *is* divinity, the innate comprehension of differentiation and union. The unity or oneness of God is therefore something which "takes place" (Jüngel) as the very life of God proceeds. Indeed, following the likes of Jenson and Pannenberg, it is only fully realized *in the economy* eschatologically. And so, while we deliberately mention the question of unity under the heading of the Father, this is only to deny what might be taken as a matter of course, just as we also did *not* discuss it under the heading of "Giving," thus tacitly moving away from a

---

only: Whitehouse, "Authority, Divine and Human," 225–43; Peters, "Authority (1)," 83–96; Winch, "Authority (2)," 97–111.

24. See esp. Jenson, "Second Locus," 172–75, re "God as Spirit," of which more below, and idem., *ST 1*, 115–24, chapter 7, "The Patrological Problem," which was discussed earlier.

25. Jenson, *ST 1*, 117, emphases original.

26. See e.g. Heron, "'Who Proceedeth,'" e.g., 161; and Orphanos, "Procession," 31.

view of the traditional Latin position, which tends to locate unity in the divine essence.[27]

Because of the eschatological fulfillment of the identity of the economic Trinity and the immanent, we cannot have neatly two subsections on "God the Father," "as Creator" (appropriating creation to his specific identity), and then as "The Eternal Father," following the analysis of Karl Barth in his *Church Dogmatics* I/1, §10. *At this stage* of the history of the church, and so the history of theology as she seeks to understand her faith, the presentation of God is still *in via*, "along the way"—although it has to be added immediately, the Christian affirmation is that *as* God *has* shown himself to be, and *is* now, *so* he ever *shall* be. *This* is essentially the significance of the covenant God, who keeps faith with Israel, and who keeps faith with *the* Israelite, Jesus, by raising him from the dead. Just so, God has promised himself as the Giver: and so he has proven himself to be, *ab initio*, *ex nihilo*, and again and again. But this is not the whole of his Story.

B.3.2—The Holy Spirit as Gift

Something there is that is perennially elusive about the Holy Spirit (for who indeed may "catch the wind"?). Hence the welter of images in both Scripture and tradition that are used to depict her. It is just this variety which has created another problem, the personal nature of the Spirit, since many symbols are of a material kind only. Every human being knows what it means to be a child and what it means correspondingly to be parent, even if they themselves are not one personally. To be human means to be not self-generated. Thus the models of "Son" and "Father" are part and parcel of our immediate human experience (even where that experience happens to be a negative one). But how to cope with "Spirit"? That is the question.

On the face of it "gift" is rather an impersonal term, but closer inspection produces some surprises.[28] For a gift to be just that, gift, there

---

27. Heron, "'Who Proceedeth'"; yet compare the justifiable revision of this de Régnon thesis, on which Heron seems to rely, by the likes of Ayres. All the same, acknowledging this justifiable revision does not thereafter imply we should seek the divine unity otherwise than suggested here, as it "takes place."

28. See again Augustine, *Trinity*, book V, chapter 3, §§12 and 13, where Augustine settles also upon the term "gift" as the most suitable "name" for this third divine person; and NB §16, 200: "There is a difference between calling something a gift and

needs exactly to be both a giver and a recipient. It is an intensely *relational* term, therefore, binding the two parties together. It also captures forcibly the *character* of the relationship between these parties: it is one of openness and sheer gratuity—of "freedom in love" and "love in freedom." Augustine's *vinculum caritatis* is justifiably a powerful expression. And so, thirdly, applying *personal* characteristics to the Spirit is not that strange or out of place, as the general ambience is a profoundly personal one (that between Father and Son). Indeed, viewing the Spirit *also* in explicitly personal terms serves to *intensify* the nature of God's personhood. One is reminded of C. S. Lewis' description of the doctrine of the Trinity as "Beyond Personality."[29] If the heart of the image of God in which the creature is made is the personal, then how much more the Creator himself! In which case, that freedom and love which is God's is all the *greater*, due to the necessary *added* openness of him/her[30] who *is* Spirit, *whose own personal consent is required as the gift to be given by another and to be received by yet another, as they delight in and through each other.*[31]

All these intensely personal and relational features of the One who is Gift in Love between Father and Son were the fruit of profound Scriptural exegesis by the early church Fathers.[32] Yet, as we saw in chapter 6 re-

---

calling it a donation; it can be a gift even before it is given, but it cannot be called a donation unless it has been given." *Just so the Recipient Son*—derived not from these considerations of Augustine but from the version of Spirit Christology being pursued here. And see Weinandy, *Reconceiving*, 81–85.

29. Lewis, "Beyond Personality," 130–88. In adopting this line of discussion here, we are not seeking to *prove* the personal nature of the Spirit, only to show what some of the implications might be having once granted her personality on other grounds.

30. See Jenson, "Eighth Locus," 174–78, re the sophiology of Sergius Bulgakov, "the masculine/feminine principles" of Gen 1:27. To ring such changes, we have adopted feminine grammar for our part in this text. Compare Heron, *Holy Spirit*, viii, re "the boundaries of language," and his own adoption of "it."

31. For which see Staniloae, "Procession," 184–86: not only are we to speak of an "I–Thou" relationship, but a three-way "I–Thou–He/Another" interaction, which gives "the fully personal character of the Holy Trinity," each with their respective *idiotēs* and all among their various, reciprocal interrelations. This is parallelled exactly by Richard of St. Victor, "Trinity," 386–93: for love to be truly *supreme* means *sharing* among these *three*.

32. See notably Wilken, "Is Pentecost the Peer of Easter?", who canvasses the work of Origen, Athanasius, Hilary of Poitiers, Didymus the Blind, Ambrose, and Augustine, all of whom eventually conflate key texts, resulting in viewing the Spirit "in the language of reciprocity, participation, and mutuality," "of the gift of love who is poured out," "since he is given, received, and possessed," so that the Holy Spirit may fulsomely "dwell among the faithful." For a good summary of this view of the Spirit's identity as

garding the necessary context of worship to affirm Jesus' identity as fully divine, so too was it the church's ongoing experience through its evolving liturgy (notably "in baptism, in the calling down of the Holy Spirit in the great prayer over the bread and the wine in the Eucharist, in the laying on of hands during the ordination of bishops, to name the most obvious rites"[33]), which also contributed to this very exegesis. Consequently, the GGR model sits well within this tradition depicting the Spirit's *proprium*, whose identity properly resides among the worshipful experience of God's people just as he dwells eternally with the Father and the Son.

And just as the discussion of God's unity took place under the heading of "the Father," so this question of God's *personhood* is deliberately tabled in this subsection. For the one metaphysical statement of God in the Bible is that "God is Spirit"—which, following Hegel, Jenson, et al.,[34] means the lively freedom of the personal, consciously acting and interacting in the ongoing flow of history, and so inscribing a story or enacting a script or performing a score.[35] But for such a history to be truly fulfilling and not merely tragic,[36] for it to be the faithful realization of that which is most fulsomely personal, and so the triumph of the gospel over nihilism, it needs an explicitly *trinitarian* explanation and a *transcendent* foundation: hence the GGR model. Moreover, through the gift of the Holy Spirit to men, women and children, our personal human stories also may become fulfilled, coming fully to themselves.[37] But where lies "the capacity" (Barth) to receive such a gift? God's Story requires telling a third time.

Love and Gift, see notably, Levering, *Engaging the Doctrine of the Holy Spirit*. That said however, our own agreement with Jenson and Pannenberg regarding the *necessary reciprocal relationships* among the divine persons creates an alternative view, establishing "*equal causality* among *all three* persons" (Habets Review). Just so, the need for the Spirit's own "personal consent" (as above), as well as the divine sheer *epektatic* Futurity Who *is* Holy Spirit.

33. Ibid., 160.

34. See again Jenson, "Second Locus," 172–75, and idem., "Eighth Locus," esp. 167–70.

35. See generally, Hauerwas and Jones, *Why Narrative?*, esp. part I, 21–110; and Loughlin, *Telling God's Story*. And see Begbie, *Music*, again, re the sense of "resolution."

36. See esp. "From Mask to Person: the Birth of an Ontology of Personhood," in Zizioulas, *Being as Communion*, 27–49, which stresses the role of Greek drama. The classic discussion of tragedy remains Steiner's *The Death of Tragedy*.

37. See Jenson, *TI*, 176–79, cited earlier at note 55, chapter seven, for God as Event whose personhood is "eschatologically independent," making that of humans precisely "*dependent*," whose personal coherence is "by virtue of a future event, the triumph of Jesus," i.e. *an event other than themselves*—"who [therefore] do not have the capacity

B.3.3—The Son as Recipient

The heart of the gospel narrates how Jesus "emptied himself, even unto death, death on a cross" (Phil 2:8). Our entire study has sought the implications of such a thing for our understanding of the One who would do such a thing—and moreover on our behalf. What kind of Lord is it who becomes *forma servi* on behalf of his creatures! Christian theology is either *theologia crucis*, or alternatively, not authentically Christian at all.

The dialectic of "surrender" and "fullness," as of "absence" and "presence," moreover, has created a view of God that is eminently dynamic. Add to this the form of dynamism we have termed *ecstatic–cum–epektatic*, and God's "actuality" (N.B. Barth's German, *die Wirklichkeit*, CD II/1, chapter VI) becomes an ever more expansive affair. Add again the Augustinian idea of *totus Christus* and God becomes "all in all" (Eph 1:23, etc.). But what is specifically meant by "recipient"?

T. F. Torrance writes, "the relation between the actuality of the incarnate Son in space and time and the God from whom He came cannot be spatialized."[38] Again, "if traditional Greek concepts are to be used, it must be said that God is not contained by anything but rather He contains the entire universe, not in the manner of a bodily container, but by His *power*."[39]

"Space," then, is seen not according to some volumetric view as a receptacle, but in terms of that dynamic sphere in which bodily agents interact and engage with one another.[40] Similarly, the Son of God as Recipient actively engages with his Father through the "medium/sphere/space" (χώρα/*chōra*) (Basil of Caesarea)[41] of the Holy Spirit—but in such a way

---

to possess themselves" (Jüngel). This entire subsection is indebted to Gunton, "The Spirit as Lord," 169–82.

38. See Torrance, esp. "The Problem of Spatial Concepts in Nicene Theology," in *Space, Time and Incarnation*, 1–21, at 3.

39. Ibid., 11, emphasis original.

40. For a delightful expansion of the spatial ideas of this subsection as I apply them to the Recipient Son, see Rae, "Spatiality of God," 70–86.

41. See again "De Spiritu Sancto," XXVI, 62, in *NPNF VIII*, 39 (emphasis original), where he says: "It is an extraordinary statement, but it is nonetheless true, that the Spirit is frequently spoken of as the *space/place* of them that are being sanctified, and it will become evident that even by this figure the Spirit, so far from being degraded, is rather glorified." For it is the "distinct manner of subsistence" (Rahner) or identity of the Holy Spirit that he/she is the "medium" of complete reciprocity whereby the Trinity dwells with men and women and they with/in the Trinity. Even more than this, as Lossky expresses it, "the Holy Spirit *effaces* himself, as Person, before the created

that there is full and free *perichoresis* among the three identities. There is thus established by the Incarnation–and–Atonement a trinitarian "coordinate system" which is "open-ended," the Trinity being itself a *"field of relationships"* which may be depicted according to the model of GGR, "the God in whom we live and move and have our being" (Acts 17:28), and where heaven and earth meet together, fulfilling the rich OT notion of Temple (as we saw in chapter 4 above, re John 1:1–18, and thereafter onto Rev 21–22).

Within such a scheme, Jesus is to be viewed as the distinctive, proper, active, and effective moment of the divine "donation" as it reaches its successful goal. Love is now satisfied because now received and delightfully responded to in freedom; indeed, true freedom is here realized in full and authentic "correspondence"/"co-response" (Jüngel). To be sure, love is now shown to be as well a matter of interdependence, or dependence even, and so of *vulnerability*. But this is precisely the *pathos* of the Living, Loving God: *he may give himself away*. We recall Jüngel's most compressed assessment of the nature of this divine love, its sheer selflessness arising out of its fulsome self-relatedness, cited above (notes 24 and 47, chapter nine), and MacKinnon's "reckoning with the actuality of limit, of *peras* or boundary" (note 57, chapter nine).

In addition, because we are talking of *divine* donation, there is ever room or place for more, a profusion of gracious love, to be received (*and surrendered!*) again and again. Just so, the shifts in Jesus' life from conception, the Jordan, and on through Golgotha to resurrection/ascension, and on through the church to the Parousia itself. This is the Recipient Christ who ever *makes room* within himself for the likes of humankind—indeed, in whom inheres *all* creation (Col 1:15–20), as it receives existence itself from him whose will grants it to all (Rev 4:11). This is the triune God who graciously *shares* his *own* life and love with the world, whose destiny is the full and free participation of created being in the divine being itself: "In that Day, you will know that I am in my Father and you in me and I in you" (John 14:20).

Lastly, it is exactly at this point, between the previous paragraph's ever more expansive shifts of Jesus' identity (as they *appear* so to be) and the final section on the Immanent Trinity, that we need to introduce

---

persons to whom he appropriates grace. . . . He substitutes himself, so to speak, for ourselves; for it is he who cries in our hearts, 'Abba, Father!' as St Paul puts it" (Lossky, *Mystical Theology*, 172, emphasis added; and see the concluding remarks, 173). What is so of the economy is prototypically the case of the immanent Godhead.

comments regarding the inherent anticipatory nature of God's being (following the likes of Pannenberg and Jenson).[42] For it is on the basis of who the triune God *will be* (we may express it in no other way) that he may faithfully enact "in advance" his identity, so that the economy reveals truly but far from exhaustively a genuine form of God's proleptic reality. It is not so much that the NT church "read back" those christological moments, which declare the identity of Jesus, from ascension to conception, or that the mystery of the rule of God grows secretly as a seed in the midst of the world only to burst open for all to see at the Eschaton. Rather, God himself, via the *inherent* **reciprocity** *among the persons* in their perichoretic dynamic, "retrojects" his very self into the midst of his fallen world to recreate it *from within* ever new out of his own Future. Hence Jesus is able to bear time's Eschaton, which he ever *receives* from the Holy Spirit, his proprium *being* the divine Futurity (as per Jenson), and so be the One he shows himself to be in his person, moment by sequential moment, since he is "always" poised "between the times" (of his two Comings), only "awaiting" its "Appearing/Unveiling." (Just so, for example, we encounter the possibility of the Transfiguration, being a glimpse of Jesus' "*real* glory," even during his *earthly* life; and supremely John 11:25, "I am the resurrection and the life," since the Day of Yahweh is proleptically here *in the middle* of human history, embodied, in person.) Indeed; this self revelation of the Word is even there "already" for those with the eyes of faith to see from the moment of Adam and Eve's nakedness being graciously covered by God's own garments. And yet, finally, we have to acknowledge "the Lamb slain from before the foundation of the world" (Rev 13:8). Such in truth is the fullness of God's glory (John 1:14, 16) and just so the possibility of our due human doxological response. So too the possibility that the GGR model may indeed depict the dynamics of the immanent Trinity itself.[43] And since according to contemporary cosmol-

---

42. See Jenson, *ST 1*, 66, emphasis original: "Since the Lord's identity is constituted in dramatic coherence, it is established not from the beginning but from the end, not at birth but at death, not in *persistence* but in *anticipation*."

43. See von Balthasar's preface, *Mysterium Paschale*, viii–ix: ". . . relating the event of the Kenosis of the Son of God to what one can, by analogy, designate as the eternal "event" of the divine processions . . . [and so] approach the mystery of the divine "essence." That essence is forever "given" in the self–gift of the Father, "rendered" in the thanksgiving of the Son, and "represented" in its character as absolute love by the Holy Spirit. . . . All the contingent "abasements" of God in the economy of salvation are forever included and outstripped in the eternal event of Love. And so what, in the temporal economy, appears as the (most real) suffering of the Cross is only the

ogy both space and time are inextricably linked, we may close with a few remarks using this very model to summarize this section.

It was concluded already in chapter 9, sections 3.1 and 3.2 under "The Living God's Fullness of Loving Time—and GGR" (pages 162–163), that:

> "to give *ecstatically*, to give again and again out of oneself, in a continuously overflowing manner, a sheer effulgence, as the Father does, for that is Who He *Is*—that means the Gift of the true Future is One of Unbounded Possibility. All of which also means that the Recipient is no mere terminus, no end—period/full-stop. Nor yet a mere infinite "deferral" (as some postmodern might say), on account of the *telos* remaining. Rather, they are (once more) true End without End. And just so is God that *epektatic* triune being, whose eternal life knows no limits whatsoever, whose whence and whither are precisely pure infinitude during love's true "donation." And mentioning "love" offers us the final aspect of the *fullness of time's intention*: the offer of a due "space" wherein One may *care for* Another; time's possibilities are those during which Another seeks One's *attention*, via *desire*. The resulting care-ful address among these *is* love's infinite future, eternal time's plenitude/pleroma of "mutual lively regard" (Aquinas). Just so is there the triune *faithfulness*, of *each One desirously attending to the Other* across all eternity.

When such a view of eternal temporality is integrated with the view above of the Son's Receptivity—of his *powerful agency* among the trinitarian perichoretic dynamic, which has the *capacity* precisely to "receive" or "envelop" the "field" of God's love Who *is* Holy Spirit, the *vinculum caritatis* Who *is* the *chōra* or "sphere" (so Basil again) of Love itself (so B.3.2), the Love Who *is* Unboundedness, the *epektatic fullness* of Futurity—then the triune God's eternal being-in-becoming is one of extraordinarily profound movement, a movement of both *duly everlasting yearning* and yet also *fully sated resting stillness*, End without End.[44]

---

manifestation of the (Trinitarian) Eucharist of the Son: he will be forever the slain Lamb, on the throne of the Father's glory, and his Eucharist—the Body shared out, the Blood poured forth—will never be abolished, since the Eucharist it is which must gather all creation into his body. What the Father has given, he will never take back."

44. If current cosmology suggests time and space are linked functions of movement, of velocity, and of agency, then we may speculate (perhaps) these factors reflect analogously the divine being's attributes of "omnipresence and unity," the triune God's Fully Spacious and Lively Intimate Presence, his "Roominess" we might say, characterized as we emphasize.

AB.1—Excursus on Reiterative Eventfulness as Eternal Trinitarian Historicality

Poised between these remarks on the divine economy (which perforce have had to anticipate to some degree reference to the immanent Trinity) and our concluding comments on the immanent Trinity itself, what might be the theological fruit of reflecting in faith as we "sit right on the very edge" of the created space-time universe as this appears to be unfolding? How might the nature of the triune God appear as that nature supremely reveals itself in this unfolding theater, climaxing with the Creator becoming a creature in Jesus? For such is that very nature, according to all that we have tried to say, that the fullness of eternal temporality resides there, of which our present human experience of created space-time is but a reflective facet.

This much is first to be declared: that our present tragic human history—together with each of our own little tragedies—shall indeed be consumed and transformed by the fire of the divine love into God's own trinitarian comedy. Everything we have related of the Christian Story compels us to acknowledge this. Consequently, the church's Eucharistic response (in the practice of word, prayer, and sacrament, and its interpretation) to our participation in this Story of Jesus, as our covenanted sharing in the baptismal death, burial, resurrection and ascension of Jesus is renewed and enlivened by the grace and power of the Holy Spirit in the sacrament of the Eucharist, is itself essentially to initiate a trinitarian form of speech.[45] But this speech, this conversation among covenant partners, as we humans learn the divine triune Song, takes place, takes time; it itself inhabits—or better "resides/dwells"—among the divine Subjects as their own perichoretic communion enacts the triune being; the Trinity *per se* grants us humans "space" *among* the Godhead—and not just *any* "space" but in joyous *Eucharistic* communion, the *delight* of Father-and-Son. Just so is the church's true worship even here and now an eschatological foretaste of the new creation; but *only* as this is deliberately and specifically a *trinitarian* undertaking, a divinely graced human *performance* in,

---

45. To reinforce the echoes: recall the German subtitle of Jüngel's *Gottes Sein ist im Werden*, viz. *Verantwortliche Rede* = answering/answerable/responsible/responding speech; and see again also Vanhoozer, *Drama of Doctrine*, and Jennings, *Beyond Theism*.

with and through Jesus Christ, the Mediator, in the Holy Spirit from and unto the Father.[46]

What this then leads to is an understanding similar in form but also in the end radically opposite to St. Augustine's *Confessions*—where praise is the means of the soul's *overcoming* of time, of *escaping* the restlessness of change, to inhabit the supposed changelessness of the Divine.[47] For now, following both a revised Gregory of Nyssa and Robert Jenson, not only is the human participation in the triune deity a life of continuous change from "one degree of glory unto another," but so too is the trinitarian nature of deity an epektatic one, where God is "new every morning" in the enduring Emergence of the New (as A.2.2 and A.3 above, and 3.1 in chapter 9 depicted). What the model of GGR is suggesting (which suggestion, we recall, is derived directly from the economy of salvation as a perception of its grammar) is an articulation indeed of continuous End without End, with a glimpse of an anticipatory metaphysic coupled with a sense of perichoretic temporality,[48] as intimate as it is "distant," as infinite as it is "limited" or endowed with *peras*.[49]

AB.2—Freedom's Reality

Yet exactly at this point more needs to be said directly in relation to how this is possible, in relation to the divine triune actuality. In a word,

---

46. See again Begbie, *Music*, generally, but notably, 155–75, chapter 6, "Repetition and Eucharist."

47. See again the thesis of Kirby, "Praise," 333–50.

48. For how such a term as "perichoretic temporality" might be filled out in its richness, as well as B.3.3 above, see one more time Begbie, *Music*, notably chapter 5, "Music, time and eternity," esp. 148–54. Nor are the consequences of this notion incidental. Much as one must respect Molnar's dogged insistence on the sovereign freedom of the immanent triune God, the perichoretic nature of the Trinity's eternal temporality being proposed here obviates—or seems to obviate—most, if not all, his common criticisms: see Molnar, *Divine Freedom*, e.g., 61–81, and "Perils," 454–80. For any "anticipatory" dynamic "works" all the way "back" from End to Beginning, the intra divine relations being fully *reciprocal*. And linking up with the next section, his notion of "freedom" would appear to be rather abstract, trying to get "behind" the *actual expression* of that freedom in the election of Jesus Christ, *as determined* by the Trinity—which is actually all we have to go on.

49. This brief subsection does not attempt to do justice to the profound metaphysics of historicality in keeping with our introductory aim, although clear suggestions have been intimated. Further material may be found in e.g., Montgomery, "Christian Philosophy of History," 182–97, Rae, *History and Hermeneutics*, and especially Quash, *Theology and the Drama of History*.

freedom! Yet, what a squandered word this has become. "Although I do not hope" (T. S. Eliot) to redeem it fully—for who might be "competent" of such a task despite the Pauline affirmation (2 Cor 3:5 in context, 2:14— 6:13)—some concluding remarks on a richer appreciation of the word "freedom" are in order here.

As twenty-first-century consumers, imbued with modernity's legacy of humanist autonomy, we westerners can almost not avoid the call to freedom's exercise of "choice," of liberalism's desire to speak and move and associate "unhindered," and so to insist upon *my* "rights," etc. Indeed, the last creature to ask questions of the water is the fish: such too is our own cultural pond's profound ambiguities and consequent ambivalence. Yet what might the renaissance of trinitarianism offer, in hope, instead— and notably via the model of GGR?

Divine "freedom" is that characteristic feature of the singular form and quality of the relations among the three divine Persons, each according to their respective, particular identities, such that their total *perichoresis*, their complete kenotic openness towards the Other, their sublime intimacy and due distance fulfils what only the holiness of God may perfectly consummate: eternal love and life, in the fullness of pure desire and delight. Here "freedom" is a collective term and denies any individualism even as it affirms the specific *proprium* of the "individual." Here "freedom" specifies a due place and a due time, the "space," the "field," which grants all possible eventualities according to the dynamic we have in this study termed "donation." Here "freedom" is both the condition of possibility and the outcome of the divine "intention" to *be* and *enact*, consistently, with utter integrity, this "donation" in all its faithful and delightful fullness. We may say then that "freedom" in the divine case is intrinsically both a transcendent phenomenon and a teleological one. "Freedom" is the willingness and ability to deliver on one's promises, whatever the obstacles, whatever the cost; "freedom" is the holy determination to realize One's true intent, and so authentically to become as One is. The tragedy of the human is to aspire to transcendence *apart from* "the Lord who is Spirit," to seek to *possess* a freedom, in contrast precisely to *receiving* it *as* the gift *of* each other *to* each other *before* Another *unto* their mutual supreme Good and commonweal. One way can only lead to death; the other Way leads and will, and will ever, lead to Life, Life in all its fullness.[50]

50. As forms of corroboration (rather than as sources), see Begbie, *Music*, 179– 270, Webster, "Evangelical Freedom," 215–26, and Hart, "Christ and Nothing," 1–19,

C—The Immanent Trinity

That God is triune is demonstrated, we have claimed, by and with the events of his economic activity. That this is no "shadow image of God," but truly the revelation of *himself* has been the whole point of so much rigorous theological endeavor down the centuries: hence Rahner's now classic *Grundaxiom*, etc. There are, however, some final remarks to note. The very revelation of God's sovereign freedom demands *that* his nature be triune even apart from such a history of salvation, indeed, apart from creation at all. But *how* such a thing might be, we simply may not tell. To speculate on the essential nature of God apart from the economy is to misunderstand what the economy itself has shown, that God is *personal*, that he has *determined* to present humanity with his chosen intention in the human being Jesus, Word–become–flesh. Nor is there any going back on such an intention: his "Yes" is his eternal Word; and its denial would contradict an integral part of what divine personhood means, *hesed* and *'emet* (so John 1:14's "grace and truth"), as the covenanted Hebrews experienced it.[51]

The Hebrew experience brings us to a further point. The trinitarian expression of God's nature is given in and through Jesus; all rests on him, on this particular individual. Just as we have called upon Augustine's notion of *totus Christus* to depict this particular person's (primarily) future orientation, so too is there a past dimension to be considered. For this human being appeared in a precise cultural and historical context. His individual humanity, and therefore the specific contours of God's personal

---

together with brilliantly, "The Pornographic Culture," 83–91, for the causes and consequences of reducing "liberty" to "license" and "freedom" to *arbitrium* or "sheer will." This section on "Freedom's Reality" is finally also corroborated by Colin Gunton's last text before he died, *Act and Being*. He asks at the end of a subsection on "The Freedom of God," 104–8: "Is freedom an attribute or a form or mode of God's action? Indeed, what kind of distinction should we draw between the two? We have seen that attribute is best understood in terms of action, in God's case the action in which God is who he is." The answer is presented in the last chapter, "Hypostasis and Attribute," 134–47, where the distinctions among the triune Persons are elaborated according to 2 Cor 13:14, with its three specific yet necessarily interrelated forms of God's singular free and freeing act of love, now extended towards creation. Such a depiction echoes nicely this section on Freedom's Reality/Actuality (German, *Wirklichkeit*, for which see again Barth's CD, chapter VI, with which Gunton himself naturally interacts in his text).

51. For those readers who wish to explore further the consequences of this way of speaking, see Dempsey, *Trinity and Election*, which pursues the debate among Molnar, McCormack, Hunsinger, and others.

intent, are to be found in terms of the institutions and traits, the ethos and worldview of his native people.⁵² Glimpses of God's trinitarianism therefore are to be found within Israel's history. Otherwise St. Paul could not have argued as he did in Galatians chapters 3 and 4, for example, nor could he have exegeted the wilderness experience as in 1 Cor 10. In other words, the ever expansive form of God's ecstatic–cum–epektatic nature according to the model of GGR has its seeds not just in the early christological moments of Jesus' own life. There are truly traces of the Trinity from the earliest days, the days of Abraham, and according to the Yahwist and Priestly historians, even before him, in the stories of Gen 1–11. But *only* with the benefit of *hindsight* may we say this; we are not reviving any general theory of *vestigia trinitatis*!

The reason for speaking in this way is this. The GGR model and our revised depictions of Christian deity need to be situated quite specifically in the context of the *given history* of revelation, which in the Bible extends from the accounts of Creation to the Eschaton. Only so may it be said that the "economic" Trinity is *eschatologically* God himself, the "immanent" Trinity. But this is not to reduce God in some general fashion to the level of creation, even creation in all its redeemed fullness. The dynamic of *love's* ever greater possibilities—especially in humanity's future redeemed condition and the true realization of human freedom in God's triune "home," wherein there is ever more fruitful "room"—forbids us to foreclose: the Omega, who is God *in se*, is ever and only End without End; but so too is God truly Alpha, in the fullness of his triune anticipatory reality. Such is the Immanent Trinity, who eternally and reiteratively gives himself to himself, the One who lives and loves *fully* and *freely* possessing himself—which becomes the basis for his gracious self-dispossession on our behalf, so that we human creatures, incapable of ourselves to possess ourselves, whose being is unto death, may nevertheless receive a share in the fullness of this divine life and love.

All of which, and once again in dependence upon the Hebraic appreciation of reality, leads us to our final consideration. What *did* those Roman generals make of it: marching into the Jerusalem temple courts

---

52. See Torrance, *Mediation*, who emphasises this Israelite matrix to Jesus' person and work ; and especially Work, "The Mission of Scripture," 125-213. This details the role of the Tanakh as firstly "the required text" for "Israel's schooling" and then supremely for Jesus' Messianic "human formation" and "identity". Scripture/Tanakh *is* "the voice of the Father who sent him," and which Jesus "faithfully obeys" and so "fulfills;" "the Bible is the very language of the Messiah."

and on into the inner sanctuary—only to find it empty; bare; naked—*seeing nothing?* Their subsequent destruction of the temple is not the most significant response—for YHWH himself is the final and most complete iconoclast, such is His Name! The strong prohibitions of the first three commandments govern all else—and still govern our relationship with the One who will be who he will be (Exod 3:14). God is *ever* the *mystery* of the world—albeit its and our "positive mystery" (Jüngel), in loving self-communication and its welcome "home." For there is ever the "zealous" divine intent to dwell eternally among humanity despite everything to the contrary (just so Rev 21–22). In which case, what might be our most appropriate response to such a One, in all his trinitarian fullness of eternal being and life? Wherein our own most authentic human co-response?

The last scriptural entry, the book of Revelation, the Apocalypse, also tenders the answer: in a word, worship. The only genuine trinitarian thinking gives way in the final analysis to the doxological, to existence drenched ("baptized") by εὐσέβεια/*eusebeia*.[53] To that effect, we note again the oft used practice of the Creed's being *sung* (see note 15, chapter six). Similarly, Robert Jenson concludes his *Systematic Theology* volume 1 likening the trinitarian dance to a fugue and volume 2 with "The End is music." But not even Monteverdi's Mass "In Illo Tempore" (1610), whose Creed is quite exquisite, nor a von Biber, whose *Missa Bruxellensis* (1700) is similarly extraordinary, may quite catch the Beauty of the Lord. For this we need to move away from the Latin West, with its Benedictine emphasis on "Listening" (however valid that of course is),[54] and settle at the feet of one Andrei Rublev, and his icon of the three angels of Mamre/the Trinity (1410).[55] Here our means of perception is necessarily a work of

---

53. N.B. Torrance's conclusions, *Trinitarian Perspectives*, 102, repeating this word Athanasius was so fond of; see too Anatolios, *Athanasius*, 83–86.

54. St. Benedict's Rule, so influential in the spirituality of the Latin West, begins the Prologue with, "Listen, O my son . . ." "It is interesting indeed that this Latin word, *ob-sculta*, has the same root, and indeed almost the same meaning, as the Latin word, *ob-oedire*, which makes our English obedience. There is a very important connection between true listening and deep obedience; both suggest a turning in order to receive more fully that which is being given" (Vest, *Preferring Christ*, 5). See too de Waal, *A Life-Giving Way*, 1–7, who echoes the intent listening, the turning and returning, of the child to their heavenly Father, thus embarking one on their journey of continuous growth in heartfelt devotion and obedience.

55. Two useful and non-technical introductions on how to pray with such an icon as Rublev's are Nouwen, *Behold*, and Castle, *Gateway*.

visual art,[56] one which invites us from the entrance at the bottom into the circle of God's holy, loving hospitality, in worshipful contemplation and adoration, which is the due human reflection of that fullness of trinitarian "mutual regard" (Aquinas) which bathes in "the radiance" of each person's "supreme light" (Richard of St. Victor)—"the delirium of arrival" (Milbank), in whose "embrace a host is a guest and a guest is a host" (Volf), a veritable "perichoretic dance" (Fiddes), a sustained, convivial "conversational fugue" (Jenson). Such is the true destiny and dignity of the human: to "bear [by receiving] the image of the One from Heaven" (St. Paul).

Figure 10: Rublev's Icon of the Trinity (1410)

---

56. See Nichols, *Art of God Incarnate*, esp. "The Artwork and Christian Revelation," "Sketch for a Christology of the Image," and "The Eyes of Faith," 105–52. It is also significant we have two essays on art in two collections on the Trinity: Brown, "The Trinity in Art," 329–56; and Horne, "Art: A Trinitarian Imperative?," 80–91.

Questions for Reflection

28. The Holy Scriptures speak again and again of the vital importance of hearing well, of listening intently, and then of retaining richly what has been heard, of pondering upon all this deep within the heart. Thereafter, any due listening requires due obedience (see note 54 above), a fruitful expression as proof even of having received what is heard. In this respect, "those who have ears to hear, let them hear" is the natural summary of all the parables, especially the one of the Sower and his seed (Mark 4 // Luke 8 // Matt 13). Yet the ear is not the only means of access to spiritual reality; other senses have their rightful role to play. Icons grant the eyes their due role; sacraments give touch and taste their role also, as does incense entice smell. All in all: "I appeal to you therefore, brothers and sisters, in view of God's mercies, to present your bodies as a living sacrifice, holy and acceptable to God, which is your spiritual/reasonable worship. Do not be conformed to this world, but be transformed by the renewing of your mind, so that you may test and approve what God's will is—his good, pleasing and perfect will." Romans 12:1–2 is the sum of any overall spirituality.

    And the goal, the *telos* of any and all of this is just this: our "freedom" in the Beloved. So, one final reflection to ponder. Our receiving, via the full gambit of the bodily senses, our participation in the triune Life and Love precipitates a form of freedom of which the world has virtually no inkling. Why do you think our own Western culture has rightly so prized freedom and yet has so little understanding of its true nature? As part of any answer, ponder the occurrences of the word "intent/intention" and "intends" above, in chapter 9, section 3:1 and 1.3, and chapter 10, sections A.2.2, AB.2, and C, plus the commentary on the three figures of chapter 7.

TWO POEMS AS CONTEMPLATIVE RESPONSE

IF I SHARE THESE two poems, the second of which comprises a triptych, it is to prompt others to ponder and contemplate for themselves lives saturated within the very Being of the Trinity, whose Life and Light, Love and Freedom embraces and permeates "all things," not least those beloved creatures made in the divine Image. This is the Gift of the Incarnation, the completed mission of the Son, who shares the Father's Holy Spirit with us.

Reflecting (on) *In the Self's Place*

How *did* you traverse that distance
    between my ego and myself,
Lover of my Soul?
    What possessed you to go the distance?

What tenderness now beckons
    to cross myself the bridge that spans
within my mind and heart—once adrift,
    but now tethered by Your grasp.

Closer to me than I am to myself,
    Dear Lover, how *do* you find the place
that lately foreclosed any opportunity
    of openness—or even sorrow?

Yet at Your Advent, ever Present,
    there resound loosened tongues

of cosmic confession and praise—
    that wondrously embraces even me!

For saturated by Your radiance,
    my senses stand accused
by the lure of Your gaze, joyously
    laid bare before the beauty of Your face.

And thus you enfold All within
    your Memory and your Call
      —Fully Yourself—
and our due fulfillment, duly settled,
    semperaneous desire, *ever* due . . .

truly gifted perichoretic receptivity

This poem is a response to Jean-Luc Marion, *In The Self's Place: The Approach of Saint Augustine*. With the title, "Reflecting (on)," a number of things are in play: it is a reflection, pure and simple; it also catches the profound sense of Augustine's "image of God" that is understood as a "mirror" or "glass" (1 Cor 13:12a), seeking to share in that process whereby the self "reflects"/progressively learns to "reflect" God's Glory, which is in fact to share in the triune God's own self-glorification (as per notably the Fourth Gospel), all of which is his *De Trinitate* as well. Hence the final bold and utterly pregnant last line (for which see my own thesis and now *The Lion, the Dove, and the Lamb*), as well as the sequence of stanzas. For there is the fact of Marion's "Approach": both Augustine and Marion necessarily come at this entire business from a *multitude* of angles/"theses," since in the end, *any* due "reflection" is necessarily multifaceted, just as in the end, it may ever *only* be "*an* approach." And so Marion's chapters unfold as a series of theses—viz. the "Conclusion," pages 307–12.

As for the sequence of stanzas: they do not follow exactly the sequence of chapters with their subject matter(s). While the first stanza echoes chapter 1, the fullest sense of that chapter's dual "confession" has to wait until stanza 4. But then that stanza actually hails chapter 5's memorable conclusion re "Time, or the Advent." In the meantime, we have first up chapter 2's complex recounting of the history of Descartes' *Mediations* on the *Cogito* and their interaction with Augustine's very different *Confessions*. The difference is due to *Confessions'* essential premise being *not* the human ego at all (with its deemed desire for its own certainty: see especially Michael Hanby's *Augustine and Modernity*, which also contrasts Augustine and Descartes, and their respective legacies) but God, whose gift of himself to the human is ever "closer to us than we are to ourselves"—albeit with an intensity and an interiority that ever *eludes* our "grasp," and may only be "received" at all at all, as the "self" comes to itself (or individuates itself, we might say contemporaneously; as it learns to integrate its own facets; and compare: love of God, love of neighbor, love of self//love of self, love of neighbor, love of God, pages 277ff.)—but while necessarily dealing with/having certain vital "*distances*" dealt with. All of which combines stanzas 2 and 3, leading back to stanza 4 and chapter 1 and the double nature of confession.

Yet, there is too the important—not to say "crucial"!—pun with the word "possession" to consider: for it is Love's essential nature to dispossess itself, even as it thereby truly "possesses," is in due relation with, the loved one—Song of Songs 2:16, 6:3, 7:10, NB the progression. And note Eberhard Jüngel's depiction of (Divine) Love: "the event of the unity of life and death for the sake of life"; "the event of a still greater selflessness in the midst of such great self-relatedness"; whereby "only love therefore has the power to integrate both possession (life) and loss (death) in favor of true personal existence: self-identity and selflessness are brought together in love's embrace to create a new way of being." Just so, the "distances" echoed here *mix together* those of chapter 2 and those of sin and the Cross's Atonement (but to what extent are the "distances" undergone and experienced by Augustine themselves the result of "sin"? So; "distances" both moral and metaphysical, including the *temporal*—chapter 5's *distentio animi*, which is firstly to be transmuted into *extensio*, and this too into an ever "advancing, deferred desire": ref Gregory of Nyssa's *epektasis*, both Gregory's and Augustine's deriving from Phil 3:13). Which atoning "bridge" "spans" nothing less than the Cosmos itself (Col 1:15–20; Eph 4:9–10), that utter gulf between the Holy God and fallen human being (e.g., Isa 6; Micah 7:18–19; Mark 15:34), and so that between Life and death, situating "nothingness"/"perishabililty" within the triune God himself, giving it its *topos*, bearing it (Jüngel again).

Resulting in each Christian's right to indeed "cross themselves," with the sign of the Cross and its Blessing! (See, e.g., John 1:12 for this "right".)

But only as and when there is due "confession"—stanza 4 eventually!

All of the above is undergirded by and predicated upon chapter 3, "Truth, or the Saturated Phenomenon," which comes to the fore in stanza 5. This is an impossibly compressed stanza! It tries to address the dense argument of Marion's phenomenology of saturated Being/Truth, of the overwhelming sense that the Divine intentionality towards creatures/the rest of reality is blazingly too much—is literally *ecstatic!*—when duly appreciated. Yet that acknowledgment can only occur when there is also the sense of faith and reciprocating love towards the other/Other—which in the end, eventually, echoes Augustine's famous line on the beauty of God, "so ancient and so fresh" (*Confessions*, 10.27.38: *sero* [late: cf. stanza 3!] *te amavi, pulchritudo tam antiqua et tam nova*): "It is the vision of an indescribable loveliness that calls our hearts out of darkness, breaking down the barriers of false love, rightly ordering those desires and impulses by which we live."[1] Under such a "gaze," the due result is the confession to joyously love "the beauty of all beauties" (*pulchritudo pulchrorum omnium, Confessions*, 3.6.10).

And then the final upshot: the situatedness of the human self—which in fact *is* no "place," *has* no "settled" place. NB the French title, *Au lieu de soi*, which also means "instead of the self" (p. xx), as well as "over there." For "there" in the end, eventually, can only equal the Divine Self Itself, which is the only "natural" "place" or *locus* or *chōra* (χώρα) wherein the human may truly/faithfully/authentically "dwell" (μένειν/*menein*), may indeed *become* "settled" (page 270)—which nonetheless is ever fresh and new and *Living*, and so hardly any "weighted settlement" at all. Yet what then have we "said" or proposed with this entire reflection? For NB too this human situatedness is only "achievable" on account of the Trinity's *own* perichoretic nature, whereby each is "within" the Others' "place/space," enabling thereby humans too to become "accommodated," to have "room" therein.

(In the course of reviewing this poem, "weighted" was changed for "settled," even if both terms are used by Marion in his text (viz. page 270). One reason is the sheer *Liveliness* of the triune God's perichoretic dynamic precludes any "weighted settlement" for the human self in the Spirited Divine Self. Another reason is due to Augustine in book 3 of *Confessions* (from which we also had the quote "the beauty of all beauties," *pulchritudo pulchrorum omnium*) describing "pride's" initial *"weight"*—for

---

1. Williams, *Wound of Knowledge*, 74.

"pride" is Augustine's primordial sense of sin as well. Consequently, it might confuse the "weight" of Love's ineffable Beauty as this "draws" and "pushes" one into God to then describe the human self's true "dwelling/resting place" as "weighted" rather than "settled.")

For *Who is* this deity, this triune God, whose Life and Being and Truth and Reality (*Wirklichkeit*—Barth), whose Light and Love and Beauty is to be reflected in our souls, who is sheerly Beyond us and "all things" (Nicene Creed)? And yet again, his *own* triune embrace (just so the Unoriginate "Memory"—and see §§12-13, pages 74-87—and the Unsurpassable "Call"; see pages 251-2 re the structure of books 11, 12, and 13 of *Confessions* at J. J. O'Donnell's suggestion) of all things and our selves—notably on account of the Incarnation, the "motor" of all things trinitarian—is such that our faith in him, in our "definite acknowledgment, recognition and confession" (Barth, *CD* IV/1, § 63, his definition of faith), grants us, due to this grace, such a place indeed.

But *What* a place! "Where" is indeed "the Heaven of Heavens"! What is the Name of this God but *idipsum*, who Himself dwells "there," "*is*" there! To which/to whose *drawing* becomes "the veritable place of self," the distance of the ego to self in the God who is Fully and Only Fully Himself, "who is and who was and who is to come" (Rev). And just so, my love, my "desire" for this One *draws* me ever into this triune-and-Incarnational God, in whose Image I/we therefore ever become—even as this God is ever himself before me, preceding me, and ever coming after me... *Such* is *His* Desire! NB the echoes of T. S. Eliot, "With the drawing of this Love and the voice of this Calling" (*Little Gidding*); for only such a drawing and a calling, *as* Gift, the Divine "*lure*," grants strength enough to the human will, and so ignites any "desire" on our part—chapter 4.

Which confession, which reflection therefore, becomes my Life: "truly gifted perichoretic receptivity."

1 — Timely Meditation

Lately have I loved you
wanton with your gifts
thrifty with my self
For your time is seldom mine
& my time always tied
by strings & desires on my agenda

Yet all times & seasons have their due
early or late they come,
come knocking,
seeking entry to gainsay ownership
of selves bound by false marks
of occupation—their own

There within my space & time
ever closer than my very self
lies a deeper probing heart
given over to ways of freeing knots,
loosing needs of self-importance
currying no favors

Your desire alternatively prodigal
marked by hands & feet open still
an economy of love eternally bestowing
properties of life never acquired,
only receivable by willing emptiness

finally known
  owning all
    coming soon

2 — Spatial Sensibility

Immensity cloistered in a cradle of straw
its prickles anticipating sharper points to come,
a mother's arms encompass the tiny form,
whose destiny embraces both wooden work
and myriad cosmic schemes sublime:

To encircle by this plan all that was lost
while granting further freedom to roam again—
yet centered now on that still point to be found
wherever the heart is focused on that tree.

For they sought to outrun his scanning eye,
to establish spheres of rule all their own.
Hither and thither and realms in between
they sped like escaping comets from the sun
to become drifting wanderers—formless, alone.

Yet whither can one go from such a Presence,
whose drawing love attracts all created things
within its boundless scope and gathering arm
to so reflect an eternal weight of glory.

Then shall we enter that refulgent room
where hearth and throne conspire to flow
rivers of fire upon each head and lips
to kiss scarred feet and seal pierced brow
with countless crowns of gold and orbs held high

And all discordant music shall be stilled
and every concentric place be filled
with fathomless sound at the last trumpet call.

3 — Circumincessio

To ponder the Way of the Word:
Word within a world, world within the Word,
divinizing matter, energizing space & time
with a holiness of breath-filled Spirit
who embraces all within her womb:

rebirthing joyful freedom of love & life
perichoretic powers of vulnerability & might,
wooing compassion & enabling nobility
the fruit of a Wordless world one Sabbath rest
and the children's status graciously restored:

just so, the goal arrives at its source,
Father's fount & root of all being—
yet ever more expansive now, pressing on
farther up & farther in
reflecting promises fulfilled over & over,
deeper & deeper the images transform
pure archetypes before
newly unbounded, limitless:
to so pursue that naked, loving gaze

And all shall know in that Day of universal song
"I am in my Father and you in me and I in you"
returning all attention to wonder at that Name.

TM

1. Augustine: *O tardum gaudium meum*, Confessions, 2.2.2, and *sero te amavi*, 10.27.38. Yet "late" and "lately" have subtly different resonances. E.g. the latter: "recently" begs the question of what one has been doing/not doing beforehand...? This then precipitates the awareness that we are always "slow"/"late" to respond to God's call—on account of our slothful (forgetful?) sinfulness. Yet God graciously *persists* (Matt 20:1–16)—"ever new." Just so, this very threefold poem may come into existence also in "response"—as "memory" is duly "recalled" and "attended to": Augustine again. So that essentially and finally, *we* are ever "late"—i.e. behind—*God's* prevenient grace and love, to whom we may only therefore ever *respond*. [See Eberhard Jüngel's principles of *Nachdenken* and *Verantwortliche Rede* as genuine theological method.] Hence: these poems necessarily *begin here*, for *God* is ever only There, ever always..."before".
   Furthermore, only *TM* is vocative (you/your), in present time, the others not

2. wanton: ref. Luke 15 and the prodigal son – and compare line 19

4–6. "Time," and its slippage, is of the essence for Augustine: within *mens*, mirroring God's eternity; humanity's "escape" via *praise*—which might/should be controverted?! Re "your time": 2 Pet 3:8; Jenson on Ps 119:89–90 in *ST1*, page 217: "the eternity of Israel's God is his faithfulness"—which exactly contrasts!

6. desires: everything according to Augustine is a question of the *object* of our desires, plus their use and/or enjoyment
   agenda: typical use of "business/corporate" language in everyday speech: to what effect?

7. ref. Ecc 3:1–8
   due: suitable irony!

9. come knocking: ref. Rev 3:20, but also ...

10. seeking: links up with knocking and Luke 11:9–13, but with reversal of roles, human and divine
    ownership: see line 12 "own" below

11. bound by false marks: cp. line 26! "Show me your credentials!," "how impressive is your CV?!". Also, what we *are*—"selves"—is often defined nowadays merely by what we *do*—*occupation*, next line. See Augustine's *Confessions*, which ala Stroup is exquisitely about the "construction" of selfhood—yet a rather different one.

12. occupation: multiple references—to contemporary culture's rulership (ownership!) by the business/economic model, of work; "residency" vs. HSp—and esp. how we "fill our *time*." Not that this is merely a response to economic rationalism; rather a reaction/rejection of something much deeper, the entire Enlightenment's programme of materialism and secular reason that has issued in "capitalist economics and liberal politics." See Milbank's reading of Augustine in *Theology and Social Theory: Beyond Secular Reason*, 1990. Just so: the idolatry of such "ownership" vs. *confessional praise of the true God*

14. virtual quote from Augustine, *Confessions*, 3.6.11, as closer // deeper in line 15—*tu autem eras interior intimo meo*

16. given over: ref. Greek, *paradidomai*
    knots: "bound" above; also a (sub-conscious) echo of Augustine, *Confessions*, 2.10.18, as well as Donne's "Batter my heart three Person'd God"

17. needs: our "knots" are often predicated upon false "needs"—*All you love is need*—and desires, all of which echoes Augustine's premise, both re structure and content, re 1 John 2:16/*Confessions* 10.30.41

18. both "no partiality" of Acts and stressing grace vs. human "merit"

19. desire: Song of Songs 7:10, etc; plus *quintessentially Augustinian* again
    alternatively prodigal: Luke 15 again

20. ref. Rev 5:6, 13:8, Col 1:24. "open" also contrasts with closed "selves" of second stanza

21. economy: Greek *oikonomia* of course! NB also that God's version is in such contrast to our contemporary preoccupation with the monetary economy and global business culture and corporate power

20–1. echo Eberhard Jüngel, Jürgen Moltmann, von Balthasar, et al.

22. properties: multiple references again. See "occupation" above, et al.

    acquired: our crazed contemporary consumer culture again! We humans may only *be* by not *having/getting*, rather "being there for the other" (Jüngel) as in the Trinity . . . and the next line . . .

23. receivable: ref. GGR model, and Donald MacKinnon re *peras*; ref. also Phil 2:6–11.

    willing: both senses

    emptiness: once more, the sheer kenotic nature of *each* triune Person, each in their *own* manner

24. originally 4 stanzas of 6 lines each, but now split to depict a cadence: Gal 4:9, the truth behind 1 Cor 4:8, maranatha!

    owning all: Beatitudes and 1 Cor 3:22–23

The eschatological undergirds all three poems, as does the impinging of eternity on time (as in T. S. Eliot's *Four Quartets* as well)—which is the substance of Christian eschatology via the Incarnation-and-the-atonement (see e.g. T. F. Torrance's, *Space, Time and Incarnation*, and *Space, Time and Resurrection*), and which is the crux of *Confessions*' entire opening paragraph: see Kirby's claim.

SS

1. immensity cloistered: direct quote from John Donne, *La Corona*

    cradle of straw and line 2: strong echoes of Martin Luther

    As with *TM*, so here we necessarily begin with the most awesome of "spatial" mysteries: the Incarnation, plus then this Very One's crucifixion, with Nothingness' *topos* thereby within the triune divine being (so Eberhard Jüngel after Karl Barth, and von Balthasar's Holy Saturday theology), and see "weightlessness" below.

3. encompass: frequent imagery of Donne's based on "circles" etc.; also word frequently used in Celtic prayers (see e.g. de Waal ed., *The Celtic Vision*), especially of God's protection—so the "caim" ritual form: ref. too Phil 2:6–11, *morphe*, and Karl Barth's

trinitarian theology: freedom, form, freedom-in-the-form; also ref. the Christmas carol!

4. wooden work: carpentry and the Cross; and see comments re crucifixion above

5. ref. Eph and Col

6. encircle: Donne again—synonym of "embrace"
plan: one translation of *oikonomia*

7. granting: freedom is a gift, *not* a right, contrary to so much contemporary culture
further: redemption is more than simply creation restored

8. center: Donne yet again!
still point: e.g. T. S. Eliot, *Four Quartets*—it is noteworthy that much of the *Four Quartets* deals with the question of time and history, using ideas of remembrance, the four elements, etc. A question: were they a subconscious force/source for the creation of these three poems? Probably . . .

9. tree: ref. back to wooden work, and early Christology (see e.g. Acts 5:30, 10:39, 13:29 and Gal 3:13)

10. scanning eye: ref. the evil, violent ones often found in Pss, who nonetheless are known and seen by Yahweh

11. spheres of rule: circle imagery and false "kingdom" theology—"realms"

13. another image à circles
sun: Son naturally (Malachi 4:2)

14. wanderers: pun, as etymologically planets = "wanderers," but now "drifting" due to no gravitational center/focus . . . and so "formless": ref. Gen 1 and Karl Barth, where form = Logos (could have been "weightless" following Nietzsche, which is taken up line 18, since weight = glory in Hebrew, *kabod*), and Jer 4:23
alone: Hell = isolation (see C. S. Lewis's *Great Divorce*), and Nietzsche re "hollowed out being".
formless, alone: contrast line 3 where mother-and-child implies intimate relationship, and the child = Logos/*the* form, albeit "tiny" (at this stage)

15. ref. Ps 139 (yet also Amos 9:1–4).

16. gravitational/solar system/central sun/Son imagery again

17. boundless: such is God's nature ala Gregory of Nyssa and Jenson
    gathering arm: Isa 40:11 and therefore *all* Second Isaiah, esp. the cosmology/theology of history;
    arm: see line 3 re "mother's arms..."

18. ref. 2 Cor 3–4, and C.S. Lewis's *The Weight of Glory*

19. eschatology again
    enter: ref. back to *TM* lines 10–12
    room: ref. Revelation's closing chapters and John 14 and Fourth Gospel's use of *menein* and *mone* (anticipates *Circ* line 21 and so ref. also to Augustine's idea that God's eternity is his unique and specific home/house)

20. hearth and throne: hearth is a homely, family fireplace, while throne biblically (Ezek, Dan, Rev) is a cosmic fireplace: our God is *both* "Abba Father" *and* "Yahweh Sabaoth"
    conspire: echoes also seven(fold) Spirit(s) in Rev

21. each head: Acts 2, etc.
    lips: Isa 6 and Acts 2:11; ref. also Luke 1 and 2 and its "Power, Presence, Praise" pattern, which is repeated in Acts 1 and 2, so that human lips so anointed issue in Praise

22. scarred feet: ref. Rev 5:6, John 20 and Thomas
    feet: ref. John 13's washing
    seal: ref. HSp and cauterization, i.e. healing the mocking crown of thorns with its "sharpness" (as well as "nails," line 2)

23. our crowns given over unto His, Rev 4:10, etc.

24. music: as image of time/eternity (e.g. Augustine) implies "the music of the *spheres*," etc. Taken up again in the last poem as well stilled and filled: echo of the hymn "I cannot tell," v.4

25. God is the center of every place/space—by definition!

26. fathomless: in this second poem re *space*—and so how filled? Answer: "ecstatically/epektatically"!
    sound: traditional trait re theophany—and so eschatology yet again
    last = final, and so finally here *is* a *due* note...

Circ

Title: Latin for *perichoresis*, originally a ref. to the two natures of Christ totally interpenetrating within the one Person; carried over to depict the mutual indwelling of the Persons of the Trinity; and applied again here.

1. ponder: ref. Luke 2:19, 51, and often in the Psalms re God's "works/deeds"; ponder/wonder: an inclusion to this poem
   Way: Mark's theology of discipleship, chs 8–10 (*hodos*) and so thereafter Lucan journey motif, chs 9–19 (and ref. Phil 2:6–11), and esp. Karl Barth, *CD* IV/1, §59.1, "The Way of the Son of God into the Far Country," as *specifically* the way of sovereign free grace in Jesus.
   All in all, the journey (through space–time, no less, individually and collectively) from pondering to wondering/contemplation/ gazing *is* the *entire* divine–human point.

2. Creator becomes a creature, the Story Writer a character within his own story, yet sustains all things still (Heb 1:2–3, Col 1:15–20)—yet again anticipates the *denial* (sic) line 9 with sin's consequences.

3. divinizing matter: ref. Eastern Orthodox theology [mc^2 = e also via light as symbol of Divine]

5. embraces: maternal imagery of God and ref. back to SS line 3

6. ref. John 3:3,5
   joy: characteristic of Luke's theology
   freedom of love and life: ref. Karl Barth, *CD* II/1, ch.VI, *die Wirklichkeit Gottes*, "God's Perfections" or attributes

7. perichoretic: see title—but now ironic, for what *is* a divine attribute after all on account of the revelation of God in Jesus?! *Both* vulnerability *and* might are *equally* divine; and so are equally to be interpenetrating/ed

8. wooing: ref. Hosea (and so A. Heschel, Jürgen Moltmann, et al) enabling nobility: ref. Karl Barth, *CD* IV/2 §64, esp. "the royal man"; NB Eberhard Jüngel's essay, *Karl Barth: A Theological Legacy*, 1986, ch.4
   Finally, lines 7 and 8 parallel each other: vulnerability // wooing

compassion, and might // enabling nobility; *but also* vice versa—perichoretic again!

9. fruit: ref. John 15:1–16 in context!
Wordless world one Sabbath rest: ref. von Balthasar's trinitarian theology, e.g. *Mysterium Paschale, Theo-Drama*.

10. While the general flavor is more of Eastern Orthodoxy, this line encapsulates the doctrine of justification, seen to exemplify Reformed Latin theology. However, see the Finnish view of the early Luther, following Mannermaa, showing Jesus' presence in faith *is* his work of justification, which converges delightfully with the notion of *theosis*.

11. having focused esp. on the Son and HSp in first 2 stanzas, we now come to the Fr, yet "the other two" are still represented: "image" and line 18 (after Robert Jenson)
just so: typical Robert Jenson phrase, just as the ideas throughout the stanza reflect his theology, which in turn is derived greatly from Gregory of Nyssa in particular and Eastern Orthodoxy in general: so lines 11–13 re root and source. Phil 3:13–4, *epektasis*, reference my thesis and used in *LDL* also.
goal/source: cf. Irenaeus' "recapitulation" theology, as well as much patristic thought re *processio/reditus*

14. direct quote from C. S. Lewis, *Last Battle*, pages 160ff; ref. again to neoplatonic themes as well

15. reflecting: 2 Cor 3:18
promises: Galatians, Martin Luther, Jürgen Moltmann, Wolfhart Pannenberg, et al. For what kind of deity is "free" to deliver on his promises?!

16–9. image: *imago Dei* and Jesus Himself (2 Cor 4); eschatologically, even *eternally* à Gregory of Nyssa: what is made in the image of God, who is the archetype, is now ever "expanded"/"stretched," as both God and creature are caught up into the *epektatic* nature of "triune infinity" (Robert Jenson, *God of the Gospel*, ch.5, and *LDL*)

17. pure archetypes: cf. Plato's "Ideal Forms"/"Pure Ideas"

19. pursue: see Gregory of Nyssa, *Life of Moses* (e.g. II, 162–4); also an alliterative bookend with "ponder," just as "wonder" forms a rhyming one to conclude
    naked: double entendre—the lot of a crucified victim; and, transparent: so ref. Mark 10:21 etc., in context, teaching for disciples on the Way, Mark 8–10.
    gaze: contemplation was/is the entire point for classical trinitarian exercises, either those of Augustine or Bonaventure

20-1. See John 14:20, in context of vv.15–23
    universal song: Augustine's *carmen universitatis*, which after Plato is seen as an imitation of eternity, is now "on that Day" truly reflecting this, since the Johannine Jesus *is* I AM in flesh, fully acknowledged/known and shared/participated in (ref. *TM* line 24)

22. Returning: because previously *was not* so returned due to sin, which is exactly self-centered/self-attending; does it also echo the patristic notion of *reditus*? Or Irenaeus . . . ? Most probably.
    attention: Augustine's *distentio animi*, now ever "extended" (pun!) to truly embrace/encompass/"encircle" eternity's "duration" (via memory and anticipation). But this may only be experienced/known in "wonder" (so Gregory of Nyssa, and Augustine re "praise"), rather than conceptually/in human, discursive speech—even by renewed "vestiges"! "Attention" is also Simone Weil's great charism.
    Name: = "Father, Son and Holy Spirit"—just in case one has not by this time realized it. (see yet again Phil 2:11)

All three poems together form a perichoretic study in time, space and the Trinity, as effected by the Incarnation–and–atonement through Jesus of Nazareth, stressing both eschatological and eternal motifs.

Bibliography

Abraham, William J. *Canon and Criterion in Christian Theology: from the Fathers to Feminism*. Oxford: Clarendon, 1998.

Alston, William P. "Substance and the Trinity." In *The Trinity: An Interdisciplinary Symposium on the Trinity*, edited by Stephen T. Davis et al., 179–201. Oxford: Oxford University Press, 1999.

Anatolios, Khaled. *Athanasius*. The Early Church Fathers. London and New York: Routledge, 2004.

———. *Retrieving Nicaea: The Development and Meaning of Trinitarian Doctrine*. Grand Rapids: Baker Academic, 2011.

Aquinas, Saint Thomas. *Summa Theologiae: A Concise Translation*, edited by Timothy McDermott. Allen, TX: Thomas More, 1989.

———. *Summa Theologica*. Translated by Fathers of the English Dominican Province. London: Burns Oates & Washbourne, 1911ff.

Athanasius, Saint. *On the Incarnation: The Treatise De Incarnatione Verbi Dei*. Translated and edited by a religious of C. S. M. V. London: A. R. Mowbray, rev. ed. 1953.

Auerbach, Erich. *Mimesis: The Representation of Reality in Western Literature*. Princeton: Princeton University Press, 1968.

Augustine, Saint. *Confessions*. Translated with an introduction and notes by Henry Chadwick. Oxford: Oxford University Press, 1991.

———. *The Trinity*. Introduction, translation and notes, by Edmund Hill, OP. New York: New City Press, 1991.

Ayres, Lewis. *Augustine and the Trinity*. Cambridge: Cambridge University Press, 2010.

———. "The Fundamental Grammar of Augustine's Trinitarian Theology." In *Augustine and his Critics: Essays in Honour of Gerald Bonner*, edited by Robert Dodaro et al., 51–76. London and New York: Routledge, 2000.

———. *Nicaea and its Legacy: An Approach to Fourth-Century Trinitarian Theology*. Oxford: Oxford University Press, 2004.

Badcock, Gary D. *The House Where God Lives: Renewing the Doctrine of the Church for Today*. Grand Rapids: Eerdmans, 2009.

Bailey, Kenneth E. "Exegesis of Luke 11:5–13." In *Poet and Peasant* and *Through Peasant Eyes: A Literary-Cultural Approach to the Parables in Luke*, 119–41. Grand Rapids: Eerdmans, combined ed.1983.

Balthasar, Hans Urs von. *The Glory of the Lord: A Theological Aesthetics*, vol.VII. *Theology: The New Covenant*. Translated by Brian McNeil, CRV. Edited by John Riches. Edinburgh: T&T Clark, 1989.

———. *Mysterium Paschale: The Mystery of Easter*. Translated with an Introduction by Aidan Nichols, OP. Edinburgh: T&T Clark, 1990.

———. *Theo-Drama: Theological Dramatic Theory, Vol.I: Prolegomena*. Translated by Graham Harrison. San Francisco: Ignatius, 1988.

———. *Theo-Drama: Theological Dramatic Theory, Vol.IV: The Action*. Translated by Graham Harrison. San Francisco: Ignatius, 1994.

———. *Theo-Drama: Theological Dramatic Theory, Vol.V: The Last Act*. Translated by Graham Harrison. San Francisco: Ignatius, 1998.

Barnes, Michel René. "Rereading Augustine's Theology of the Trinity." In *The Trinity: An Interdisciplinary Symposium on the Trinity*, edited by Stephen T. Davis et al., 145–76. Oxford: Oxford University Press, 1999.

———. "The Visible Christ and the Invisible Trinity: Mt. 5:8 in Augustine's Trinitarian Theology of 400." *ModTh* 19/3 (2003) 329–55.

Barth, Karl. *Church Dogmatics*. 4 Vols. Edited by G. W. Bromiley and T. F. Torrance. Edinburgh: T&T Clark, 1956–75.

———. "The Humanity of God." In *The Humanity of God*, 33–64. The Fontana Library of Theology and Philosophy. Translated by John Newton Thomas and Thomas Weiser. London: Collins, 1961.

Bartholomew, Craig G., and Michael W. Goheen, *The Drama of Scripture: Finding your Place in the Biblical Story*. Grand Rapids: Baker Academic, 2004.

Bauckham, Richard, et al, eds. *The Epistle to the Hebrews and Christian Theology*. Grand Rapids: Eerdmans, 2009.

———. *God Crucified: Monotheism and Christology in the New Testament*. Didsbury Lectures, 1996. Carlisle: Paternoster, 1998.

———. *Jesus and the God of Israel: God Crucified and Other Studies on the New Testament's Christology of Divine Identity*. Grand Rapids: Eerdmans, 2008.

Beale, G. K. *The Temple and the Church's Mission: A Biblical Theology of the Dwelling Place of God*. New Studies in Biblical Theology 17. Downers Grove, IL: IVP Academic, 2004.

Begbie, Jeremy S. *Theology, Music and Time*. Cambridge Studies in Christian Doctrine. Cambridge: Cambridge University Press, 2000.

Bennett, Jana Marguerite. *Water Is Thicker Than Blood: An Augustinian Theology of Marriage and Singleness*. Oxford and New York: Oxford University Press, 2008.

Billings, J. Todd. "John Calvin's Soteriology: On the Multifaceted 'Sum' of the Gospel." *IJST* 11/4 (2009) 428 47.

———. *Union with Christ: Reframing Theology and Ministry for the Church*. Grand Rapids: Baker Academic, 2011.

Black, A. Bryden. *God's Address—Living with the Triune God: A Scripture Workbook in the Style of Manuduction to Accompany The Lion, the Dove, & the Lamb*. Eugene: Wipf & Stock, 2017.

Blaising, Craig. "Creedal Formation as Hermeneutical Development: A Reexamination of Nicaea." *Pro Ecclesia* XIX/4 (2010) 371–88.

Bloom, Harold. *Shakespeare: The Invention of the Human*. New York: Riverhead Books, 1998.

Boersma, Hans. *Heavenly Participation: The Weaving of a Sacramental Tapestry*. Grand Rapids: Eerdmans, 2011.

———. *Nouvelle Théologie and Sacramental Ontology: A Return to Mystery*. Oxford: Oxford University Press, 2009.

Boff, Leonardo, OFM. *Trinity and Society*. Translated by Paul Burns. Maryknoll: Orbis, 1988.
Bosch, David J. *Transforming Mission: Paradigm Shifts in Theology of Mission*. American Society of Missiology Series, No.16. Maryknoll: Orbis, 1991.
———. *Witness to the World: The Christian Mission in Theological Perspective*. Marshalls Theological Library. London: Marshall, Morgan & Scott, 1980.
Braaten, Carl E. and Robert W. Jenson, eds. *Christian Dogmatics, Vols 1 & 2*. Philadelphia: Fortress Press, 1984.
———. *In One Body through the Cross: The Princeton Proposal for Christian Unity*. Grand Rapids: Eerdmans, 2003.
———. *The Ecumenical Future. Background papers for* In One Body through the Cross. Grand Rapids: Eerdmans, 2004.
Bradley, James. "Across the River and Beyond the Trees: Feuerbach's Relevance to Modern Thought." In *New Studies in Theology 1*, edited by Stephen Sykes and Derek Holmes, 139–61. London: Duckworth, 1980.
Bray, Gerald. *Creeds, Councils and Christ*. Leicester: Inter-Varsity, 1984.
Brown, David. "The Trinity in Art." In *The Trinity: An Interdisciplinary Symposium on the Trinity*, edited by Stephen T. Davis et al., 329–56. Oxford: Oxford University Press, 1999.
Brown, Peter. *Augustine of Hippo: A Biography*. London: Faber & Faber, 1967 / New ed. Berkeley and Los Angeles: University of California, 2000.
Buckley, James J. "Intimacy: The Character of Robert Jenson's Theology." In *Trinity, Time, and Church: A Response to the Theology of Robert W. Jenson*, edited by Colin E. Gunton, 10–22. Grand Rapids: Eerdmans, 2000.
Castle, Tony. *Gateway to the Trinity: Meditations on Rublev's Icon*. Slough: St Paul Publications, 1988.
Chadwick, Henry. *The Early Church*. The Pelican History of the Church. Harmondsworth: Penguin, 1967.
Childs, Brevard S. "The Early Reception of the Hebrew Bible: The Septuagint and the New Testament." In *The Struggle to Understand Isaiah as Christian Scripture*, 1–31. Grand Rapids: Eerdmans, 2004.
Coakley, Sarah. *God, Sexuality, and the Self: An Essay 'On the Trinity'*. Cambridge: Cambridge University Press, 2013.
———. "Re-Thinking Gregory of Nyssa: Introduction—Gender, Trinitarian Analogies, and the Pedagogy of *The Song*." *ModTh* 18/4 (2002) 431–43. The entire edition is devoted to Gregory of Nyssa.
———. "The Trinity and Gender Reconsidered." In *God's Life in Trinity*, edited by Miroslav Volf and Michael Welker, 133–42. Minneapolis: Fortress, 2006.
Coffey, David. *Deus Trinitas: The Doctrine of the Triune God*. New York and Oxford: Oxford University Press, 1999.
Colle, Ralph Del. *Christ and the Spirit: Spirit Christology in Trinitarian Perspective*. New York and Oxford: Oxford University Press, 1994.
Colyer, Elmer M. *How to Read T. F. Torrance: Understanding his Trinitarian & Scientific Theology*. Downers Grove: Inter-Varsity, 2001/Eugene: Wipf and Stock, 2007.
Confessing the One Faith: An Ecumenical Explication of the Apostolic Faith as it is Confessed in the Nicene-Constantinopolitan Creed (381). Faith & Order paper No.153. Geneva: WCC, New Revised Version, 1991.

Congar, Yves M. J., OP. *I Believe in the Holy Spirit: Vol.1, The Holy Spirit in the 'Economy' – Revelation and Experience of the Spirit; Vol.2, He is Lord and Giver of Life; Vol.3, The River of the Water of Life (Rev 22:1) flows in the East and in the West.* Translated by David Smith. New York: Seabury and London: Geoffrey Chapman, 1983.

Culpepper, R. Alan. *The Gospel and Letters of John.* Nashville: Abingdon, 1998.

Daniélou, Jean, SJ. *Gospel Message and Hellenistic Culture. A History of Early Christian Doctrine before the Council of Nicaea,* vol. 2. Translated, edited and with a Postscript by John Austin Baker. London: Darton, Longmann and Todd, 1973.

———. *The Origins of Latin Christianity. A History of Early Christian Doctrine before the Council of Nicaea,* vol. 3. Translated by David Smith and John Austin Baker. London: Darton, Longman and Todd, 1977.

Davies, Brian. *The Thought of Thomas Aquinas.* Oxford: Clarendon, 1992.

Dempsey, Michael T., ed. *Trinity and Election in Contemporary Theology.* Grand Rapids: Eerdmans, 2011.

DeWeese, Garrett J. *God and the Nature of Time.* Ashgate Philosophy of Religion Series. Aldershot: Ashgate, 2004.

Dionysius, *The Divine Names* and *The Mystical Theology.* Translated by C. E. Rolt. London: SPCK, 1940.

Dunn, James D. G. *Baptism in the Holy Spirit.* SBT Series 2, 15. London: SCM, 1970.

———. *Christology in the Making: A New Testament Inquiry into the Origins of the Doctrine of the Incarnation.* London: SCM, 1980.

———. *Did the First Christians Worship Jesus? The New Testament Evidence.* London: SPCK, 2010.

———. *Jesus and the Spirit: A Study of the Religious and Charismatic Experience of Jesus and the First Christians as Reflected in the New Testament.* London: SCM, 1975.

Eliade, Mircea. *The Myth of the Eternal Return: or, Cosmos and History.* Translated by Willard R. Trask. Princeton: Princeton University Press, 1954.

Emery, Gilles, OP. *The Trinitarian Theology of St Thomas Aquinas.* Translated by Francesca Aran Murphy. Oxford: Oxford University Press, 2007.

———. *Trinity in Aquinas.* Translated by Robert Williams, et al. Naples, FA: Sapientia Press, 2nd ed. 2006.

Farrow, Douglas. *Ascension and Ecclesia: On the significance of the Doctrine of the Ascension for Ecclesiology and Christian Cosmology.* Grand Rapids: Eerdmans, 1999.

———. et al. "Robert Jenson's *Systematic Theology*: Three Responses." *IJST* 1/1 (1999) 89–104.

Fee, Gordon D. *The First Epistle to the Corinthians.* The New International Commentary on the New Testament. Grand Rapids: Eerdmans, 1987.

———. *God's Empowering Presence: The Holy Spirit in the Letters of Paul.* Peabody, MA: Hendrickson Publishers, 1994.

Ferguson, E. "Progress in Perfection: Gregory of Nyssa's Vita Moysis." *Studia Patristica* 14 (1976) 307–14.

Fiddes, Paul. "Overcoming Nothingness." In *The Creative Suffering of God,* 261–67. Oxford: Clarendon, 1988.

Fitzgerald, Allan D., gen ed. *Augustine through the Ages: An Encyclopedia.* Grand Rapids: Eerdmans, 1999.

Flett, John G. *The Witness of God: The Trinity, Missio Dei, Karl Barth, and the Nature of Christian Community.* Grand Rapids: Eerdmans, 2010.

Fout, Jason A. Review of *God is Not a Story*, by Francesca Aran Murphy. *IJST* 13/4 (2011) 475–78.

Gallusz, Laszlo. *The Throne Motif in the Book of Revelation: Profiles from the History of Interpretation*. Library of New Testament Studies 487. London: Bloomsbury T&T Clark, 2014.

Garcia, Mark A. "Imputation as Attribution: Union with Christ, Reification and Justification as Declarative Word." *IJST* 11/4 (2009) 415–27.

Gioia, Luigi, OSB. *The Theological Epistemology of Augustine's* De Trinitate. Oxford Theological Monographs. Oxford: Oxford University Press, 2008.

Goldingay, John, and David Payne. *A Critical and Exegetical Commentary on Isaiah 40–55, Vols I & II*. The International Critical Commentary on the Holy Scriptures of the Old and New Testaments. London & New York: T&T Clark, 2006.

Grant, Robert M. *Greek Apologists of the Second Century*. London: SCM, 1988.

Green, Bradley G. *Colin Gunton and the Failure of Augustine: The Theology of Colin Gunton in Light of Augustine*. Distinguished Dissertations in Christian Theology 4. Eugene, OR: Pickwick Publications, 2011.

Green, H. Benedict, CR. *Matthew, Poet of the Beatitudes*. JSNT Supplement Series 203. Sheffield: Sheffield Academic, 2001.

Greenman, Jeffrey P., et al., eds. *The Sermon on the Mount through the Centuries: From the Early Church to John Paul II*. Grand Rapids: Brazos, 2007.

Gregory of Nyssa. *From Glory to Glory: Texts from Gregory of Nyssa's Mystical Writings*. Selected and with an Introduction by Jean Daniélou, SJ, translated and edited by Herbert Musurillo, SJ. Crestwood, NY: St Vladimir's Seminary, rev. ed. 1979.

Grillmeier, Aloys, SJ. *Christ in Christian Tradition, vol.1, From the Apostolic Age to Chalcedon (AD 451)*. Translated by John Bowden. London and Oxford: Mowbrays, rev ed 1975.

Gunton, Colin E. *Act and Being: Towards a Theology of the Divine Attributes*. Grand Rapids: Eerdmans, 2003.

———. *Becoming and Being: The Doctrine of God in Charles Hartshorne and Karl Barth*. Oxford Theological Monographs. Oxford: Oxford University Press, 1978.

———. "The History. Augustine, The Trinity and the Theological Crisis of the West." In *The Promise of Trinitarian Theology*, 31–57. Edinburgh: T&T Clark, 1991/rev ed. 1997.

———. "The Spirit as Lord: Christianity, modernity and freedom." In *Different Gospels: Christian Orthodoxy & Modern Theologies*, edited by Andrew Walker, 169–82. London: Hodder & Stoughton, 1988.

———. "Towards a Theology of Mediation: Aspects of the Early History." In *The Triune Creator: A Historical and Systematic Study*, 41–64. Grand Rapids: Eerdmans, 1998.

———. ed. *Trinity, Time, and the Church: A Response to the Theology of Robert W. Jenson*. Grand Rapids: Eerdmans, 2000.

Guroian, Vigen. "And I Look for the Resurrection . . ." In *Nicene Christianity: The Future for a New Ecumenism*, edited by Christopher R. Seitz, 203–12. Grand Rapids: Brazos, 2001.

Habets, Myk. *The Anointed Son: A Trinitarian Spirit Christology*. Princeton Theological Monograph Series 129. Eugene, OR: Pickwick Publications, 2010.

———. Review of *Engaging the Doctrine of the Holy Spirit* by Matthew Levering. *ModTh* 34/4 (2018) 677–79.

———. *Theosis in the Theology of Thomas Torrance*. Ashgate New Critical Thinking in Religion, Theology and Biblical Studies. Farnham, UK: Ashgate, 2009.

Hanby, Michael. *Augustine and Modernity*. London and New York: Routledge, 2003.

Hankey, Wayne J. "The Place of the Psychological Image of the Trinity in the Arguments of Augustine's *De Trinitate*, Anselm's *Monologion* and Aquinas' *Summa Theologiae*." *Dionysius* 3 (1979) 99–110.

Hanson, R. P. C. *The Search for the Christian Doctrine of God: The Arian Controversy 318-381*. Edinburgh: T&T Clark, 1988.

Hart, David Bentley. "The Angel at the Ford of Jabbok: On the Theology of Robert Jenson." In *In the Aftermath: Provocations and Laments*, 156–69. Grand Rapids: Eerdmans, 2009.

———. *The Beauty of the Infinite: The Aesthetics of Christian Truth*. Grand Rapids: Eerdmans, 2003.

———. "Christ and Nothing (No Other God)." In *In the Aftermath: Provocations and Laments*, 1–19. Grand Rapids: Eerdmans, 2009.

———. "The Pornographic Culture." In *In the Aftermath: Provocations and Laments*, 83–91. Grand Rapids: Eerdmans, 2009.

Hauerwas, Stanley, and L. Gregory Jones, eds. *Why Narrative? Readings in Narrative Theology*. Grand Rapids: Eerdmans, 1989.

Hays, Richard B. *Echoes of Scripture in the Gospels*. Waco: Baylor University Press, 2016.

Hector, Kevin W. "God's Triunity and Self-determination: A Conversation with Karl Barth, Bruce McCormack and Paul Molnar." *IJST* 7/3 (2005) 246–61.

Hengel, Martin. *Judaism and Hellenism: Studies in their Encounter in Palestine during the Early Hellenistic Period*, 2 vols. Translated by John Bowden. London: SCM, 1974.

———. "The Prologue of the Gospel of John as the Gateway to Christological Truth." In *The Gospel of John and Christian Theology*, edited by Richard Bauckham and Carl Mosser, 265–94. Grand Rapids: Eerdmans, 2008.

———. *The Son of God: The Origin of Christology and the History of Jewish-Hellenistic Religion*. Translated by John Bowden. London: SCM, 1976.

Heron, Alasdair I. C. *The Holy Spirit: The Holy Spirit in the Bible, in the History of Christian Thought and in Recent Theology*. Foundations for Faith: An Introduction to Christian Doctrine. London: Marshall Morgan & Scott, 1983.

———. "'Who Proceedeth from the Father and the Son': The Problem of the *Filioque*." *SJT* 24 (1971) 149 66.

Hill, Edmund, OP. *The Mystery of the Trinity*. London: Geoffrey Chapman, 1985.

Hill, Wesley. *Paul and the Trinity: Persons, Relations, and the Pauline Letters*. Grand Rapids: Eerdmans, 2015.

Hodgson, Leonard. *The Doctrine of the Trinity*. Welwyn: James Nisbet, 1943.

Horne, Brian L. "Art: A Trinitarian Imperative?" In *Trinitarian Theology Today*, edited by Christoph Schwöbel, 80–91. Edinburgh: T&T Clark, 1995.

Horton, Michael S. "Union and Communion: Calvin's Theology of Word and Sacrament." *IJST* 11/4 (2009) 399–414.

Hunsinger, George. *How to Read Karl Barth: The Shape of His Theology*. New York and Oxford: Oxford University Press, 1991.

———. "*Mysterium Trinitatis*: Karl Barth's Conception of Eternity." In *Disruptive Grace: Studies in the Theology of Karl Barth*, 186–209. Grand Rapids: Eerdmans, 2000.

———. "Robert Jenson's Systematic Theology: a review essay." *SJT* 55 (2002) 161–200.

Hurtado, Larry W. "The Binitarian Pattern of Earliest Christian Devotion and Early Doctrinal Development." In *The Place of Christ in Liturgical Prayer: Trinity, Christology, and Liturgical Theology*, edited by Bryan D. Spinks, 23-50. Collegeville: Liturgical Press, 2008.

———. *Lord Jesus Christ: Devotion to Jesus in Earliest Christianity*. Grand Rapids: Eerdmans, 2003.

Jennings, Theodore W., Jr. *Beyond Theism: A Grammar of God-Language*. New York and Oxford: Oxford University Press, 1985.

Jenson, Robert W. "D. Stephen Long's Saving Karl Barth: An Agent's Perspective." *Pro Ecclesia* XXIV/2 (2015) 131-33.

———. "Eighth Locus – The Holy Spirit." In *Christian Dogmatics, Vol.2*, edited by Carl E. Braaten & Robert W. Jenson, 101-78. Philadelphia: Fortress Press, 1984.

———. *God According to the Gospel: The Triune Identity*. Philadelphia: Fortress Press, 1982.

———. *On Thinking the Human: Resolutions of Difficult Notions*. Grand Rapids: Eerdmans, 2003.

———. "Response to Watson and Hunsinger." *SJT* 55 (2002) 225-32.

———. "Second Locus – The Triune God." In *Christian Dogmatics, Vol.1*, edited by Carl E. Braaten & Robert W. Jenson, 79-191. Philadelphia: Fortress Press, 1984.

———. *Systematic Theology: vol. 1 The Triune God, vol. 2 The Works of God*. New York and Oxford: Oxford University Press, 1997/99.

———. *Theology as Revisionary Metaphysics: Essays on God and Creation*. Ed. Stephen John Wright. Eugene, OR: Cascade Books, 2014.

———. *Unbaptized God: The Basic Flaw in Ecumenical Theology*. Minneapolis: Fortress, 1992.

———. "What is the Point of Trinitarian Theology?" In *Trinitarian Theology Today*, edited by Christoph Schwöbel, 31-43. Edinburgh: T&T Clark, 1995.

John Paul II, *Man and Woman He Created Them: A Theology of the Body*. Translation, Introduction, and Index by Michael Waldstein. Boston: Pauline Books, 2006.

Jüngel, Eberhard. *The Doctrine of the Trinity: God's Being is in Becoming*. Monograph Supplements to the Scottish Journal of Theology 4. Translated by Horton Harris. Edinburgh: Scottish Academic Press, 1976.

———. "The Emergence of the New." In *Theological Essays II*, 35-58. Translated by Arnold Neufeldt-Fast and J. B. Webster. Edited with an Introduction by J. B. Webster. Edinburgh: T&T Clark, 1995.

———. *God as the Mystery of the World: On the Foundation of the Theology of the Crucified One in the Dispute between Theism and Atheism*. Translated by Darrell L. Guder. Edinburgh: T&T Clark, 1983.

———. *God's Being is in Becoming: The Trinitarian Being of God in the Theology of Karl Barth. A Paraphrase*. Translated by John Webster. Grand Rapids: Eerdmans, 2001.

———. *Gottes Sein ist im Werden. Verantwortliche Rede vom Sein Gottes bei Karl Barth. Eine Paraphrase*. Tübingen: J. C. B. Mohr, First edition, 1964.

Jungmann, Josef A. *The Place of Christ in Liturgical Prayer*. Translated by A. Peeler. London and Dublin: Geoffrey Chapman, 1965.

Kasper, Walter. *The God of Jesus Christ*. Translated by Matthew J. O'Connell. London: SCM, 1984.

———. *Jesus the Christ*. Translated by V. Green. London: Burns & Oates, 1976.

Kelly, J. N. D. *Early Christian Doctrines*. London: Adam & Charles Black, 4th ed 1968.

Kerr, Fergus. *Theology after Wittgenstein*. Oxford: Basil Blackwell, 1986.

Kierkegaard, Søren. *Spiritual Writings: Gift, Creation, Love – Selections from the Upbuilding Discourses*. Selected, translated, and with an introduction by George Pattison. New York & London: Harper, 2010.

Kirby, W. J. T. "Praise as the Soul's Overcoming of Time in the *Confessions* of St Augustine." *Pro Ecclesia* VI/3 (1997) 333–50.

Knight, Douglas. "Jenson on Time." In *Trinity, Time and Church: A Response to the Theology of Robert W. Jenson*, edited by Colin E. Gunton, 71–79. Grand Rapids: Eerdmans, 2000.

Kuschel, Karl-Josef. *Born Before All Time? The Dispute over Christ's Origin*. Translated by John Bowden. New York: Crossroad, 1992.

LaCocque, André, and Paul Ricoeur. "Exodus 3:14. The Revelation of Revelations." In *Thinking Biblically: Exegetical and Hermeneutical Studies*, 307–61. Translated by David Pellauer. Chicago and London: University of Chicago Press, 1998.

LaCugna, C. M. "Re-Conceiving the Trinity as the Mystery of Salvation." *SJT* 38 (1985) 1–23.

Langdon, Adrian. "Confessing Eternity: Karl Barth and the Western Tradition." *Pro Ecclesia* XXI/2 (2012) 125–44.

Lash, Nicholas. "Ideology, Metaphor and Analogy." In *Theology on the Way to Emmaus*, 105–119. London: SCM, 1986.

Leamy, Katy. *The Holy Trinity: Hans Urs von Balthasar and His Sources*. Eugene: Pickwick, 2015.

Leithart, Peter J. *Athanasius*. Foundations of Theological Exegesis and Christian Spirituality. Grand Rapids: Baker Academic, 2011.

Levering, Matthew. *Engaging the Doctrine of the Holy Spirit: Love and Gift in the Trinity and the Church*. Grand Rapids: Baker Academic, 2016.

———. *Scripture and Metaphysics: Aquinas and the Renewal of Trinitarian Theology*. Challenges in Contemporary Theology. Oxford: Blackwell, 2004.

Lewis, C. S. "Beyond Personality: or First Steps in the Doctrine of the Trinity." In *Mere Christianity*, 130–188. London and Glasgow: Fontana, 1955

Long, D. Stephen. "Responses to Reviewers: Identifying What Matters Most." *Pro Ecclesia* XXIV/2 (2015) 154–61..

Lonergan, Bernard, SJ. *The Triune God: Doctrines. Collected Works of Bernard Lonergan: The Robert Mollot Collection 11*. Translated from *De Deo Trino: Pars Dogmatica* (1964) by Michael G. Shields; edited by Robert M. Doran and H. Daniel Monsour. Toronto: University of Toronto Press, 2009.

———. *The Way to Nicea: The Dialectical Development of Trinitarian Theology*. Translated by Conn O'Donovan from the first part of *De Deo Trino*. London: Darton, Longman & Todd, 1976.

Lossky, Vladimir. *The Mystical Theology of the Eastern Church*. Translated by the Fellowship of St. Albans and St. Sergius. Cambridge and London: James Clarke, 1957.

Loughlin, Gerard. *Telling God's Story: Bible, Church and narrative theology*. Cambridge: Cambridge University Press, 1996.

Louth, Andrew *The Origins of the Christian Mystical Tradition: from Plato to Denys*. Oxford: Clarendon, 1983.

Lubac, Henri Cardinal de, SJ. *Corpus Mysticum – The Eucharist and the Church in the Middle Ages*. Translated by Gemma Simmonds, CJ, with Richard Price and

Christopher Stephens. Edited by Laurence Paul Hemming and Susan Frank Parsons. *Faith in Reason: Philosophical Enquiries*. London: SCM, 2006.

MacDonald, Neil B. *Karl Barth and the Strange New World within the Bible: Barth, Wittgenstein, and the Metadilemmas of the Enlightenment*. Milton Keynes: Paternoster, rev. ed. 2001.

MacKinnon, Donald M. "'Substance' in Christology—a cross-bench view." In *Christ, Faith and History: Cambridge Studies in Christology*, edited by S. W. Sykes and J. P. Clayton, 279–300. Cambridge: Cambridge University Press, 1972.

———. *Themes in Theology: The Three-fold Cord. Essays in Philosophy, Politics and Theology*. Edinburgh: T&T Clark, 1987.

Macleod, C. W. "Allegory and Mysticism in Origen and Gregory of Nyssa." *JTS* 22 (1971) 362–79.

McFague, Sallie. *Metaphorical Theology: Models of God in Religious Language*. London: SCM, 1983.

McGrath, Alister E. *Christian Theology: An Introduction*. Oxford: Blackwell, 4th ed. 2007.

———. *The Genesis of Doctrine: A Study in the Foundations of Doctrinal Criticism. The 1990 Bampton Lectures*. Oxford: Basil Blackwell, 1990.

———. *Luther's Theology of the Cross: Martin Luther's Theological Breakthrough*. Chichester: Wiley-Blackwell, 2nd ed 2011.

———. *The Making of Modern German Christology: From the Enlightenment to Pannenberg*. Oxford: Basil Blackwell, 1986.

———. *T. F. Torrance: An Intellectual Biography*. Edinburgh: T&T Clark, 1999.

———. *Understanding Doctrine: Its Purpose and Relevance for Today*. London: Hodder & Stoughton, 1990.

Marion, Jean-Luc. *In The Self's Place: The Approach of Saint Augustine*. Translated by Jeffrey L. Kosky. Stanford: Stanford University Press, 2012.

Marshall, Bruce D. *Christology in Conflict: The Identity of a Saviour in Rahner and Barth*. Oxford: Basil Blackwell, 1987.

Martin, Jennifer Newsome. *Hans Urs von Balthasar and the Critical Appropriation of Russian Religious Thought*. Notre Dame: University of Notre Dame Press, 2015.

Martin, Ralph P. *A Hymn of Christ: Philippians 2:5-11 in Recent Interpretation & in the Setting of Early Christian Worship*. Downers Grove: Inter-Varsity, 3rd ed. 1997.

Martin, Ralph P., and Brian J. Dodd, eds. *Where Christology Began: Essays on Philippians 2*. Louisville: WJK, 1998.

Mazzocco, Mariel. "The Secret Dynamism of Divine Simplicity." *ModTh* 34/3 (2018) 434–443.

Mersch, Émile. *The Theology of the Mystical Body*. Translated by C. Vollert. St. Louis and London: Herder, 1951.

———. *The Whole Christ: The Historical Development of the Doctrine of the Mystical Body in Scripture and Tradition*. Translated by J. R. Kelly. London: D. Dobson, 1949.

Molnar, Paul D. *Divine Freedom and the Doctrine of the Immanent Trinity: In Dialogue with Karl Barth and Contemporary Theology*. London and New York: T&T Clark, 2002.

———. "The Perils of Embracing a 'Historicized Christology'." *ModTh* 30/4 (2014) 454–80.

———. *Thomas F. Torrance: Theologian of the Trinity*. Great Theologians Series. Farnham, UK: Ashgate, 2009.
Moltmann, Jürgen. "The Church in the trinitarian history of God." In *The Church in the Power of the Spirit: A Contribution to Messianic Ecclesiology*, 50–65. Translated by Margaret Kohl. London: SCM, 1977.
———. *The Crucified God: The Cross of Christ as the Foundation and Criticism [criterion] of Christian Theology*. Translated by R. A. Wilson and John Bowden. London: SCM, 1974.
———. *The Trinity and the Kingdom of God: The Doctrine of God*. Translated by Margaret Kohl. London: SCM, 1981.
———. *The Way of Jesus Christ: Christology in messianic dimensions*. Translated by Margaret Kohl. London: SCM, 1990.
Montgomery, John W. "Toward a Christian Philosophy of History." In *Where is History Going?*, 182–97. Minneapolis: Bethany Fellowship, 1969.
Motyer, J. A. *The Day of the Lion: The Message of Amos*. The Bible Speaks Today: OT Series. London: Inter-Varsity, 1974.
Murphy, Francesca Aran. *God is Not a Story: Realism Revisited*. Oxford: Oxford University Press, 2007.
Nichols, Aidan, OP. *The Art of God Incarnate: Theology and Image in Christian Tradition*. London: Darton, Longman and Todd, 1980
———. *Figuring out the Church: Her Marks, and Her Masters*. San Francisco: Ignatius, 2013.
———. *No Bloodless Myth: A Guide through Balthasar's Dramatics. Introduction to Hans Urs von Balthasar*. Washington, DC: Catholic University of America Press, 2000.
North, Christopher R. *The Second Isaiah: Introduction, Translation and Commentary to Chapters XL-LV*. Oxford: Clarendon, 1964.
Nouwen, Henri J. M. *Behold the Beauty of the Lord: Praying with Icons*. Notre Dame: Ave Maria, 1987.
O'Leary, Joseph Stephen. *Questioning Back: The Overcoming of Metaphysics in Christian Tradition*. Minneapolis: Winston, 1985.
Olson, Roger. "Trinity and Eschatology: the Historical Being of God in Jürgen Moltmann and Wolfhart Pannenberg." *SJT* 36 (1983) 213–27.
Orphanos, Markos A. "The procession of the Holy Spirit according to certain Later Greek Fathers." In *Spirit of God, Spirit of Christ: Ecumenical Reflections on the Filioque Controversy*, edited by Luckas Vischer, 21–45. London: SPCK and Geneva: WCC, 1981.
Pannenberg, Wolfhart. "Analogy and Doxology." In *Basic Questions in Theology. Collected Essays, vol.1*, 211–38. Translated by George H. Kehm. Philadelphia: Westminster, 1983.
———. "The Appropriation of the Philosophical Concept of God as a Dogmatic Problem of Earliest Christian Theology." In *Basic Questions in Theology. Collected Essays, Vol. II*, 119–83. Translated by George H. Kehm. Philadelphia: Westminister, 1983.
———. "Eternity, Time, and the Trinitarian God." In *Trinity, Time, and Church: A Response to the Theology of Robert W. Jenson*, edited by Colin E. Gunton, 62–70. Grand Rapids: Eerdmans, 2000.

———. *Jesus – God and Man*. Translated by Lewis L. Wilkins & Duane A. Priebe. London: SCM, 1968.

———. *Metaphysics and the Idea of God*. Translated by Philip Clayton. Grand Rapids: Eerdmans, 1990.

———. *Systematic Theology*, Vols 1–3. Translated by Geoffrey W. Bromiley. Grand Rapids: Eerdmans, 1991/94/98.

Patte, Daniel. *Discipleship According to the Sermon on the Mount: Four Legitimate Readings, Four Plausible Views of Discipleship, and their Relative Values*. Valley Forge: Trinity International, 1996.

Pelikan, Jaroslav. *Credo: Historical and Theological Guide to Creeds and Confessions of Faith in the Christian Tradition*. New Haven and London: Yale University Press, 2003.

———. *The Christian Tradition: A History of the Development of Doctrine. Vol.3 – The Growth of Medieval Theology (600–1300)*. Chicago and London: University of Chicago Press, 1978.

———. *The Christian Tradition: A History of the Development of Doctrine. Vol.4 – Reformation of Church and Dogma (1300–1700)*. Chicago and London: University of Chicago Press, 1984.

Perrin, Nicholas. *Jesus the Temple*. Grand Rapids: Baker Academic, 2010.

Peters, R. S. "Authority (1)." In *Political Philosophy*, edited by Anthony Quinn, 83–96. Oxford Readings in Philosophy. Oxford: Oxford University Press, 1967.

Pitre, Brant. *Jesus and the Last Supper*. Grand Rapids: Eerdmans, 2015.

Placher, William C. *Narratives of a Vulnerable God: Christ, Theology, and Scripture*. Louisville: WJK, 1994.

Placher, William C. Review of *God is Not a Story*, by Francesca Aran Murphy. *ModTh* 24/3 (2008) 511–13.

Quash, Ben. *Theology and the Drama of History*. Cambridge Studies in Christian Doctrine. Cambridge: Cambridge University Press, 2005.

Rae, Murray A. *History and Hermeneutics*. London: T&T Clark, 2005.

———. "The Spatiality of God." In *Trinitarian Theology After Barth*, edited by Myk Habets and Phillip Tolliday, 70–86. Princeton Theological Monograph Series 148. Eugene, OR: Pickwick Publications, 2011.

Radner, Ephraim *The End of the Church: A Pneumatology of Christian Division in the West*. Grand Rapids: Eerdmans, 1998.

Rahner, Karl. *Foundations of Christian Faith: An Introduction to the Idea of Christianity*. Translated by William V. Dych. London: Darton, Longman and Todd, 1978.

———. *The Trinity*. Translated by Joseph Donceel. London: Burns & Oates, 1970.

Richard of St Victor. "Book Three of The Trinity." In *The Twelve Patriarchs, The Mystical Ark, Book Three of The Trinity*, 373–97. The Classics of Western Spirituality. Translation and Introduction by Grover A. Zinn. London: SPCK, 1979.

Rist, John M. *Augustine: Ancient Thought Baptized*. Cambridge: Cambridge University Press, 1994.

Roberts, Christopher C. *Creation and Covenant: The Significance of Sexual Difference in the Moral Theology of Marriage*. London and New York: T&T Clark, 2007.

Roberts, Richard H. "Barth's Doctrine of Time: Its Nature and Implications." In *Karl Barth – Studies of his Theological Methods*, edited by S. W. Sykes, 88–146. Oxford: Clarendon, 1979.

———. "Karl Barth." In *One God in Trinity: An analysis of the primary dogma of Christianity*, edited by Peter Toon & James D. Spiceland, 78–94. London: Samuel Bagster, 1980.

Robinson, Dominic. *Understanding the "Imago Dei": The Thought of Barth, von Balthasar and Moltmann*. Farnham, UK: Ashgate, 2011.

Rogers, Eugene F., et al. Book symposium: Reviews of *God, Sexuality, and the Self*, by Sarah Coakley. *ModTh* 30/4 (2014) 552–99.

Rosato, Philip J, SJ. *The Spirit as Lord: The Pneumatology of Karl Barth*. Edinburgh: T&T Clark, 1981.

Rusch, William G. *The Trinitarian Controversy*. Translated and edited by William G. Rusch. Sources of Early Christian Thought. Philadelphia: Fortress Press, 1980.

Sanders, Fred. *The Triune God*. New Studies in Dogmatics. Grand Rapids: Zondervan, 2016.

Sanders, Fred, et al. "A Name, Names, and Half a Name." Review(s), as a symposium, of *The Divine Name(s) and the Holy Trinity, vol.1 Distinguishing the Voices*, by R. Kendall Soulen. *Pro Ecclesia* XXIII/1 (2014) 22–80.

Schillebeeckx, Edward. *The Church with a Human Face: A New and Expanded Theology of Ministry*. Translated by John Bowden. London: SCM, 1985.

Scola, Angelo Cardinal. *The Nuptial Mystery*. Ressourcement: Retrieval and Renewal in Catholic Thought. Translated by Michelle K. Borras. Grand Rapids: Eerdmans, 2005.

Siecienski, A. Edward. *The* Filioque: *History of a Doctrinal Controversy*. Oxford Studies in Historical Theology. Oxford: Oxford University Press, 2010.

Smail, Tom. "Editorial." *Theological Renewal* 8 (1978) 2–6.

———. *The Giving Gift: The Holy Spirit in Person*. London: Hodder & Stoughton, 1988.

———. *Like Father, Like Son: The Trinity Imaged in our Humanity*. Milton Keynes, UK: Paternoster, 2005.

Smith, Gordon T. "The Sacraments and the Embodiment of Our Trinitarian Faith." In *Trinitarian Theology for the Church: Scripture, Community, Worship*, edited by Daniel J. Treier and David Lauber, 185–203. Downers Grove: Inter-Varsity Academic, 2009.

Soskice, Janet Martin. *The Kindness of God: Metaphor, Gender, and Religious Language*. Oxford: Oxford University Press, 2007.

———. *Metaphor and Religious Language*. Oxford: Clarendon, 1985.

Soulen, R. Kendall. *The Divine Name(s) and the Holy Trinity, vol.1 Distinguishing the Voices*. Louisville: WJK, 2011.

Spinks, Bryan D., ed. *The Place of Christ in Liturgical Prayer: Trinity, Christology, and Liturgical Theology*. Collegeville: Liturgical Press, 2008.

Staniloae, Dumitru. "The procession of the Holy Spirit from the Father and his relation to the Son, as the basis of our deification and adoption." In *Spirit of God, Spirit of Christ: Ecumenical Reflections on the* Filioque *Controversy*, edited by Luckas Vischer, 174–86. London: SPCK and Geneva: WCC, 1981.

Stead, Christopher. *Divine Substance*. Oxford: Clarendon, 1977.

Steiner, George. *The Death of Tragedy*. London: Faber & Faber, 1961.

———. *Real Presences: Is there anything in what we say?* London: Faber & Faber, 1989.

Stott, John. *The Message of the Sermon on the Mount: Christian Counter-culture*. The Bible Speaks Today: NT Series. Leicester: Inter-Varsity, 1978.

Strom, Mark. *Reframing Paul: Conversations in Grace and Community*. Downers Grove: Inter-Varsity, 2000.
Stroup, George W. "The Narrative Structure of Christian Faith." In *The Promise of Narrative Theology*, 170–98. London: SCM, 1984.
Swain, Scott R. *The God of the Gospel: Robert Jenson's Trinitarian Theology*. Downers Grove: IVP Academic, 2013.
Thiselton, Anthony C. *The First Epistle to the Corinthians: A Commentary on the Greek Text*. The New International Greek Testament Commentary. Grand Rapids: Eerdmans, 2000.
Thompson, Marianne Meye. *The God of the Gospel of John*. Grand Rapids: Eerdmans, 2001.
Torrance, Alan J. *Persons in Communion: Trinitarian Description and Human Participation*. Edinburgh: T&T Clark, 1996.
Torrance, James B. *Worship, Community and the Triune God of Grace. The Didsbury Lectures 1994*. Carlisle: Paternoster, 1996.
Torrance, Thomas F. "Athanasius: A Study in the Foundations of Classical Theology." In *Theology in Reconciliation*, 215–66.
———. *Atonement: The Person and Work of Christ*, ed. Robert T Walker. Milton Keynes: Paternoster, 2009.
———. *The Christian Doctrine of God, One Being Three Persons*. Edinburgh: T&T Clark, 1996.
———. "The Epistemological Relevance of the Holy Spirit." In *God and Rationality*, 165–92. London: Oxford University Press, 1971.
———. *The Ground and Grammar of Theology*. Belfast: Christian Journals Limited, 1980.
———. ed., *The Incarnation: Ecumenical Studies in the Nicene-Constantinopolitan Creed* Edinburgh: Handsel, 1981.
———. *Incarnation: The Person and Life of Christ*, ed. Robert T Walker. Milton Keynes: Paternoster, 2008.
———. "The Integration of Form in Natural and in Theological Science." In *Transformation and Convergence in the Frame of Knowledge: Explorations in the Interrelations of Scientific and Theological Enterprise*, 61–105. Belfast: Christian Journals Limited, 1984.
———. "The Legacy of Karl Barth (1886–1986)." *SJT* 39 (1986) 289–308.
———. *The Mediation of Christ. The 1982 Didsbury Lectures*. Carlisle: Paternoster, 1983.
———. "The Mind of Christ in Worship: The Problem of Apollinarianism in the Liturgy." In *Theology in Reconciliation*, 139–214.
———. "The Paschal Mystery of Christ and the Eucharist." In *Theology in Reconciliation*, 106–38.
———. "The Roman Doctrine of Grace from the Point of View of Reformed Theology." In *Theology in Reconstruction*, 169–91. London: SCM, 1965.
———. *Space, time and Incarnation*. London: Oxford University Press, 1969.
———. *Space, time and resurrection*. Edinburgh: Handsel, 1976.
———. *Theology in Reconciliation: Essays towards Evangelical and Catholic Unity in East and West*. London: Geoffrey Chapman, 1975.
———. *The Trinitarian Faith: The Evangelical Theology of the Ancient Catholic Church*. Edinburgh: T&T Clark, 1988.

———. *Trinitarian Perspectives: Towards Doctrinal Agreement*. Edinburgh: T&T Clark, 1994.

Vanhoozer, Kevin J. *The Drama of Doctrine: A Canonical Linguistic Approach to Christian Theology*. Louisville: WJK, 2005.

Verkuyl, Johannes. "Ways and Means." In *Contemporary Missiology: an Introduction*, 205–25. Translated and edited by Dale Cooper. Grand Rapids: Eerdmans, 1978.

Vest, Norvene, Oblate OSB. *Preferring Christ: A Devotional Commentary and Workbook on the Rule of St. Benedict*. Trabuco Canyon, CA: Source Books, 1990.

Vickers, Jason E. *Invocation and Assent: The Making and Remaking of Trinitarian Theology*. Grand Rapids: Eerdmans, 2008.

Vischer, Lukas, ed. *Spirit of God, Spirit of Christ: Ecumenical reflections on the* Filioque *Controversy*. London: SPCK and Geneva: WCC, 1981.

Waal, Esther de. *A Life-Giving Way: A Commentary on the Rule of St. Benedict*. Contemporary Christian Insights. London and New York: Continuum, 1995.

Watson, Francis. "'America's Theologian': an appreciation of Robert Jenson's Systematic Theology, with some remarks about the bible." *SJT* 55 (2002) 201–23.

———. *Paul and the Hermeneutics of Faith*. London and New York: T&T Clark, 2004.

Webster, John B. *Eberhard Jüngel: An introduction to his theology* Cambridge: Cambridge University Press, 1986.

———. "Evangelical Freedom." In *Confessing God: Essays in Christian Dogmatics II*, 215–26. London and New York: T&T Clark, 2005.

Weinandy, Thomas G., OFM Cap. *The Father's Spirit of Sonship: Reconceiving the Trinity*. Edinburgh: T&T Clark, 1995.

White, Thomas Joseph, ed. *The Analogy of Being: Invention of the Antichrist or the Wisdom of God?* Grand Rapids: Eerdmans, 2011.

Whitehouse, W. A. "Authority, Divine and Human." In *The Authority of Grace: Essays in Response to Karl Barth*, 225–43. Edinburgh: T&T Clark, 1981.

Wilken, Robert Louis. "Is Pentecost the Peer of Easter? Scripture, Liturgy, and the *Proprium* of the Holy Spirit". In *Trinity, Time, and the Church: A Response to the Theology of Robert W. Jenson*, edited by Colin E. Gunton, 158–77. Grand Rapids: Eerdmans, 2000.

———. *The Spirit of Early Christian Thought: Seeking the Face of God*. New Haven and London: Yale University Press, 2003.

Williams, Rowan. *Arius: Heresy and Tradition*. London: Darton, Longman and Todd, 1987/rev. ed. Grand Rapids: Eerdmans, 2002.

———. *The Wound of Knowledge: Christian Spirituality from the NT to St. John of the Cross*. London: Darton, Longman and Todd, 1979.

Winch, Peter. "Authority (2)." In *Political Philosophy*, edited by Anthony Quinn, 97–111. Oxford Readings in Philosophy. Oxford: Oxford University Press, 1967.

Work, Telford. "The End of Scripture: God's Word in Faithful Practice." In *Living and Active: Scripture in the Economy of Salvation*, 215–314. Grand Rapids: Eerdmans, 2002.

———. "The Mission of Scripture: A School for All the World." In *Living and Active: Scripture in the Economy of Salvation*, 125–213. Grand Rapids: Eerdmans, 2002.

Wright, Christopher J. H. *The Mission of God: Unlocking the Bible's Grand Narrative*. Downers Grove: Inter-Varsity, 2006.

———. *The Mission of God's People: A Biblical Theology of the Church's Mission*. Grand Rapids: Zondervan, 2010.

Wright, N. T. *Jesus and the Victory of God. Christian Origins and the Question of God*, Vol.2. London: SPCK, 1996.

———. "Jesus Christ is Lord: Philippians 2:5–11." In *The Climax of the Covenant: Christ and the Law in Pauline Theology*, 56–98. Edinburgh: T&T Clark, 1991.

———. *The New Testament and the People of God. Christian Origins and the Question of God*, Vol.1. London: SPCK, 1992.

———. "The One God of Israel, Freshly Revealed." In *Paul and the Faithfulness of God. Christian Origins and the Question of God*, Vol.4, 619–773. Minneapolis: Fortress, 2013

Wright, Stephen John, and Chris E. W. Green. *The Promise of Robert W. Jenson's Theology: Constructive Engagements*. Minneapolis: Fortress, 2017.

Yeago, David S. "The New Testament and the Nicene Dogma: A Contribution to the Recovery of Theological Exegesis." *Pro Ecclesia* III/2 (1994) 152–64.

Young, Frances M. *From Nicaea to Chalcedon: A Guide to its Literature and Background*. London: SCM, 1983.

Ziegler, Geordie W. *Trinitarian Grace and Participation: An Entry into the Theology of T. F. Torrance*. Minneapolis: Fortress, 2017.

Zimmerli, Walther. *I am Yahweh*. Translated by Douglas W. Scott. Edited with an Introduction by Walter Brueggemann. Atlanta: John Knox, 1982.

Zizioulas, John D. *Being as Communion: Studies in Personhood and the Church*. London: Darton, Longman and Todd, 1985.

———. *Communion and Otherness: Further Studies in Personhood and the Church*. Edited by Paul McPartlan. London: T&T Clark, 2006.

———. *Lectures in Christian Dogmatics*. Edited by Douglas H. Knight. London and New York: T&T Clark, 2008.

Index of Names

Anatolios, Khaled, 55, 57, 88, 189
Arius, 55–63
Athanasius, 48, 51–64, 86, 88, 141–44, 160, 189
Augustine, xiv, 7, 49, 77, 78, 89–112, 114, 116, 123, 126–33, 139, 155, 163, 168, 177–78, 185, 187, 193
Ayres, Lewis, 55–57, 89, 99, 103–11, 155, 177

Bailey, Kenneth E., 42
Balthasar, Hans Urs von, 102, 118, 132, 134, 157, 161, 163, 175, 182, 202, 206
Barnes, Michel René, 89, 91
Barth, Karl, xix, xx, 3, 45, 64, 65, 69, 70, 72, 74, 87, 90, 95, 96, 114, 117, 118, 121, 124, 126, 132, 136, 148, 152, 153–58, 164–65, 169–71, 174–75, 177, 179, 180, 187, 196, 202–3, 205
Bartholomew, Craig G., 34
Basil of Caesarea, 60, 66–68, 93, 130–31, 154, 159, 180, 183
Bauckham, Richard, 14, 48, 144
Begbie, Jeremy S., 130, 163, 179, 185–86
Boersma, Hans, 79, 147
Billings, J. Todd, 142
Boethius, 114, 176
Bradley, James, 118, 134

Calvin, 142
Coakley, Sarah, 70, 159
Colle, Ralph Del, 151

Daniélou, Jean, 54, 55
Dunn, James D. G., 14, 32

Emery, Gilles, xiv, 150

Fee, Gordon D., 35, 47

Gallusz, Laszlo, 28
Gregory Nazianzen, 60, 67, 83
Gregory of Nyssa, 60, 64, 68, 70, 124–25, 132, 158–60, 173n15, 185, 194, 204, 206, 207
Gunton, Colin E., 110, 117, 118, 122, 142, 180, 187

Habets, Myk, xxiii, 142n9, 151n3, 179n32
Hart, David Bentley, 117, 152, 186
Hengel, Martin, 14, 24, 53
Hill, Wesley, 23n6
Hunsinger, George, 132, 133, 137, 153, 164, 173, 175, 187
Hurtado, Larry W., 14, 143

Irenaeus, 16, 20, 55, 62, 72, 206

Jennings, Theodore W., 115, 184
Jenson, Robert W., 138 citations from 10 publications
Jüngel, Eberhard, xx, 58, 90, 95n15, 117, 118, 129n117, 152–65, 171–76, 179–80n37, 181, 184–86, 189, 194, 200
Jungmann, Josef A., 142–43, 149

Kasper, Walter, 31, 66, 95, 111, 170

Kirby, W. J. T., 91, 185

Leithart, Peter J., 63, 133, 172n11
Levering, Matthew, xiv, 150, 179
Lonergan, Bernard, 14
Loughlin, Gerard, 179
Luther, 30, 95, 157, 202, 206

McGrath, Alister E., 13, 30, 54, 117n75, 148, 157
Marion, Jean-Luc, 106, 124, 127, 163, 166, 192-96
Martin, Ralph P., 20
Moltmann, Jürgen, 111, 157, 161, 162, 202, 205

Neill, Stephen, 15, 25
Nichols, Aidan, 78, 134, 190

Origen, 54-55, 178n32

Pannenberg, Wolfhart, 15, 51, 62, 118n77, 119n84, 122, 128, 130-31, 152n7, 154-55, 171, 176, 179n32, 206
Pelikan, Jaroslav, 56, 145n15

Quash, Ben, 163n52, 185n49

Rae, Murray A., 180n40, 185n49
Rahner, Karl, 66n32, 68-70, 92, 110, 119, 173n16, 180n41, 187

Sanders, Fred, 16, 45, 78n59, 166n62
Soskice, Janet Martin, 1-2, 70-71
Soulen, R. Kendall, 27n10, 36n18, 45n7 and 9
Steiner, George, 58, 179n36, 189
Stroup, George W., 91, 95, 201

Tertullian, 53-54
Torrance, Alan J., 146n17
Torrance, James B., 147
Torrance, T. F., 2, 61, 63, 65n31, 69, 83n67, 84-87, 120, 130n120, 140-48, 152, 160n41, 169-70, 180, 188n52, 189n53, 202
Thiselton, Anthony C., 47

Vickers, Jason, 49, 66, 170

Watson, Francis, 19, 135
Webster, John B., 96, 153, 154, 156, 165, 171, 186
Weinandy, Thomas G., 151, 178
Wilken, Robert Louis, 55, 78, 178-79
Williams, Rowan D., 63, 126, 159
Wright, Christopher J. H., 45, 160
Wright, N. T., 20, 34, 36, 47, 49
Wright, Stephen John, 134

Zizioulas, John D., 114, 179

Index of Subjects

accidents, see too substance, 52, 90, 94
anabasis, see too *katabasis*, 143, 146, 147, 160
analogy, 74, 90, 99, 105–10, 111, 116, 151, 154, 182n43
apologists, 53, 55
archē (source/fount/root, monarchy), 25, 54, 68, 102, 113–14, 121, 155, 175, 206

baptism, 10, 21, 32–33, 35, 40, 61, 67n34, 78n60, 83, 149, 170, 170n4, 179, 184

chōra (space/sphere), 87, 130, 131, 155, 163, 176, 180, 183, 184
church, xiii, 13, 14, 17, 26, 30, 32, 35, 45, 49, 56–59, 61–62, 65, 74–76, 77–84, 96, 120, 136, 140, 142, 143, 144–48, 149, 151, 170, 177, 181, 184
Constantinople, council of, xiii, 13–14, 59–60, 66, 77, 81
correspondence/co-response, 74, 81, 143, 154–56, 165, 171, 181

day of the Lord/Yahweh, xiv, 19, 182
doctrine, 13, 15, 16, 35, 49, 52, 53, 55–56, 58, 59, 89, 92, 116, 119, 120, 132, 136, 154, 158, 166, 171, 178, 179, 206
dogma, 3, 13–15, 17, 49, 57, 68
dualism, 62, 64–66, 78–79, 133, 144

economy (of salvation), 16, 33–34, 53–54, 68, 70, 77, 79, 85, 87, 93, 96, 121, 135, 139, 148, 159–60, 162, 165, 176, 181–87, 197, 201
ecstatic/*ecstasis*, 158–62, 172, 175, 180, 183, 188, 195, 204
election, 28, 136, 155–56, 158n34, 185, 187
epektasis/epektatic, 158–62, 172, 175, 179, 183, 185, 188, 204, 206
eschatology, 20, 40–42, 50, 69, 76, 78–79, 82, 84, 92, 112, 119, 121, 131, 133–36, 137, 158, 172–73, 176–77, 179, 182, 184, 188, 202, 204, 206, 207
eucharist, 79, 81, 149, 165, 166, 179, 183–85
eusebeia, 57n14, 189

faith, faithfulness, rule of faith, xii, 7, 15, 17, 27, 46, 49, 53, 56, 57, 61, 77, 80, 82, 91, 92, 107, 109, 119, 120, 134–35, 138, 146, 147, 154, 163, 164, 165, 170, 172, 177, 179, 182, 186, 188, 195
father, 9–10, 13–16, 19–20, 23n6, 24, 26, 27, 32, 38–49, 53, 54–55, 57–69, 74, 80, 85, 86, 87, 88, 92, 94–100, 102, 103, 105, 113–17, 121, 122, 123, 124, 125–26, 129–31, 140–47, 151–66, 169, 170, 171, 172, 175–77, 178–85, 188, 192
field, trinitarian relations as, 128, 130, 142, 143, 147, 154, 181, 183, 186

freedom, divine and human, xxi, 28, 66, 74, 87, 115-17, 119, 121, 135, 149, 154-55, 158-59, 164-65, 171-72, 175-76, 178-79, 181, 185-86, 187-88, 191, 192, 198, 199, 203

GGR, model of, 10, 150-67, 170-76, 179, 181, 182, 183, 185, 186, 188, 202
godforsakenness, death on the cross, 107, 164, 185
God's being:
  in act, 67, 68, 85, 86-87, 96, 121, 125, 135, 152-53, 170-73, 180, 184, 185, 186
  as event, 10, 121, 151-53, 156, 159, 160, 161, 164, 169-71, 174, 180, 182n43, 184, 187n50, 194
  as movement, 87, 146, 147n20, 151, 152, 153, 155, 161, 175, 183
  as double movement, 160-62, 180

history (historicality), see too economy, theodrama, 13, 18-19, 22, 34, 53, 61, 75, 78, 79, 98, 110, 111, 117-18, 119, 123, 126, 137, 139, 141, 145, 151, 157-60, 163, 164-65, 169, 171, 173, 174, 177, 179, 182, 184-85, 187, 188, 203, 204
Holy Spirit, see too spirit Christology, xiv-v, 9-10, 14-16, 20, 26, 27, 30, 31-34, 35, 40-41, 43-45, 48-49, 53, 54, 55, 59, 60, 61, 65, 66-67, 68, 69, 72, 74-88, 91, 96-103, 105, 113-16, 119, 120, 121-24, 125-26, 128, 130-31, 142-49, 151-67, 169, 170, 176, 177-79, 180, 183, 186, 192, 195, 199
homoousios, homoousion, 14, 57, 59-66, 85, 90, 114, 133
hope, 34, 41-42, 83-84, 116-17, 128, 134-35, 138-39, 165, 173, 174, 186

hypostasis, 52, 54-55, 59, 62, 67-68, 87, 90, 93-95, 115, 122n99, 124, 126, 132, 187n5
hypostatic union, 68, 120, 142

identity, 10, 13-15, 18, 19, 20, 22, 23, 26, 27, 30-31, 48, 61, 63, 66, 68, 76, 88, 91n7, 95, 96, 99, 113-17, 119, 122, 130, 133, 135, 137, 138, 141, 144, 153, 154, 158, 162, 168, 171, 175, 177, 178-79, 179, 180, 181-82, 188n52, 194
idiotēs, 76, 165n57, 178n31
incarnation, 16, 25, 26, 57n14, 60-61, 64n29, 66, 68, 69, 71, 74, 78n59, 83, 101, 106, 107n37, 140-43, 146, 147, 156n20, 157, 160, 162, 165, 167, 171, 181, 190n56

katabasis, see too *anabasis*, 143, 146-47, 160
kenosis (forma servi), see too godforsakeness, 20-24, 36, 102-3, 161, 165, 180, 182n43, 186, 202

limitless(ness), 124-25, 132, 162-63, 164, 199
love, of God, in selflessness and selfrelatedness, 134-35, 156, 161, 194

mediator/mediatorial, 16, 48, 53, 64, 101, 107, 140-47, 185
metaphysics (philosophy), 51-53, 55-57, 58, 62, 63, 65, 90, 95, 101, 112-15, 118, 119n84, 125, 129, 133-37, 150, 153, 172, 175, 179, 185, 194
model, 1-4
music, 58, 130, 143, 179, 185-86, 189, 198, 204

name of Yahweh/the Lord, 18, 23, 27, 36, 38, 40-42, 45, 50, 165, 167, 189
Nicaea/Nicea, council of, 13, 14, 55, 56, 59-60, 64, 81

nicene creed, 13, 14, 15, 45, 56, 58, 59–61, 64, 66, 69, 77–84, 85, 92, 140, 148, 189
nothingness (*nihil*, *Nichtige*), 64, 156–57, 164, 171, 172, 174, 175, 177, 194, 202

ousia, 52, 59, 63n24, 67, 86, 90, 93, 96, 113–15, 124–26, 132, 159

perichoresis, 84–87, 121, 126, 130, 132, 135, 161, 171, 181, 183, 184, 185, 186, 190, 193, 195, 196, 199, 205
perishability (*peras*), 156–57, 164–65, 181, 185n48, 194, 202
personhood, personal, 2, 9, 15, 24, 26, 33, 45, 47, 54, 55, 66, 67, 68, 71n46, 72, 84, 85, 87, 90–91, 93, 94–96, 98, 99, 102, 103–10, 111–12, 113–16, 120, 121, 122, 123, 129, 130, 133, 139, 140–41, 147, 151, 153, 154, 155, 156, 161, 162, 164, 170n5, 173, 175, 176, 177–79, 187, 194
predicate, 52, 94, 125, 172, 173n15
proprium, 68, 76n56, 102, 115, 117, 130, 154, 162n50, 179, 182, 186, 222

relation, relationality, of the trinity, 3, 23n6, 27, 39, 44, 48, 50, 61, 63n26, 64, 68, 74, 76, 84, 86, 87, 90, 92, 94–96, 98, 99, 103–4, 111, 114–16, 121–24, 126, 129, 130, 135n131, 136, 138, 140–41, 152, 155, 167–68, 176, 178, 179n32, 181, 185n48, 186, 194

sabellianism, 54, 93
spirit christology, 31–34, 44, 151
subject, subjectivity, 47, 52, 90, 93, 102, 103, 111–12, 117, 123, 126, 145, 155n19, 162, 173, 174, 176, 184
substance, 52, 54, 59, 63n24, 64, 90, 93–96, 99, 104, 105, 111, 114, 133, 145, 153, 155, 174n20

temple, 26, 36, 72, 77, 79, 151, 181, 188–89
temporality, time, 33, 65, 82, 83, 94, 98, 106, 115n68, 117–26, 126–31, 132, 136, 140, 157, 158, 162–65, 171n9, 172, 173–74, 182, 183, 184, 185, 185n48, 193, 197, 202
theodrama, drama, 13, 27, 34, 34n16, 54, 57, 116, 118, 120, 134, 135, 137, 139, 145, 147, 157n27, 163n52, 171, 174n20, 175, 179n36, 182n42, 184n45, 185n48 and 49
totus christus/Whole Christ, 78–79, 151, 167, 180, 187

vinculum caritatis, 99, 178, 183

worship, see too *eusebeia*, 14, 24n7, 28–31, 39, 45–48, 49, 50, 56–58, 60–61, 67, 84–85, 108, 115n65, 120, 142–44, 146, 147, 149, 179, 184, 189, 190